Stern:
THE MAN and HIS GANG

Zev Golan

Yair Publishing

Photographs courtesy of the Jabotinsky Institute in Israel, Tel Aviv, except Stern's manuscript poem: author's collection; Lehi transmitter, recruit training, Lehi convention, portraits of Torenberg, Lengsfelder, Ben-Dov, Gepner, Ravitz, and Heruti: Lehi Heritage Society archives, Lehi Museum, Tel Aviv; Eldad: courtesy of Arieh Eldad; Segal: courtesy of Amisar Segal; Svorai: courtesy of Tova Svorai; Memorial Day 2011 photo by Yosef Lior, courtesy of Lehi Heritage Society.

Design and Layout: Benjie Herskowitz
Cover photo: Stern's hat and shaving utensils in the room in which Stern was killed, now part of the Lehi Museum in Tel Aviv.
Photograph by Mike Horton. T-shirt courtesy of Zionist Freedom Alliance.

ISBN 978-965-91724-0-5

Published by Yair Publishing
8 Rechov Stern, Tel Aviv, Israel

Printed in Israel

Lehi was fire.
You try to talk about it today
and you can't even touch it.

Benjamin Gepner, 97,
the oldest living Lehi veteran

Also by Zev Golan:

*Free Jerusalem: Heroes, Heroines and Rogues
Who Created the State of Israel*

*God, Man and Nietzsche: A Startling Dialogue
between Judaism and Modern Philosophers*

In Hebrew

The Shofars of the Revolt

*Awake o' Israel: the Life and Thought
of the Late Rabbi Moshe Segal*

The Shabtai Zvi Diaries

Translation from the Hebrew

The First Tithe by Israel Eldad

Contents

Photographs following page 144

Introduction

Many years ago in a history class at a university in the United States—Yeshiva University, of all places—a lecturer dismissed the successful revolt of the Irgun against the British in the 1940s, which led to the creation of the State of Israel, as immoral and unnecessary. When asked about the Stern Group, he turned red and exclaimed, "They were animals!" Given that most of the students had never heard of either the Irgun or the Stern Group, the information imparted by the history teacher at this Jewish university did not arouse much controversy; only two students argued or asked for clarifications, which the teacher did not provide. (He has since become a respected member of the Jewish establishment in America.)

A few months later Menachem Begin, former Commander in Chief of the Irgun, was elected prime minister of Israel. Despite worldwide consternation and fears that he was a fascist tyrannical militant dictator-to-be, Begin proved a gentleman who did not fire the political civil-service appointees of his Labor party predecessors, regularly consulted the political opposition, and insisted his ministers be present to listen to parliamentary criticism of government policy. He began the first-ever urban renewal programs in Israel, which involved Israel's poor and discriminated-against Sephardic communities in their own cultural and economic rejuvenation. He signed a peace treaty with Egypt and offered local Arabs autonomy in their own affairs.

In Israel, following Begin's election, Irgun and Stern Group veterans were for the first time recognized by the state and their martyrs accorded the status of heroes. After Begin took office, everybody had heard of the Irgun, even in Yeshiva University. But the Sternists were still something different. The Irgun was an army. Its very name—Irgun Zvai Leumi—means National Military Organization. Every country has an army and

7

many people know someone who has at one time been a soldier. But the Sternist organization was not an army. It was a...Group. Or a movement. Or a Gang. Few people know someone who was at one time a gang member—a gangster. So the mystery remained. Were they "animals"? soldiers? terrorists? freedom fighters? All of the above? Even the subsequent election of Yitzhak Shamir, former "commander" of the Sternists, to the premiership did not dispel the doubts, for unlike Begin, Shamir never really left the underground. He epitomized the fighters Abraham Stern had said would only be "discharged from the ranks with our last breath," so four decades after his underground campaign against the British Empire, Shamir barely spoke about it, or about anything else except his love for Eretz Israel (the Land of Israel).

Who was Abraham Stern—poet or warrior? Who were his comrades— hoodlums or intellectuals? How did they come together, what were their beliefs, what their thoughts as they roamed the streets of cities under foreign occupation searching for an "imperialist" soldier or cabinet minister to shoot? Were they animals or heroes? What did they do after their armed uprising forced England out of Palestine? What became of them and what of their ideas?

The author will resist the temptation to critique, condemn, or praise the subjects of this book. They have already been castigated from almost every existing political perspective and for a wide variety of often contradictory faults. They have been labeled fascists, socialists, and anarchists; traitors, fifth columnists, and separatists; imperialists and anti-imperialists; and messianic fanatics and secularist anti-messianists. They have also won praise as noble warriors, opponents of indiscriminate terror, and far-sighted statesmen. The author hopes this book will help readers make up their own minds about the ideas and deeds of the Sternists by facilitating an understanding of why hundreds of young men and women took up arms against England, left their homes and hid "underground," were sentenced to years in jail, and in some cases ascended the gallows because they joined STERN, THE MAN AND HIS GANG.

1

In the late-1930s, pirate captains ferried contraband in the Mediterranean Sea along the coast of the Holy Land. The illegal material being smuggled into the country was human; this was the Irgun's "underground railroad" over the oceans, transporting Jews escaping from Europe to the safety of their own homeland. On one occasion, the usual shore supervisor had been called to Greece to deal with a missing ship. The Irgun sent Abraham Stern, a member of its High Command, to watch the debarkation of a boatload of refugees, and he was given overall charge of the activity that night. Stern stood on a cliff and watched the operation.

The refugees' boat weighed anchor some two hundred yards offshore. The crew loaded the Jews into dinghies, which could approach the beach. Irgunists waded out and met them halfway, carrying the refugees and their bags ashore and sending the dinghies back for more. On shore, many of the refugees fell to their knees and kissed the sands of the homeland. British patrol boats discovered the landing site, sent up flares, and began shooting. The new immigrants huddled by the hundreds under the cliff, where they were protected. The cliff's top and Stern on it were visible targets and the bullets whizzed by him. Stern did not move; he continued issuing instructions, ordered the buses parked nearby abandoned, directed that the immigrants be marched to Herzliya under an armed Irgun escort, and left the hill only after all the immigrants and their Irgun handlers were safely inland.[1]

Stern seemed to court death. Like the lovers described by King Solomon in the Song of Songs, Stern and death knocked at each other's doors; they sought each other around corners and they ran through the hills around

Jerusalem; they called to each other and evaded a final embrace. When death finally came to Stern it was violent and bloody, like a line from one of Stern's own songs, not Solomon's:

> I know a night will come, or day
> when falling in battle will be my lonely lot.
> Surrounded then by crouching beasts of prey,
> and desert, and death, and the air, so heavy and hot.[2]

The British police put the photographs of Stern and his associates in Palestine's newspapers on February 3, 1942, with prices on their heads.

Who Was Abraham Stern and Why Do People Say Terrible Things about Him?

When Abraham Stern was shot at point-blank range in a rooftop apartment in downtown Tel Aviv on February 12, 1942, he was 34 years old. He was what one might call famous: his face appeared on wanted posters in every post office in the country. The British police had been hunting him and his "gang" for months.

Youth

Stern was born in Suwałki, Poland, in December 1907. His father, Mordecai, was a dentist and his mother, Leah Hadassah, was a midwife. His maternal grandfather, Raphael Grushkin, was a Jewish author and poet in Lithuania.

During one of the Russian army's retreats from Suwałki in the First World War, in 1915, the Jews abandoned the city with the troops. Stern's mother took him and his younger brother David to her aunt in the Ural Mountains. His father had been in Koenigsberg for medical treatment; when he returned to Suwałki he was taken prisoner by the Germans. He was released at the end of the war and Stern's mother and brother returned to Suwałki, leaving Abraham with his aunt because his father had written that the schools in Suwałki had not yet reopened. Both his parents felt that Stern's education was more important than their being together. Abraham therefore continued his schooling in the Urals, though since the Russian Revolution, the schools had been transformed into Workers Schools in which the children were forced to work more than study; but this was as good as it got at the time and eventually more classes were added. In addi-

11

tion, Stern studied Hebrew with a tutor. He wrote to his father not to send any more money as his mother had left him more than enough.[3]

Stern's fortunes soon changed. Communication with Suwałki was cut, their money ran out, his aunt moved to Siberia, gave birth, fell ill, the housekeeper left, and 11-year-old Abraham was charged with all her duties and more: shopping, cleaning, cooking, washing, and lugging water from a nearby river. His aunt regained her health but not her benign attitude to Stern. When an uncle visited from St. Petersberg, Stern left with him. In St. Petersberg, he was paid for his work, ate well, went to the theater and concerts often (he especially enjoyed the play *The Robbers* by Friedrich Schiller and hearing the opera singer Feodor Chaliapin), reenrolled in school, and began taking piano lessons.[4] He also joined a movement for young communists.[5]

At 13, Stern left communism and Russia behind and set off for Suwałki. He joined the masses of the dispossessed mobbing the trains; when he could not find a wagon to hide in for a free ride, he walked. He paid a Lithuanian farmer to carry him, in a sack, across the border to Poland. Finally home, Abraham encountered a family he had not seen for six years. He did not enjoy his mother's attempts to pamper him and had to learn to speak Polish again, despite being fluent in Russian and already able to quote revolutionary poetry by heart.[6]

Back in Suwałki and weathered by his experiences, Stern's leadership qualities came to the fore. He ran a Zionist youth group, edited his high school newspaper, and managed, directed, and starred in a local theater company. He did well in history and literature, failed math (supposedly because the teacher found his independent character irksome) and Latin, avoided sports, treated his friends respectfully but kept his distance, and was a favorite among the young women he knew, whom he treated chivalrously and with whom he read poetry or to whom he sent his own verses.[7]

Eretz Israel

Stern's family, being Zionist and seeing the growing anti-Semitism in Poland, helped arrange for him to transfer to a high school in Eretz Israel. He and a friend, Pinchas Robinson, left Poland together. Their ship docked in Haifa on January 1, 1926. Stern described his first days in the Holy Land:

> I arrived full of hopes and reverentially touched this land,
> mother to the Jewish people, this land upon which I in-
> tended to build a new life full of song, sun, and joy. I

reverentially blessed the land of the Patriarchs, the beloved land which my heart, together with the hearts of all Israel, pined for. I was like an innocently and foolishly happy child when I ate and drank from what is *ours*, when I walked on our land under *our* sun. And this sun laughed so gaily, the land was so pretty, that my soul filled with hope and faith in a better future.

I docked in Haifa, was in Tel Aviv, and am in Jerusalem. All of Eretz Israel. And the more I saw, the more my soul rejoiced.[8]

He and Robinson shared a room in a dormitory on the corner of Jerusalem's Yellin Street, opposite the Lemel School (near today's city center). The "gentle and quiet" Stern, as one classmate described him, was slightly out of place, a polite well-dressed European among the famously rough and informal natives. His classmates variously described him as serious, a dreamer, full of humor, a singer, and even a dancer. Ironically, one teacher urged Robinson to be more like Stern, for, he said, Stern "will never do anything out of the ordinary or crazy...."[9]

Stern spent most of his free time reading, managed to learn English in addition to the local Hebrew, and would, whenever given a chance, recite entire poems by Goethe. He and Robinson soon began organizing parties, of which Stern was the life. His expressed desire was to become a professional actor. His summer vacation was spent in the university library not far from his home. When he visited relatives in Alexandria, Egypt, that summer, he spent most of his time in their library. When he returned to Jerusalem, he frequented a local barbershop, where he was given a table in a corner at which he could read and write.[10]

Back in school, Stern felt more at home. He excelled in class (except math) but was also a prankster. He and Robinson taught their classmates salon dancing and romantic Polish songs. Stern often displayed his musical talents by playing whatever cooking utensil was at hand.[11]

He was selected to recite a poem at the annual school ball and chose Haim Nahman Bialik's "In the City of Destruction," about the April 1903 Kishinev pogrom.[12] On stage that night he declaimed the verses not as a reader but as someone living through the massacre. The audience was impressed if shocked, and he was visibly exhausted when finished, pale, and unable to speak.[13]

That summer his parents pressed him to drop his thespian goals and instead to become a lawyer. He considered this a "gray" profession, devoid of the life found on the stage and in movie theaters. He somewhat listlessly continued corresponding with an old flame in Poland and considered new ones in Jerusalem, perking up only as the new school year approached. He looked forward to starting his university studies, which he saw as an opportunity to move beyond Dostoevsky and the other Russian writers he had already devoured and explore works by Darwin, Spencer, Descartes, Spinoza, Lenin, Leibnitz, Nietzsche, and others.[14]

Roni

The 19-year-old Stern sat on the steps of Hebrew University on Mount Scopus; in his words, "all of Jerusalem spread before me, surrounded by silence, fluffy clouds in the sky above, and the entire universe in my soul."[15] One of his new classmates was 17-year-old Roni Burstein, his future wife. She asked him if he was a writer, so he asked her if she were a dentist; they hit it off immediately. In his diary he wrote of Roni's "wonderful hands" and "lips frightening in their sensuality, lips seductive in their sensuality. Promising and frightening."[16] He was amazed "she smiled so sweetly" at him. They each spent the next three months wondering if they loved each other and by the end of January 1928 had apparently answered in the affirmative. They spent their nights together in Stern's apartment, or meandering through the streets and woods of Jerusalem. Nonetheless, in his diary entries Stern continued to debate with himself whether he loved Roni.[17]

Aside from the time they spent in each other's company, Stern spent that first semester of his university studies invited often to his professors' homes for dinners and holidays; he excelled at his studies despite feeling that he was neglecting them; helped others with their Latin and Greek translations; relaxed by writing ditties of his own; and remained, in jacket and tie, the best-dressed student on Mount Scopus. He never raised his voice in argument, and he dreamed of becoming a published poet. To one of his friends he confided that he wanted to write something grand and new; his friend retorted that there is nothing new under the sun. Stern replied, "That's what you think."[18]

Stern probably had in mind a literary masterpiece; he may not yet have been aware of the truth he would soon express in one of his poems: "Yes, I am a soldier and a poet \ Today I write in ink, tomorrow in blood."[19] Soon Stern's words would blaze a new road in modern Hebrew verse; and his deeds, a new era. The summer of 1929 may have moved Stern in these directions. Until then he was reserved, polite, and studious, pervaded by a melancholy—he referred to "carrying a silent, hopeless sadness inside" and "thinking always about...that despised and cursed thing called life," convinced he was born for something other than what he was doing and dreaming of living differently, of "flying."[20] Yet he was also a jolly partygoer. After that summer, death became a recurring concept in his musings and writings. For August was bloody in Palestine in 1929.

Duty

Arab incitement against the local Jews had been growing in intensity and religious fervor for almost a year. In late August the Arabs attacked around the country. The ancient Jewish community in Hebron, south of Jerusalem, site of the tombs of the Patriarchs Abraham, Isaac, and Jacob, was completely destroyed, from babies to elderly rabbis—all were killed, hospitalized, or evacuated. The murdered families in Safed can still be visited today, eight decades later, in an old Safed mountain cemetery. In slightly over a week, 139 Jews were murdered. Self-defense or counterattacks were almost nonexistent, given that the British had earlier disarmed the Jews. The British did little to protect the Jews themselves (one British police officer, Douglas Duff, later wrote that the police were unable to do more because British policy, "difficult to excuse even as military expediency," essentially consisted of contradictory commitments made to different populations, while the British policymakers did not station enough police or soldiers in the country to prevent the resulting strife[21]).

Stern was called upon by the Hagana, a semi-legal Jewish self-defense organization, to do guard duty in Jerusalem, then later in the southern Galilee. The days were boring, whiled away by shelling nuts and chewing seeds. At night Stern and his friends faced the unknown dark expanses with no ability to defend themselves if attacked, since the local farmers did not want to share their guns,[22] and the Hagana did not issue weapons to its guards. Many young members of the Hagana said they learned then for the first time how unprepared was the organization and how inappropriate its policy of waiting to be attacked. Stern expressed these same thoughts to his fellow guards. The people who shared these views would, over the next two years, coagulate into a second Hagana organization, known first as Hagana B, then as a Nationalist Hagana, and finally as the Irgun Zvai Leumi (National Military Organization), known worldwide as the Irgun.

Stern wrote of his loneliness on guard duty, of feeling "alone and abandoned...so distant, a stranger....Everyone is far from me. Only death is near; only he has not forgotten me."[23] He naturally feared that each night of his guard duty would be his last. After a month of this anxiety he returned to Jerusalem, where he now felt "empty."[24] Roni had gone to Vienna; Stern left to visit his aunt and uncle in Alexandria. He described the train ride: "I looked out the window, and the names of the Hebrew communities caressed my ears: Be'er Yaacov, Rehovot, Gan Yavne. The clear, youthful, gay green of the orchards caressed my eyes. My soul filled with joy and happiness as I looked at this sea of green, at the blossoms, at this life." Yet this traveler's idyll in a reborn Jewish homeland is jarred by the sentence that followed: "I thought how happily I would give my life so that all of Palestine could bloom like these orchards, so that all of Eretz Israel could become a giant orchard whose fruits would provide a bright, happy future for the Jewish people….We love Eretz Israel more than our lives…we are ready to give our selves and our lives to her." Stern ended by noting that were he "a poet-prophet I would sing about the homeland's future; were I wealthy I would give all my money to the Jewish people."[25]

His Egyptian vacation was restless, spent reading, wandering the streets, and window shopping. He wrote poems he never completed.[26] He was moved almost to tears by kindnesses done him. He was unable to put into words the depth of his thanks to a friend who paid a debt for him, but he did complete a whole song for his aunt who bought him a teacup. He also noted that he could barely stand being away from "my love, Jerusalem."[27]

He returned in late November, happy to be approaching a place "of deprivation and the necessity to do without so many things in the future."[28] Stern immediately volunteered to be drafted into another stint as a guard far away from the city he loved, this time in Naharayim, south of the Sea of Galilee, just over the Jordan River, where an electric power plant was being built. By now the ambivalence in his feelings toward Roni had been resolved; he knew he loved her, his letters were full of passionate embraces and tender phrases ("Where are you, where are your gentle caresses? Where are your pleasant conversations, your smiling looks, your kissing smiles…?"[29]), yet he wrote to her that he had doubts about their future happiness. He trusted her, he wrote, but not himself, and "I do not believe in life and happiness."[30] He described the life he knew as "suffering, bitterness, disappointments, the hidden pain of doubt, hunger, tears, dark thoughts of death," and said he was afraid she would leave him.[31]

Such thoughts about himself and about life apparently plagued Stern. That winter he won a university prize for essays on drama as a development of the cultic in the Middle Ages and on Shakespeare, yet a week later, and on a day he described as beautiful, he was overcome by feelings of missing Roni and feared delving too deeply into himself and his pain, where he would find "alienation" from others and from himself.[32] One spring day he watched the sun set in the Valley of the Cross, with the valley's monastery "silent in its majesty" and sheep bells sounding on the hills, a light fog covering all, and he felt at one with the heavens, "in love with the blue expanse, and the warm pleasant depth of the infinite,"[33] yet another day he was calling himself "regular and gray" and wondering how Roni could love him, "how you could be so wrong about me?"[34] The image Stern had of himself was of a man "angry, selfish, bitter, rude, jealous," and ever wondering why Roni would love him.[35] Their letters for the next few years would be full of mutual doubt; she told him he was "better and more noble" than she and "I don't deserve you," while he argued the opposite.[36]

At Hebrew University, Stern was recognized as an exceptional student with a great academic future. His teachers took pains to find him work tutoring or teaching others. At one point, he was hired by the YMCA to teach English; he confessed to great nervousness when he discovered that he had 26 adult students in his class.[37] While his professors imagined him one day heading the classics department,[38] Stern had other ideas. He was already thinking in the terms of a note he had sent his brother in Suwałki: "May we go through all of life together, hand in hand, shoulder to shoulder, toward one goal: the realization of the dream of our people in its homeland."[39] The British had yet other ideas for the future of the Jewish homeland and redefined their policy in Palestine as meant to limit Jewish immigration, Jewish land ownership, and Jewish self-government. Stern told Roni, in a passage that can be read in reference to the problems and independence of either an individual or a people,

> Reality is not what it is and appears to be, but what force of will and longing for a goal may make it. So much in life is dependent on us—but to get anything in life, you have to seek it....to long for it with all your spiritual energies, meaning that to get it you are ready for any sacrifice....Sometimes it's difficult, all is emptiness and seemingly without consolation, with so much superfluity, irrelevance and pointlessness...but these are moments of doubts and contradictions, foggy moments. They must pass if the longing for freedom and independence is genuine and definite....No one understands

better than I the pain of longing and the loneliness and
dull pain of alienation, but as great as the loneliness and
despair grow, so they must be fought, so must we believe
in and hope not for a miracle, but that our will and pa-
tience will overcome life's difficulties.[40]

Preparedness for death and an all-consuming devotion to the Jewish
people and its homeland apparently became the dominant themes in Stern's
life at this point, as they would typify the national liberation movement
he founded a decade later. Another characteristic of his freedom-fighting
unit, which differentiated it from the Irgun and the Hagana, was its refusal
to stand on ceremony, its rejection of affectation, and its derision of military-style hierarchy. Dr. Israel Eldad, one of the movement's three leaders
after Stern was killed, writes in his memoirs that the movement did not
have regional or divisional commanders, only people "responsible" for this
or that; even he and his two associates, Yitzhak Shamir and Nathan Yalin-
Mor, did not call themselves members of a Command but of a Central
Committee.[41] Stern's was the only Palestinian underground with this characteristic, which apparently sprang from his personality. Students at Hebrew University were wont to join one of several fraternities at the time
Stern was enrolled. Aside from distinctly political clubs, one of the more
colorful groups was "El Al," which often held parties and lectures in a basement on today's Strauss Street in Jerusalem. Most of the members were
also members of Betar, a youth movement sponsored by Vladimir Ze'ev
Jabotinsky, who called for the establishment of a Jewish army and state and
the evacuation of the world's Jews to their ancient homeland. So the club
adopted predominantly pro-Jewish-independence attitudes. Stern often
attended El Al's parties, though he steadfastly refused requests to join the
club. He explained to Baruch Barkai, who asked him to join, that he knew
the members were committed to a national revival, but they wasted too
much time on "nonsense and external habits" such as symbols, titles, and
uniforms.[42] Thus it would appear no accident that Stern's own soldiers
would later be known as "anonymous soldiers without uniforms."

The Irgun

At the urging of his friend, David Raziel (a future Commander in Chief
of the Irgun), Stern joined the newly formed Irgun and participated in its
second officers' course in early 1932. He wrote then what became his most
popular song, the anthem of the Irgun and later of his own Lehi, which
begins,

Soldiers without names or uniforms are we
Surrounded by terror and death.
For the rest of our lives we are enlistees,
Discharged from the ranks with our last breath.

On red days of blood and atrocities,
On black nights dark with despair,
We'll raise our flag in the towns and the cities;
On that flag, "Protect and Conquer" will appear.[43]

The anthem's stirring tune was also composed by Stern. Roni remembered the night she first heard the song. She had been away for a year, and she and Stern arranged to meet on a street corner in a nearby neighborhood, where they hoped not to be noticed. "We were in love," Roni recalled. "We told each other of the year's events, rushing through them so as to say everything." Then Stern said he had a song and asked Roni if she wanted to hear it. He sang it for her and asked, "Do you think anyone will think it has any value?" He explained that he had written it and composed the melody. Roni knew Stern could not score music and asked if it had been written out. When he said no, she said, "Quick, we must get to my room and write it down so it won't be lost." In her room, Stern sang it a few times to enable her to write out the notes. After which Stern again inquired, "Are you sure? Tell me the truth—do you really think someone will find it worthwhile?"[44]

The song was first published in the Irgun's newspaper, of which Stern was one of the editors. The paper reflected the Irgun's views as well as Stern's; in one of his articles for the paper, Stern wrote that only cowards or the shortsighted would respond to increasing Arab armaments by recommending retreat or appeasement; "but we, who view the building of the homeland for the entire nation, in all its millions, as the purpose of our existence, for which we are prepared to sacrifice ourselves, we must stand firm day and night on behalf of the life of the nation...until victory."[45]

At the university Stern still "needed all my spiritual and physical energies to get through" his examinations.[46] He was often hungry and he was so overworked that one day shortly after the exams he even fainted,[47] but his attitude was anomalously "be strong and of good courage, don't fall in spirit, everything will be alright...that's my credo....With all my soul I believe in a better and brighter future, and I try never to lose this faith."[48]

Stern was given command of a lookout post in Jerusalem's Old City, on the roof of the Habad Synagogue (at the corner of today's Or Hahayim and the covered Cardo Streets), where he therefore spent quite a few nights in 1932-33. He taught in a new Betar Officers Training School, where the adulation of his students, who preferred to be with him in the hall rather than with other teachers in their classrooms, led to Stern's dismissal.[49] He was also one of eight students suspended from Hebrew University for three weeks (four others were suspended for a year) when friends in a club he helped found, Hulda, protested the establishment of a Peace School named for the British administration's legal advisor, Norman Bentwich. Afterward, they called the university's chancellor, Judah Leb Magnes, to task for relying on British bayonets to deal with students who disrupted Bentwich's speech. Though Stern had been out of town the day of the protest, his friends appointed him to represent them at rallies to protest their suspension. Stern said he was less upset at being suspended than with the fact that "a student with nationalist views has no place in the university," and that the university was apparently glad to be rid of such students. The protests and negotiations were successful and the students were reinstated.[50] In any event, Stern won several more academic prizes in medieval Hebrew and ancient Greek literature and graduated.[51]

Italy

In 1933, just as Roni completed her studies in Vienna, Stern left for Florence, Italy, to continue his studies.

Stern continued to mature on this trip. His self-doubts disappeared, along with his harpings on personal faults and life's futility. None of these are mentioned again in his letters. In their place is the optimism he had already expressed in his "credo" and a new-found self-reliance. Another term that appears in Stern's letters for the first time in the early 1930s, during his residence in Florence, is God. God is mentioned many times, and though it is always in passing, in expressions such as "for God's sake," "thank God," and "if God so wills," nonetheless—these phrases stand out given their previous absence.[52]

His letters are full of the idea that "things will get better," and when others failed to follow through on their commitments to him, he opined that this reinforced his earlier belief that a person should truly rely only on himself.[53] Even he was aware that he was going through "a period of personal growth and purification."[54] "I don't dream, and now I've even stopped daydreaming. All my so-called daydreams—in other words, dreamlike plans for the future—are for me strategic programs," he told his brother's future wife.[55] Stern stated that he was considering options he would not have considered in the past because it was clear that "national matters must take precedence over personal desires."[56]

If Stern felt sad, it was only because he was far from Eretz Israel. In Florence, Stern hoped to complete a quick Ph.D. on Eros.[57] Meanwhile he toured the city's artistic and architectural treasures. He was so enchanted by conductor Bruno Walter's performance of Mozart's "Jupiter" Symphony and Wagner's "The Death of Isolde" that he became a regular concertgoer. He was less impressed with performances of modern music.[58] And though he literally lost sleep after hearing Schubert's "Unfinished" Symphony in a movie theater, convinced that "new worlds had opened" to him,[59] still he put this and all the museums he visited (usually on Sundays, when admission was free, since he was living hand-to-mouth[60]) in perspective: "Overall: vanity of vanities, all is vanity," he wrote, and "My heart bleeds....All my friends are at their posts and I am here writing about tickets and concerts."[61] Florence, he said, could provide "everything, I'm not exaggerating....But Jerusalem is alive in my soul like in the past, in all the sweet glory of its heavy stones. And I never forget her."[62] He called the cultural events he was attending "externals" which provided no satisfaction as long as he was borrowing money to attend the concerts and as long as he was not in Eretz Israel.[63]

He was happiest every Monday, the day newspapers from Palestine were delivered. "Is there any greater happiness in the world than being in the homeland? Not a day or hour goes by when I don't think of Eretz [Israel]. These are not just longings! In my soul I am there!"[64]

One exception to Stern's desire for word and culture from the homeland was a visit to Florence by the Ohel theater group. Stern boycotted its performances because "I decided that a theater that is trying to instill 'proletarian culture,' such that in the course of the last five years it put on only socialist plays...is not worthy of support." Stern immediately decided to forego a performance of the Berlin Philharmonic as well, "since it would be absurd to withhold support from Ohel while supporting the Nazis."[65]

Stern spent much of his time organizing a Zionist club. He lectured every two weeks, tried almost fruitlessly to find someone who preferred learning Hebrew to assimilating, and envied those in Eretz Israel who "must be happy: you have the chance to work (even when it isn't so important) for our idea."[66] He pressed the local Jewish community to contribute toward a lunch kitchen for visiting Jewish students with no means of support. This last effort failed when the communal leaders pleaded their own needs and Stern sarcastically took up a collection for them. He was so involved with his Zionist activities that when his funds ran even lower than usual, he assured Roni by letter that she "shouldn't think it impacts negatively on my mood. You may not believe me, but my mood is good, because on the one hand material problems were never the main thing for me, and on the other hand I have great satisfaction [from my work]."[67]

Indeed, when the possibility arose of his being offered a position at Hebrew University, Stern thought it unrealistic to expect the university directors to hire someone with his political views and activities, and he had no intention of toning these down: "I won't give up my political involvement! It is the essence of my life, the core of my soul, and I would prefer to die as an 'anonymous soldier' than to live fifty years as a famous professor."[68]

In 1934 the government of Austria took violent action against one of the country's labor parties, and many of Stern's friends followed the events breathlessly. Though Stern's sympathies were with the persecuted labor activists, he upbraided his friends for their attitude, calling them to account for getting involved in the struggles of another nation instead of solving their own nation's problems. Stern's friends spoke to him of a united international effort of which Jews should be a part, whereas he insisted they not waste time while Zionism had yet to be realized and Jews suffered in Poland or were oppressed by the British in Eretz Israel. Later that year, while the Zionist movement remained polarized by internecine strife after Jabotinsky's followers were falsely accused of killing a Labor movement official in Tel Aviv, Stern wrote to Roni that he could not fathom how this could be happening "while Zionism is on the verge of oblivion. Very soon the whole Yishuv [Jewish community in Eretz Israel] and the entire nation will be aware of the death sentence being passed against us—the Jewish people—and at a time like this I find it so very hard to force myself to sit studying Greek literature."[69]

Stern was not really spending all his time on Homer. Even planned vacations with Roni were trumped by Stern's need to travel. The Irgun Commander in Chief, Abraham T'homi, had established a modus operandi for the Irgun to buy arms (legally) in Poland and ship or smuggle them, via Warsaw and Romania, to Eretz Israel. T'homi had appointed Stern to oversee the whole operation. On his trips to Warsaw, Stern "disguised" himself as a mild-mannered bookseller peddling detective stories from Eretz Israel. Soon he expanded and began importing handguns from Italy as well. Before long he had sent the Irgun its first submachine guns.

Marriage

When he and Roni finally reunited in April 1935, they spent two beautiful weeks together, until a very nervous Stern informed her that he had decided to devote his life to the Irgun; children were therefore out of the question and they should split up. In October, on one of Stern's secret forays to Eretz Israel on Irgun business, his friend Raziel tricked him and Roni into an encounter and left them to their own devices. They spent two days together, often silently, before Stern confessed he could not do without her and proposed, eight years after they had first met.[70]

They were married on the last Friday of January 1936. Stern came late to his own wedding. He had been given guard duty that day near Jaffa and arrived in Ramat Gan for the ceremony just as the canopy was being disassembled on the assumption that he had gotten cold feet. The guests watched him as he ran through the fields, skirted a herd of grazing cows, and picked wild flowers, which he presented to Roni as a bouquet.

Though not religiously observant until then, Roni remembered Stern "telling me before our marriage: Our house will be a Jewish home, you must know this now. You will observe the Sabbath, we will observe the fast days, you will light Sabbath candles, I will go to synagogue."[71] According to Roni, Stern prayed every morning and "never went to sleep without first reading from the Bible." They even fasted, in accordance with Jewish custom, on their wedding day, signifying that they were being reborn together and wiping the slate clear in atonement for past sins. (Stern's commitment was solid; on one of his journeys to Warsaw the Jewish restaurants were closed and Stern went hungry for two days.[72])

Taking Charge

The years 1936-39 are known in Israel as the "disturbances." Arabs call them the "uprising." In a little over three years, 501 Jews, mostly civilians, were murdered. Arab employees of Jewish firms also went on strike, and Arabs attacked British police and soldiers as well. The poet Uri Zvi Greenberg expressed the feeling of the Jewish community when he wrote, "every day another funeral." The establishment Jewish leadership called for "restraint" and urged Jews not to take the law into their own hands. Stern thought the burning of so much that the Jews had built and the murder of unarmed Jews in their homeland showed the bankruptcy of Zionist officialdom and its policy and the validity of the Irgun's alternative. He called it "a time for a revaluation of values, this hour of the collapse of the [Zionist] enterprise and triumph of the concept."[73] He was appointed

T'homi's deputy or aide de camp in Eretz Israel. T'homi spent most of his time procuring arms and training his troops. The troops wanted more action; they wanted to attack. Stern and Raziel co-authored an instructional book in Hebrew about guns, the first of its kind. Stern, in his private conversations, advocated training the Irgun's gun sights not on the Arab gangs but on the British Empire. T'homi, meanwhile, believed the Jews needed one united army in Eretz Israel, and he privately made plans to return to the Hagana, an organization he had left in order to help found the Irgun in 1931.

In April 1937, T'homi split the Irgun and took half its members into the Hagana; the promises he had been given by the Hagana were broken and he was quickly marginalized, his men absorbed into the Hagana without being able to influence policy. The Irgun commanders who did not follow T'homi preferred an underground army without the Hagana's political ties to the Labor party; they wanted an independent military command. Stern was among these commanders. T'homi later called him the most consistent of them; according to T'homi, Stern had decided that the Irgun should be a revolutionary combat organization, not an army, and this was the only justifiable reason to see the ranks split.[74]

When Moshe Rosenberg became Commander in Chief of the Irgun following T'homi's departure, Stern was on his High Command. Stern was put in charge of propaganda. He continued traveling to Europe, from where he warned that the hour was more critical than war—it was the eve of war.[75] He forged contacts and coordinated arms shipments with the Polish government and army. The idea was for the Poles to train forty thousand Polish Jews, who would launch an armed invasion of Eretz Israel by sea. In June 1938, Stern reached an agreement with the Polish consul in Jerusalem to allow the Irgun to run training camps in Poland and encourage Polish Jewish youth to emigrate to the Holy Land. Poland committed to giving the Irgun guns and locations for the camps; Poland also promised to try, when diplomatically possible, to pressure England to allow Polish Jews into Eretz Israel. In July, Stern was back in Poland setting up the camps, planning the courses with his associates there, and secretly "drafting" Polish members of Betar into the Irgun. Stern had no qualms about negotiating with a Polish government that was at the very least imposing economic hardships on its Jews, and at the worst, wanted these Jews out of Poland. Unlike the socialist anti-Zionist Bund party, which fought for Jewish rights in Poland, or assimilated Polish Jews who did not want to leave, and unlike American Jewish leaders who thought a "transfer" of Jews to Eretz Israel would be an immoral violation of their freedom to live where they liked, all Stern's feverish activity was based on his analysis of a confluence of interests: the Poles wanted the Jews out, the Jews needed to get out before a quickly approaching disaster, and the struggle to free the homeland needed them.

Jabotinsky was irked by the independent underground cells being organized within his Betar movement. In February 1939 Raziel agreed to unite Betar and the Irgun and thus make the Irgun subservient to Jabotinsky's Revisionist political party. Stern and most of the Irgun commanders opposed this move, as they had previously opposed the idea that the army should take orders from the Labor party. Stern knew Raziel's arrangement would not last, since the Irgun had to be an independent revolutionary army, but Stern did not break publicly with Jabotinsky. When someone made a toast to "Irgun Commander Stern," he replied, "Jabotinsky is the Commander of the Irgun, make your toast to him." When another called him a leader, Stern demurred, saying, "I am not a leader, I am only a soldier in a reborn Hebrew army determined to free its ancient homeland."[76]

But Stern was setting out on his own path. He opened a club in Warsaw named The Jordan, where the locals could come for relaxation and education. Unlike the official Zionist establishment, Stern did not conceal his goals; on one of the clubhouse's walls was a huge poster of Eretz Israel under the banner: "The Jewish State." In August 1938 Stern's local assistant, Lily Strassman, founded a newspaper that she and Stern named the Polish equivalent of "Liberated Jerusalem." They had intended to have as subtitle on the paper, "The Journal of the Armed Struggle for a Jewish State," but the Polish Interior Ministry denied them permission. In March 1939 Stern and Strassman held a press conference in Warsaw at which Stern declared that the Irgun intended to stop armed Arab attacks on Jews in Eretz Israel by means of armed reprisal attacks. In May, Stern helped turn occasional Irgun bulletins in Warsaw into a Yiddish daily, which he and its founding editor, Samuel Merlin, called *Di Tat* (The Deed); Yalin-Mor was Merlin's assistant, then his partner.

In Eretz Israel, too, Stern was working on "propaganda." The Irgun began issuing broadsides in mid-1938, some of which he wrote. According to one Irgunist, Azriel Bensenberg, they began publishing reports of their activities because no one else would: One night Stern, Raziel, and Aharon Heichman met Bensenberg after an attack and Stern told him he had made history—this was the first time Jewish youths had attacked inside Arab territory. "The next day," Bensenberg recalled, "we searched through the newspapers—there was nothing. Nothing! The Arabs had not shot at us, the British were not notified, so there was nothing, and even on our side no one was talking about it. We said, if you make such an effort—and it was an effort—and you act and succeed, and there is no news item anywhere, it is as if you did nothing. After that we publicized every action by posting broadsides on the walls."[77]

That summer, another Irgun newspaper was formed, called *Masu'ot* (Torches), for which Stern wrote under the pen name Elazar Ben-Yair. Elazar Ben-Yair had been the commander of rebel forces at Masada during the Jewish revolt against Rome in the year 70. By adopting his name, Stern was drawing an historical connection between the ancient zealots who fought for Jewish independence and the modern freedom fighters, as well as signaling that the modern fighters were as committed to liberty as their forefathers, who had committed suicide rather than be slaves to the approaching Romans. After Stern's articles began appearing under this name, his comrades in arms began calling him Yair (pronounced Ya-ēr), and this became not only his nom de plume but also his nom de guerre. Proceeding on the media front, in February 1939 Stern initiated an English-language Irgun paper called *Sentinel*, and in March he helped write the first broadcasts of an Irgun radio station.

On May 17, 1939, the British issued another in a series of White Papers redefining their policy in Palestine. Each successive paper had whittled away at the British commitment to assisting in the creation of a Jewish national home in Palestine and shrunken the territory considered "Palestine" for this home.[78] Now the British essentially forbade land sales to Jews in most of the country and instituted drastic quotas on the number of Jews allowed to immigrate—no more than a total of 75,000 over the next five years—after which an Arab majority was to be given control over Jewish immigration policy. An emotional Yalin-Mor brought Stern, who was in Warsaw, an early report from the newswires and expected to hear a barrage of angry curses; instead Stern was unmoved, calling this the only possible development. He did note that all the establishment Jewish organizations that had expected to benefit from a long friendship with England were now left out in the cold. Conceivably they would realize the only recourse was to be rid of British rule altogether. Yalin-Mor understood Stern's attitude was more appropriate than his own and headlined *Di Tat*, "Neither Surprised Nor Demoralized."[79]

David Raziel was arrested by the British police in May, a few days after the White Paper had been issued. A week after the White Paper, the Irgun began responding to a slew of Arab attacks on Jews with deadly reprisals.

This went on for two months or so. The new Irgun acting commander, Hanoch Kalay, called Stern back from Poland to be his deputy, in charge of propaganda, intelligence, foreign diplomacy, and other tasks. Stern expressed himself in more than one way regarding the Arabs. One person remembers Stern saying that after the British were expelled from the country, the Jews would be able to talk to the Arabs. Another remembers Stern saying that the Jews would be able to deal with the Arabs. This latter phrase is ambiguous and perhaps the former conversant had misunderstood what Stern meant by it. For Stern okayed for publication in his underground paper a text by Yaacov Orenstein criticizing *Haaretz* for reporting that a man was attacked by "his neighbors" rather than saying outright "Arabs," and for editorializing elsewhere in favor of limiting national sovereignty in order to promote international harmony. Orenstein wrote that the purpose of such an editorial is to convince local Jews that Hebrew sovereignty will need to be limited so as to enable the creation of an Arab state: "This will not happen! The Hebrew nation will be the sole sovereign in this land. And the question of foreigners will be resolved through population transfers."[80] And since Stern wrote, among other things, that anyone who occupied the country and intended to remain in it needed to be fought—the Jews of Eretz Israel needing to "fight for a sovereign Israel in borders to be set by the sword of conquest"[81]—he had to acknowledge that, living in a predominantly Arab Middle East, the Jews could not expect to be free from the need to fight for generations.

Indeed, Stern and Raziel had earlier, in late 1938 or early 1939, sent an Irgunist, David Sitton, to Lebanon and Syria to meet with ethnic minorities threatened by the pan-Arab movement. Sitton was a journalist and could travel freely, without the need for a false identity. He made it as far as the Syrian border with Iraq and found representatives of the Assyrian, Kurdish, Druse, Maronite Christian, Metawali (a Shi'ite sect), and Shi'ite Moslem communities expressing support for the Irgun's retaliatory bombings against Arab attacks organized by the British-appointed mufti of Jerusalem, Haj Amin el-Husseini. The Assyrian activist Yousef Malik warned Sitton that "the massacre of my people [in Simel, Iraq, in 1933] should be a warning of what is to come for you Jews in Palestine," since, he said, "Arab-Moslem nationalism knows no compromises; the Moslems will not agree to the existence of non-Moslem peoples in the region." Malik further warned, "If you rely on the British government, you will come to a bitter end, because it will betray you just as it betrayed us."[82] The Maronite Patriarch Antoun Arida told Sitton that he considered the continued exist-

ence of the Christian and Jewish minorities in the Middle East dependent
on the existence of a Jewish state in Palestine allied with a Christian Lebanon.[83] (Sitton's Shi'ite contact, Suleiman Khaider, helped smuggle rifles and
pistols to the Irgun and then to Lehi. In the summer of 1940 he snuck across
the Lebanese border with Palestine. He was provided by Lehi with false identity papers in the name of Shlomo Mizrachi so he could move about Tel Aviv.
He even spent the Day of Atonement fasting in a synagogue with his Lehi
associates. Eventually Lehi asked him to return to Lebanon, where he continued to provide logistical support to Lehi agents.[84]) Two or three weeks after Sitton returned to Jerusalem he was arrested at his newspaper's offices
by the British. Months later, he and hundreds of other suspects like him
were incarcerated in the Sarafand Detention Camp, located inside a huge
British army base in the center of the country. Ironically, he was told by
his Irish guards, "Just like you, we are fighting them [the British]," and "We
know your war is just." One guard told him, "We have no doubt that the
day is not far off when you and we will succeed in shaking off the chains
of oppression. The British won't be the ruler of nations anymore."[85]

At some point in 1939 it became clear to Stern that Raziel and he were
at odds not only about the Irgun's subservience to Jabotinsky and the Re-
visionists but also, far more seriously, about its subservience to Britain.
Stern got hold of a copy of a letter sent by Raziel in the final days of 1938
to Arthur Giles, chief of the British Criminal Investigation Department
(CID) in Palestine. Raziel sought to assure Giles that he, Raziel, was not
"an enemy of Great Britain in Palestine." He professed his "love" for British culture and noted England's "friendly attitude towards my people." One
can only imagine Stern's distress as he read this missive from the Commander in Chief of the Irgun explaining to the top British detective in Palestine that Zionism was "not an adversary to England," and that the opposition of certain British newspapers and officials to Zionism was the
result of "a regrettable misunderstanding" or of their ignorance. A Jewish
state, Raziel wrote, would be surrounded by Arabs and of necessity would
always rely on a European power for support. "We criticize the methods of
the government," Raziel continued, "but we do not intend to uproot the
rule."[86] Stern saw that he and Raziel were headed in opposite directions.

By June 1939, with Raziel in jail, the Irgun under Stern's direction began to attack British targets. They began modestly, perhaps because of their
limited means, by attacking the communications network—first, they blew
up telephone booths in Jerusalem, Tel Aviv, and Haifa. Then they exploded
a bomb in a post office, timed to go off when no civilians would be hurt.

The target of the Jewish forces was changing from members of Arab gangs involved in attacking Jewish schools and hospitals to the British who were occupying Eretz Israel. Stern set the target and he personified the new urban revolutionary. A decade earlier he had dreamed in his poems that

> We live underground!
> Between damp basement walls,
> Beneath a bulb's pale light,
> on a floor on which the rain falls.
>
> In the dark underground we
> have been blinded by a dream:
> The floor's puddle is—the Sea of Galilee;
> the bulb's light—a sunbeam.[87]

He wrote:

> As my father carried
> a prayer shawl to Sabbath synagogue,
> I carry sacred pistols...
>
> Blessed be he who believes and cursed be he who denies
> the religion of Redemption and the war of liberation.[88]

When an Irgun soldier was killed assembling a bomb in August 1939, Stern wrote,

> Hebrew mother, hold your tears,
> You raised a young yet great son,
> A stalwart Jew, revenge and liberty were his wares
> A generation sees itself and its desire—in his person.[89]

Prison

On August 31, 1939, the members of the Irgun's High Command met in a third-floor apartment at 6 Aharonovitch Street in Tel Aviv, around the corner from today's Dizengoff Circle. Present were Hanoch Kalay, Aharon Heichman, Haim Lubinsky, and Stern; Raziel was in jail. Also present that night was Yaacov Eliav, who had come to give a report on recent operations in Jerusalem. Stern had asked Roni to pack him a suitcase so he could leave for Warsaw in the morning. By morning, Warsaw was being bombed by

German aircraft. World War II had begun. Coincidentally, the British had burst into the Irgun apartment a few hours earlier and arrested the entire Command. Those present had time to burn or flush most of the incriminating documents, but even those who climbed out a window were quickly tracked and apprehended.

At the time the Command was arrested, Stern was probably the most prominent of the commanders, certainly the most independent, ideological, and intense.

But Stern was one among equals. Only after their chief Raziel was released when he decided to halt operations against the British and, on the contrary, enlist in the British effort against the Germans, did this situation change. Stern argued that the Germans fit the Hebrew definition of *tsorer* (hateful foes of the Jews in the tradition of Haman, the would-be destroyer of Persia's Jews), but he insisted the British were the *oyev* (enemy) which, as long as it forcibly occupied the Jewish country, needed to be fought. A wartime truce with the British could only be justified if the British committed England to further the aims of Jewish statehood after the war. Since the British were heading in the opposite direction, preventing Jewish land ownership and self-defense and blocking Europe's about-to-be murdered Jews from escaping to their homeland, there was no basis for cooperation with England. This had long been Stern's foreign policy and would later characterize his underground's foreign policy: seeking allies wherever they were to be found, but always on the basis of their willingness to further the overall aim of establishing a Jewish state.

Some in the Irgun argued that times were too chaotic and they would do better to do nothing, to see how the war and international politics would develop. Stern replied that a revolutionary movement that wants to save Jews from destruction cannot bide its time but must exploit every hour and situation to save them.[90]

When the rest of the Command was released from detention in June 1940, the long arguments between the commanders behind barbed wire in the Sarafand Detention Camp were followed by long arguments in Tel Aviv. Friends and associates brought Raziel and Stern together in various neutral apartments. They spent the spring and summer dueling. Raziel resigned, had second thoughts, and then was more or less deposed as Commander in Chief. Hanoch Kalay was next in line again but at his request, in June 1940, Stern became the *de facto* commander of the Irgun. On June 26, Stern's Irgun issued an internal bulletin clarifying its positions on several issues:

The Irgun lives and is engaged in an armed struggle to establish the Kingdom of Israel in its historical borders....Our defense is offense. Our war will be in enemy territory....At this time when nations are falling and countries being destroyed, to sit and do nothing except wait for the worst is a crime. Thinking that in one way or another our nation is lost is a crime. The nation will never be lost as long as it has faith and arms itself to deal with the future....This time of war obligates our forces to be ready to die or face tortures worse than death. Victory will not be won in comfort or complacency. Comfort is for the victors not the fighters....The end of our suffering is liberty.[91]

After Raziel's resignation Jabotinsky had reinstated him, but Jabotinsky died in New York in August 1940.

All the above led to Stern being anathema to just about everyone. He openly called for a Jewish state while the Zionist movement was trying not to upset the Arabs and the British; he called for the mass evacuation of Jews from Europe, as did Jabotinsky, while the Jewish socialist parties and American Jewish leaders were convinced this would only increase anti-Semitism; he called for armed resistance and the creation of a Jewish army in Eretz Israel at a time when only Jabotinsky was calling for the latter, and no one, for the former, since the Jewish establishment argued at that time that Jewish guns should be kept "pure," meaning, not used except when under attack; he called the British a foreign regime in the Jewish homeland while the rest of the Zionist movement, from right to left, considered England a friend of Zionism that had taken a few wrong steps; and he took up arms to expel the British while others hoped they would stay and tied their own political and material fortunes to British influence.

In his final two years, Stern went even further on his own path, taking several political and military steps that ensured that at his death, only a few dozen people would mourn him. He created the underground and adopted guerilla tactics and an independent foreign policy that no other Zionist movement supported.

Lehi

Since Stern's release from jail and detention, he and Roni had been living in a one-and-a-half-room apartment Roni rented for them in Tel Aviv, at 57 Pinsker Street. On September 9, Italian planes bombed Tel Aviv, killing 112 people. Stern and Roni were resting at home when the raid began.

They ran into the stairwell, Stern still barefoot. Stern covered Roni with his own body to protect her as two bombs fell on the building, and he absorbed the falling glass and metal shards. He and the building's other injured were evacuated from the ruins by civil defense personnel and moved across the street.[92]

On the eve of Rosh Hashana (the Jewish New Year) 1940, exactly one year after the Command's arrest, the schism in the Irgun was a fact. Stern's followers formed a rival Irgun with a name that was almost imperceptibly different from it but which would, a year later, come to be called the Fighters for the Freedom of Israel (henceforth: Lehi, its Hebrew acronym).[93] Stern issued the first proclamation of his new organization:

> The passing year was one of disaster and destruction: For the Jews of the world—exile. Europe is being totally destroyed. Its Jews have lost all and are imprisoned in ghettos. For the Jewish community of Eretz Israel—a year of lost direction....For the Irgun—a year of restraint...and negotiations....
>
> We take upon ourselves three tasks: (a) to unite all those loyal, proud and fighting...in the ranks of the Hebrew liberation movement; (b) to appear before the world as the single representative of the Jewish fighters and institute a policy of eliminating the Diaspora...; (c) to become as quickly as possible a force capable of taking control of the country by force of arms....
>
> To ready ourselves for these tasks the fighting force is changing its structure to that of a revolutionary underground....[94]

Stern and Raziel each sought the support of the other Irgun commanders. Moshe Segal, one of the first Jews to fulfill his religious obligations in defiance of a British ban (he had sounded the ram's horn at the Western Wall on the Day of Atonement in 1930 and had been arrested) and the leader of a religious youth movement, sat on Raziel's High Command. He remained with Raziel despite Stern's personal request. Segal's guiding principle was Jewish unity, and since Stern was the one splitting from the accepted organizational framework, Segal stayed put.[95] (Several years later, after both Raziel and Stern were dead, Segal moved to Lehi with hundreds of teenaged members and graduates of his youth movement, who were known as *Hashmonaim* (Hasmoneans), a name taken from the heroes of the Hanukah holiday.) Most of the commanders stayed with Raziel. Stern's troops numbered in the dozens. Benjamin Zeroni told Stern he was made to be a political leader not a commander in chief. Zeroni suggested he himself be in charge of operations, or perhaps Kalay. Later, Zeroni spent three nights combing the Tel Aviv beaches with Segal in an attempt to reunite Stern's organization with the original Irgun. The accord they hammered out was rejected by the Irgun. Zeroni and Kalay had no choice but to leave Stern's organization. Stern's troops were further depleted.

By the autumn of 1940 Stern's organization was low on funds. Like many a revolutionary movement before it, it chose to appropriate funds from the enemy by robbing its banks. Stern's recruits were taught that robberies were moral on two conditions: the underground members had already given all they had to the movement, and they were sure the funds would be used only for the revolution.[96] The first bank to be robbed was the Anglo-Palestine Bank, on September 16, 1940. Zeroni, at the time still in the group, surveyed the bank and planned the robbery. Yaacov Eliav of Jerusalem, and Abraham Amper and Zelig Jack, two new immigrants, also participated. One member of the group was arrested and sentenced to jail but they made away with thousands of British pounds.

Stern used the money to fund another underground paper, *Bamachteret* (In the Underground). But not only that. A few weeks after immigrants who had arrived on a ship called *Atlantic* were deported from Eretz Israel (on December 8), *Bamachteret* reported that the British police who transferred the immigrants were armed with clubs and sticks and they did not spare women, children, the elderly, or the former inmates of Buchenwald and Dachau who were among the deportees. Immediately following this news item was another: on December 19, three explosions rocked the Immigration Department in Tel Aviv on Allenby Street, burning documents and passports.[97]

Abraham Amper was ordered by Stern to identify potential fighters among Betar members and Irgunists who arrived as legal immigrants at the ports. When Israel Eldad, who eventually was to run the underground with Shamir and Yalin-Mor, arrived early in 1941, Amper met him and scheduled a meeting between him and Stern.

They met on a dimly lit corner of Rothschild Boulevard in Tel Aviv. They talked politics and reviewed articles for publication. Stern read his 18 tenets and precepts, the "Principles of Rebirth," aloud to Eldad and asked the latter to prepare a commentary. Eldad filled 46 pages of a black-covered notebook with an emotional text written as if in one breath.

In a follow-up meeting Stern took the notebook, studied it, and politely told Eldad that he would have "written it differently."[98] Less effusively, less fire, less pathos; more logic, analysis, practicality.

Stern met Shamir on another of Tel Aviv's dimly lit corners, and they, too, circled the streets as was the underground custom. Shamir remembers Stern telling him that he knew "clear as day that the police wouldn't be satisfied with arresting him but would kill him on the spot. He said this in a quiet voice, with no emotion, and added that he was sure his murder wouldn't be the end of Lehi. On the contrary, the murder would increase the movement's strength and many would join the ranks."[99] Though Stern spoke without emotion, Shamir was overcome, hoping against hope that Stern was overstating the danger.

In May 1941, the German Luftwaffe strafed an airport in Iraq, unknowingly killing Irgun Commander in Chief David Raziel, who had volunteered for a dangerous mission with the British in the area. Yalin-Mor writes that when he brought Stern the news, Stern opened a small prayer book, turned to face Jerusalem, and recited the memorial Kaddish for his friend turned rival.[100]

By July 1941, the underground was again out of money. The target this time was the National Arab Bank of Jerusalem. This time, too, the robbery went afoul and a Sternist was sent to jail.

Robbing banks, of course, was only a means, not the purpose of the underground. At one planning meeting the assassination of British Minister of State Oliver Lyttelton, based in Cairo, was discussed. One member proposed also eliminating some Jews whose activity was endangering the organization. Stern said this was out of the question and told the fighters to focus on British detectives serving in the CID. Another member proposed killing someone whom Stern also vetoed, as the proposed victim was Australian while Stern insisted on attacking only the British.[101]

Stern and his fighters began readying escape routes and safe houses to absorb prison escapees. Stern sent messages to Mizra, a detention camp on the coast, north of Acco, where several dozen of his men were behind barbed wire, urging them to escape. "Mizra, Mizra, Mizra," he would repeat at meetings, pinning great hopes on the high-quality fighters locked up there. Stern maintained an unbroken line of communication with Mizra. In addition to letters and coded messages, he dispatched an occasional pistol.

Stern sent the detainees copies of his radio broadcasts, accounts of underground operations, and honest reports of his troubles. The men inside learned of the arrests and defections outside, of those who tired of the struggle and dropped out, of those who feared for their lives and turned themselves in, of those who disagreed with this or that policy or scheme of Stern's and left him for other paths. They knew the British were hunting Stern and the local Jews condemning him. They probably did not know how hunted he was: Stern wandered Tel Aviv's streets with a suitcase that opened into a makeshift cot. One night he slept in a public bomb shelter; one night, in a stairwell. As the police dragnet spread and Jewish antagonism grew, Stern's face appeared on wanted posters. The police were offering a 1,000-pound reward for Stern, a small fortune. He had few hiding places and almost no one who was willing to shelter him for a night. He could no longer walk outside during daylight hours. The only way he could see Roni was by sending a last-minute note setting a street corner and a time to meet; Stern and Roni would walk up and down the street for an hour or so, while Amper and Jack served as armed bodyguards, one on each side of the road.[102] To encourage their beleaguered comrade, the Mizra detainees sent him a Hanukah gift late in 1941: an olive-wood Hanukah lamp with the traditional eight candle holes, one for each night of the holiday commemorating the victory of the Jewish Hasmonean freedom fighters over ancient Greece. They attached a note to the lamp: "To our days' Hasmonean, from his soldiers in captivity." As Moshe Svorai relates, Stern glowed when he received the gift and read the message. He sent a reply paraphrasing the Hanukah prayers, which thank God for the "victory of the few over the many," by noting how few they were and how many the enemies, yet conscience and necessity dictate: War, war to the end![103]

At the same time, he published a broadside that was soon pasted onto the billboards of Tel Aviv, pledging "the torches of Hebrew victory will yet be carried in the hills of Judah and Jerusalem, on Mount Tabor, Mount Carmel and Mount Hermon. Then we will surely merit the establishment of the Hebrew Kingdom in the land of the Hasmoneans and the establishment of the Temple on Temple Mount."[104]

One letter Stern received from Mizra he found frustrating, though it may have been sent with good intentions. Stern was working on a plan to take control of Mizra and release all the prisoners. The detainees wanted to know why it was taking so long and seemed a bit angry. Stern was taken aback; he read the letter several times before telling Yaacov Orenstein, in whose apartment and with whom he was opening the mail, "I don't understand them....They were only arrested and one day they'll get out of the camp, either by escaping or after our victory. Don't they understand that I've been sentenced to a different fate? I'm not going to be arrested, I'm going to be killed without any dallying." Orenstein tried to disagree but Stern insisted on changing the subject.[105]

Stern's reputation as a reckless thief and a political danger was further enhanced by a British sting operation. In the early years of the war, when the Germans were advancing, Stern believed that the Allies would lose the war. "Contacts which we may be able to form with the Axis may, therefore, be able to save the Jewish community in Eretz Israel. If not, if the Axis loses, people will say I was insane. I'll have to chance that," Stern had argued when he was in prison.[106] One of his deputies, Yaacov Polani, recalled that "at every meeting I had with him, the main subject, which consumed him, was saving Polish Jewry, especially those under German occupation....The spectacle of families with children and the elderly being uprooted gave him no rest."[107] Stern called his officers together. In an apartment near Rothschild Boulevard in Tel Aviv, he told them that the Germans will surely clear Poland of Jews. As of yet, Stern said, the Germans have not decided what to do with them, which is why one day the Germans say they are going to send the Jews to a ghetto near Lublin and the next day they say they are going to ship them to Madagascar. Stern recalled for his officers the "transfer agreement" negotiated between Labor Zionist leader Haim Arlosorov and the Germans, signed in 1933, which allowed Jews to emigrate to Eretz Israel without having to go broke in the process. The Germans honored the agreement until the beginning of World War II, even allowing Jewish representatives to run an office in Berlin until then. Stern reminded his men of his own negotiations with the Poles in the 1930s; he asked rhetorically if they thought the governing Polish parties were any less anti-Semitic than the Germans, yet the Poles provided Stern and the Irgun with military training and arms and helped Jews emigrate to Eretz Israel.[108] Stern sent a man, Naftali Lubinchik, to Lebanon to approach the Germans about transferring Jews to Eretz Israel. The emissary met with Werner von Hentig of the German Foreign Ministry, who may have passed the idea to his superior, but on the whole the Germans paid no attention. The British knew Stern was ready to make a deal with the devil to get Jews out of Europe so they set up a sting. Stern was approached about making a deal with Italy and he took the bait. The British publicized the fiasco and increased the public's hatred of Stern, who was now said to be a supporter of the Axis.

Despite the pressures, Stern almost always began conversations with his members by inquiring into the well being of a relative or another underground member. One family Stern worried about was that of Moshe Svorai, who with his wife Tova had a little girl.

The Svorais lived in a laundry room that had been converted into a small rooftop apartment at 8 Mizrachi B Street in south Tel Aviv. At night, Moshe would scratch in code on the door and Tova would open it for him. The night of January 3, 1942, Moshe came and gently pulled Tova aside.[109]

"Tova," he said, "I've brought Yair. We were propagandizing for the underground and he's got no place to sleep, he roams the streets at night with a collapsible cot in a suitcase." Tova replied, "Our house is his house and the house of any underground member who needs one."[110]

That day, two Sternists had held up a bank clerk on Ahad Haam Street in Tel Aviv. Passers-by set out in pursuit of the thieves. Underground member Joshua Becker passed the money to a waiting motorcyclist and continued running from the pursuers. When he reached a dead end street he hid in a cellar, where a British sergeant discovered him; as Becker fled the sergeant's bullets, back into the street, he saw people to his right and left falling. Becker returned the gunfire aimed at him.[111] He and his teammate were apprehended, and the Sternists lost two more fighters. Worse was that two innocent Jews had been killed by stray bullets during the chase. The public did not know if they had been felled by British bullets or Becker's.

Stern had often warned his fighters to avoid assaulting anybody but British forces. Stern and his right-hand man, Joshua Zetler, had turned down the plans for this operation. After Zetler's arrest, Stern's new deputy, Yitzhak Tselnick, sent Becker and his partner on their mission.[112] Stern was shaken by the killings and did not think it much mattered whose bullets had hit the victims. He overcame his remorse only because he felt he had to continue. But the local Jewish community hated Stern and his cohorts more than ever. Few could receive his radio broadcasts or received his underground newspapers. Even those who did had no conception of what Stern was writing about. The ideas that Stern propounded and the words he used—that the British were "foreign occupiers" of the country and that "armed struggle" was necessary in order to achieve the goal of a "sovereign Israel"—sounded to most Jews at the time like a foreign language. They therefore had no comprehension of or sympathy for Stern and his fighters.

Moshe improvised a bed for Stern, which he dismantled in the morning, but since Stern had no other place to go, he found himself putting it together every night and eventually left it in place. After breakfast Tova would excuse herself and leave Moshe and Stern at the hallway table, where they wrote the underground newspaper and broadcasts and made their plans.[113] "Faced with Yair's burning vision, all my little dreams are meaningless," thought Tova.[114]

Days Red with Blood

In late January 1942 the Sternists took the offensive against England. They mined the roof of 8 Yael Street in Tel Aviv and set off a small explosion that they hoped would bring high-ranking police officers to the scene, who would then be killed by a second explosion. Once again the plans went awry. Three lower-level police officials appeared at the scene first and were killed. Two were Jewish officers and the third was British, a man who had hanged an Irgunist named Shlomo Ben-Yosef in the Acco prison in 1938. Notwithstanding the identity of the British victim, Stern now appeared to everyone in Eretz Israel, British as well as Jewish, as a criminal or a fifth columnist. The British stopped referring to Stern's Group and began calling it the Stern Gang.[115]

One night Tova opened the door for Moshe, who, out of breath, asked if Stern had arrived. He and Stern had met in a dark alley, but a car pulled up and an Englishman demanded their identification papers. They ran in different directions and were shot at. A few minutes later there came another scratching at the door, which Tova opened for Stern, who immediately asked if Moshe had arrived. The next morning Amper scratched, coming at Roni's request. She had heard the shots a few blocks from her expected rendezvous with her husband and wanted to be sure he was still alive.

On January 27, the British police raided an apartment at 30 Dizengoff Street in Tel Aviv. Moshe Svorai, Yaacov Eliav, Zelig Jack and Abraham Amper were relaxing after a demolitions lesson. All suspicious material and arms had been removed, so the apartment was "clean." Svorai was in bed, immersed in a book, *The Memoirs of a Social Revolutionary*. Amper sat on Svorai's bed, Jack was in the next bed. Eliav was in the lavatory. British detective Geoffrey Morton knocked, then pushed open the door to the apartment, gun drawn. Morton's version of what ensued is that he yelled, "Don't stand!" Amper reached for a coat, in which Morton assumed was a gun, and Jack and Svorai sprang at him. In response, he shot and managed to fell them all before any could reach him or a weapon.[116] The survivors of the shooting tell a different and more detailed story. According to them, Morton yelled, "Hands up!" to the off-guard fighters. Behind Morton and not yet inside the apartment were two detectives whose guns were also drawn, and behind them another detective, Thomas James Wilkin. The Sternists stood and raised their arms. Svorai says Morton waved off his team with his left hand and with his right, shot Amper three times in the stomach. Amper fell and Morton shot Svorai in his left shoulder and right thigh. Svorai says Jack was then shot twice in the stomach. Jack and Amper now lay on Svorai's bed, and Svorai was on the floor. Morton shot him again, hitting his jaw.[117]

Morton's detectives flipped Amper and Jack over on the bed and Svorai on the floor, searching through their pockets. Svorai says he was kicked and remembers hearing the detectives cursing them all. He says he watched one of the detectives put a package with a pistol in it on the windowsill, near Svorai's new raincoat, where it would be found during a search. Wilkin tried to identify the injured. Morton loaded a second cartridge and shot five times through the bathroom door.[118] Eliav, however, had already climbed through the window and, holding onto the vines which grew around a water pipe, begun his descent. British police fired at him from below and hit him, causing him to fall to the earth. The police dragged him out back and beat him until, he says, he questioned their lack of shame at beating a wounded man.[119]

Morton visited Eliav in the yard. According to Morton, Eliav cursed him with gusto.[120] Wilkin came down, too, and failed to identify Eliav.[121]

The British brought the local medics an hour later.[122] Amper yelled repeatedly, "My stomach is exploding!" The medics asked Wilkin (Morton was not in the room) to allow them to take Amper and Jack to Hadassah Hospital, as their condition was critical. Svorai reports that Wilkin and other detectives present simultaneously answered no, and Wilkin also refused the medics' request to inject Amper and Jack with more sedatives, as well as their request to leave a medical report of what treatment they had administered to each of the wounded. Svorai says he heard Wilkin say it did not matter, these Jews deserved what happened to them. Two and a half or three hours after the shooting, the four wounded men were taken— according to Svorai, by hand, Wilkin denying the medics use of stretchers— to a police van and then to Jaffa Hospital.[123] Amper and Jack died four days later. Svorai and Eliav recovered and in April were sentenced by a British military court to life imprisonment.

When he was in the detention camp, Stern had written to his wife that it pained him that she was suffering because of him.[124] Now he told her:

> My child, do you think I do not know the meaning of
> pain? I tell no one but I know, I know well the meaning
> of a mournful heart. A man would need a heart of stone
> and nerves of steel to withstand the bitterness and deg-
> radation of poverty and wanderings and continual anxi-

ety for everyone and everything, the responsibility for the
lives of those who, with me, abandoned all to throw
themselves into this insane but magnificent life, this life
of battle for a better future, for the happiness even of
those who are today willing to turn us over to the hangman.

How fortunate that I have faith. Prayer from the
heart purifies the soul, strengthens the heart, and bright-
ens the world.[125]

Regarding himself he thought of the words of the Russian poet
Lermontov, "The rebel, longing for the storm \ As if in it he'll find calm,"
and told Roni, "I was happy with you, you are my joy, my calm, my repose.
With you I am placid, it is warm and bright."[126]

Yitzhak Shamir was under detention in Mizra. Stern wrote him, saying that all the experienced fighters, who were by then known to the police, were being arrested or killed. The newer fighters being given responsibility were naturally less experienced. Stern admonished Shamir he
should not sit "securely" in prison; he must do everything to break out and
rejoin the organization, as soon as possible.

Stern stayed away from the Svorai's apartment the night of the
Dizengoff Street shootings and the following night. Julie Torenberg was
assigned to accompany Stern as he strolled the streets of Tel Aviv, to give
an air of innocence to the hunted man. She met him about 9 P.M. and they
circled for hours. "Everyone was after us," Torenberg said, remembering the
early days of 1942.[127] She says they preferred neighborhoods that were not
home to the well to do; they walked "where the Jews who lived were a better sort—Congress, Peretz and Aliya Streets—where the people would not
inform on us."[128] As usual, Stern was in jacket and tie even at this hour
and on this roaming, and they appeared to be a couple out for a walk. He
asked about Julie and her family and where they had come from, and inquired about each member of his group in Tel Aviv, whether they were safe,
if they had a place to live. She told him she and her friend Nelly were looking to rent an apartment, or a room in an apartment, one that had an easily accessed exit should the need arise. But she noted that she and Nelly
were not having much success; all the landlords were suspicious because
of what had been publicized about Stern's followers. Stern expressed his
empathy. Stern asked again about the group's members. She answered that
they were getting by and provided what she thought was a good example:

when one had work he shared his food with a friend. Afterward she wondered if she had not inadvertently given Stern cause to worry that some of the members were going hungry.

Torenberg reported to him about a brochure that had been printed, supposedly in Lehi's name, tying the group to the Germans. She remembered having to describe it for him, "I didn't know if the British were the forgers, but I couldn't carry it that night, it would have been dangerous to be caught with such material." Stern asked her to read it again and ensure that he received a full report of its contents. Torenberg's 22-year-old friend Nelly Lengsfelder (then, Fisher), met them and relieved Torenberg. Nelly walked with Stern for about two hours in the middle of the night. When the hour was too late for him to continue walking, she learned that he had no safe place to sleep and offered her apartment. She slept elsewhere and returned in the morning with food. By midday she was restless because she knew her neighbor would discern the comings and goings at her apartment, so she visited again, but Stern was gone. He and his deputy Tselnick had spied Nelly's landlord snooping around and left.[129] Torenberg later found out that Stern had not had a place to sleep that night and recalled, "No greater tragedy could have befallen me than to discover that Yair had no place to go."[130]

At midnight on January 29 Stern returned to the Svorai's apartment, telling Tova he had no other option and would be moving to Jerusalem in two days. The next day, January 30, the British police put Stern's photograph in all the newspapers and he was no longer able to leave the apartment.[131]

Hisia Shapiro was Stern's "contact," who would visit him at the Svorai's early in the morning. At first she delivered not only underground messages to Stern but also groceries to Tova. As the pressure and searches increased she arrived earlier and had to skip the shopping.

Shapiro allowed herself, once, to express to Stern her anxiety over the peril he was in. She pleaded with him to take fewer risks, and argued, "Who could ever take your place?" He replied in what Shapiro recalled as perhaps the single instance he was angry, "Do not talk like that…If I die others from the ranks will take my place and continue the war. If I die, Mizra will continue."[132]

Around dawn on the icy morning of February 12, 1942, Tova and Stern heard a scratched signal. They knew Jack and Amper were dead, Moshe lay wounded in the Jaffa Hospital, and Shapiro had stopped coming because of the searches. Stern nodded his okay and Tova opened the door. Shapiro entered and explained the mail could not wait. Shapiro joined Tova in bed where they tried to keep warm in the freezing rooftop apartment. Shapiro whispered the latest depressing news to Tova: who had been arrested, what rumors were circulating outside. Stern insisted on being given the news. Shapiro reported that the ranks were thinning and one rumor had it that Stern had fled abroad.

Stern, already dressed in his gray jacket and a tie, sat at the hall table writing replies to the mail. One letter was a Jewish offer of a safe haven if he would abandon his war and hide quietly. Stern refused the offer, writing, "I am not one of those who of their own accord turn themselves in to the police." He said that if the attack at 30 Dizengoff Street had opened the eyes of his proposed benefactors and made clear to them the regime's true nature, he was prepared to cooperate with them in operations against the government.[133]

At 7:30, Stern bade Shapiro farewell. "Send all our friends my heartfelt greetings—from abroad!" he smiled as she left. Tova put breakfast on the table. Stern paced back and forth, thought he spotted one or two figures on the roof, and pressed up against a wall as Tova closed the slats of the shutters. They ate.[134]

Not far away, Detective Wilkin entered the office of his assistant, Bernard Stamp, whom Morton respected for both his analytical mind and his ability to compose well-written reports, and asked if he was ready to set off on a routine search. Stamp was glad for the opportunity to diversify the day's activities, and a small group set off for an address that had come under suspicion, 8 Mizrachi B Street.[135]

(How had the address come under suspicion? Did Tova attract attention one night when she stood on a street corner near the apartment to signal Tselnick that he should go up? Was Hisia Shapiro followed on one of her early morning visits to Stern? Or was it a slip of Moshe's tongue that set the events in motion? Alan Saunders, Inspector-General of Police in Palestine, reported to London a week later that a guard in the hospital, who had been assigned to win the confidence of Eliav and Svorai, overheard Svorai give his address to Eliav's visiting mother that morning, and that this engendered the search. This account is based on information provided by Morton, who later elaborated and wrote that while Eliav's mother waited for a bus to take her to the address, the guard drove to Morton's office and Morton sent the police to the Svorai's apartment. Batya Eliav, the mother, later told Roni that when she reached the address, all the events about to be described—the driving, search, trips back and forth to the police station and the encounter between Stern and Morton—had already taken place. Undoubtedly the hospital guard overheard Svorai's whispering, but was this before or after Wilkin and Stamp left? The British police later claimed it was before. In another report sent from Palestine to London, the British High Commissioner stated that the police knew that Stern was in the apartment and "accordingly" raided it. This is an unlikely story given the small number of police who set out and their lack of preparedness for whom they would encounter. Are all the British reports a mix of truth and falsehood?[136] An Israeli judge who considered affidavits and testimony by surviving neighbors, police officials, and Lehi members in the 1980s and 1990s ruled that the evidence he weighed showed that the British reached the apartment an hour or so before Svorai's conversation with Batya Eliav, but the judge stressed that he was giving a legal ruling in a libel case brought by Svorai, not trying to usurp the historian's role of providing a true account of what had happened more than fifty years before.[137])

There was a knock at the door. Stern hid in the closet, as he always did when the landlord, a plumber, or anyone else came by. Tova opened the door. Wilkin and his two associates entered.

She seemed to recognize Stamp, from a previous search, he thought, and she asked what they wanted; they said they had come to search and asked if she lived alone, which she said she did.[138] "Why don't you visit your injured husband?" Wilkin asked Tova, adding he had come to get some fresh clothes for Moshe.[139]

Tova left the intruders in the hallway and brought Wilkin some of Moshe's clothes. Wilkin first made small talk with comments about how Moshe's foolish war had left her and their little girl to the Fates, then raised his voice and shouted, "You are killers, thieves, all of you, all of Stern's people! You will all face a bitter end, just like Amper and Jack. We will cart you all off to the Nahalat Itzhak cemetery!" Tova answered, "Wilkin, pay attention and listen. I will yet see you all fleeing our country."[140]

The detectives brought in two neighbors to witness and attest to the propriety of the search. Though Stern's hat was in view, they paid it no attention; perhaps they thought it belonged to Moshe. Wilkin scanned the papers on the table at which Stern had been writing, went through the drawers, and stacked the articles and notes he found. Wilkin asked Stamp to search the apartment. At first everything seemed ordinary, and the detectives were not especially interested. Stamp expected to soon be saying he had found no one and nothing and they could be off. Then he came upon a shaving brush. "It was damp…I said, 'She's been having a shave!' I put it down and had a good look around after that. Somebody had used it, and her husband was under arrest."[141]

They started a more thorough search at the door. A moment later Stamp opened the closet door and searched through the clothing. His hand came into contact with Stern, who was standing well hidden behind the clothes, his head slightly bowed within the constraints of the closet's height.[142] "There we were, there he was….He was not in a position to do anything even if he wanted to," according to Stamp.[143] Stern was pulled out; the detective reached for his gun; Tova jumped in front of Stern and yelled, "You'll have to shoot me first!"[144]

Stamp ordered Stern to sit on the couch; Stern was put in the corner nearest the door.[145] Stamp ran his hands over Stern and found nothing. They could not handcuff Stern because they had not brought cuffs, not expecting to find anyone. Wilkin said they had better get Morton, walked to the door, and shouted to his driver, "Go get Geoff and tell him we've got him, or we think it's him."[146]

Stamp sat opposite the couch. One of the detective's large hands held Stern's two hands and his other held a gun over Stern's nose, aimed between his eyes. Another detective, standing at the door next to the couch, held a second pistol about six inches from Stern's head. Stern asked Tova for his shoes, which she brought him despite Wilkin's saying that she should take orders only from the police.[147] Wilkin showed the neighbors Stern's wanted picture and said, "Here's the murderer." Tova began to argue, telling the neighbors not to believe Wilkin, that Stern is really a great man who loves his people, but Stern interrupted, saying, "Tova, it isn't worth answering him."[148] Eventually five or six more detectives came, with Morton. A Jewish detective who one night eyed Tova entered, stood opposite the couch, looked hard at Stern, and walked out. Tova was taken into the kitchen to change out of her flannel robe—over which she was wearing a sweater for warmth—into a dress and coat. The two neighbors were shown the door. A detective pushed Tova toward the door, too; she called for Wilkin, the only detective whom she knew, in order to protest the rough treatment, but he was no longer in the apartment.[149] Stamp thought she was refusing to leave and promised her that nothing would happen to Stern.[150]

Tova was taken downstairs and brought to a waiting police car. Wilkin was there and he told her to get in, which she did. She saw Wilkin looking up in the direction of her home and looked up, too. Three shots were fired. Tova cried out, "Plainclothesmen are murdering Stern! They're murdering

Stern!" As they drove off, Wilkin made a "v" for victory sign to the police, a signal he repeated to every passing police car along their route.[151]

As to what happened upstairs, Morton later wrote that Stern "was bending down to tie his shoelaces...he suddenly dived under the gun of the policeman who was covering him and made a mad rush towards the open window leading on to the flat roof." Morton said that since Stern knew the room was surrounded he could not have been trying to escape, so Morton concluded that he was trying to detonate a device that would kill everyone in the room. "In order to prevent another shambles, I shot him dead."[152]

Morton's account was called "hogwash" by the policeman whose gun was trained on Stern. Stamp reported that when Morton entered the room, he said to Stamp, "You missed your chance, didn't you?" According to Stamp, Morton laughed when he asked what Morton meant. Wilkin was dismissed. The other detectives stayed. "Morton said something like, 'That's it,' I can't recall the words. He went over to Stern, who was sitting there. He pulled him to his feet. Dragged him...sort of pushed him, spun him around, and Morton shot him." Morton shot him once, Stamp says, and Stern went down. Detective Alec Stewart fired, too; Morton said, "Don't be a bloody fool, Stewart, that's enough." Stamp understood that Morton meant that he had already killed him.[153]

Stamp called Morton's claim that he feared Stern was going to blow them up "ridiculous." "It's laughable. If he [Stern] was going to do that, why didn't he do it? We were in the place long before the main body of police came along....I think we'd have been blown into a few pieces....Why should he sit there?" Stamp's view was that Stern "was wrongly killed. He was the right man; he was wrongly killed. He should never have been—murdered, you can call it; that's what I'd call it. He was killed by the police force, he was unarmed, [with] no chance of escape."[154]

Indeed, the British censor went to work on the day's newspapers and in blue pencil deleted from the planned copy all references to Stern having been "murdered," then inserted new text not written by the reporters—that Stern had been shot trying to escape.[155]

That Stern was "shot dead while trying to escape" is the story telegrammed to London that night by the commanding officer of forces in Palestine. Two days later the War Office was cabled that Stern was killed while resisting arrest. A recipient wrote on the telegram, "The Stern Gang has been liquidated."[156]

That may have been a bit of an exaggeration. "Under Yair's orders we rose to initiate the greatest revolution in our nation's life since we were exiled from our land—to 'forever wrest the homeland from foreign hands,' and to 'renew Hebrew mastery over the redeemed land,'" wrote Yalin-Mor in a clandestine pamphlet published by the underground in 1944. "After two thousand years of Exile, Yair again ignited the flaming desire for freedom."[157]

2

A Revolution Rooted in Jewish History

Abraham Stern, called Yair, was the individual who epitomized the beginning of the Jewish revolt against England. His namesake, Elazar Ben-Yair, was the individual who epitomized the end of what is known in history as the "Great Revolt" against Rome, almost two thousand years earlier.

The revolt against Rome was ignited by much the same causes as the modern revolt against England. Rome had occupied the country of the Jews, then called Eretz Israel or, alternately, Judea, and ruled with a heavy hand, crucifying Jews throughout its reign. In the year 66, Rome allowed or instigated offenses to Jewish religious sensibilities, and the Jews rose to defend their religious and political independence. England, too, occupied the same country, now called Eretz Israel or, alternately, Palestine, ruled with a heavy hand, and in 1928 proscribed Jewish rights to prayer at the Western Wall; then later, rights to immigrate or own land.

The Romans sent a legion to enforce order in Eretz Israel; the Jews, fighting for independence in their own land, defeated the Roman legion in Beth Horon, twin villages just north of Jerusalem, near today's Highway 443. The Romans sent tens of thousands of troops to quell the rebellion. Two years after the revolt had begun the Jewish cities in the Golan Heights and Galilee were subdued. The Romans had Jerusalem surrounded but the fighters inside held on. In fact, the Jews were hurt more by internecine strife than by the Roman siege. The fighters were divided into two main militias, the Sicarii and the Zealots. Some were also called Birionim. In addition, some of the Jews belonged to a "peace camp" that wanted to come to terms with Rome. The Romans breached the walls of the city in the summer of 70, and three weeks later took the city and burned the Jewish Temple on Mount Moriah, which was and still is also known as the Temple Mount (in today's Old City of Jerusalem).

At the beginning of the revolt four years earlier, Sicarii fighters had defeated Roman soldiers garrisoned at Masada in the Judean desert, near the Dead Sea. After the fall of the capital, Jerusalem, many Sicarri escaped southward to Masada. Some ten thousand Roman soldiers laid siege to this mountaintop haven in 72. In early 73, the Romans succeeded in breaching the walls and taking the mountain. But almost all the Jews were dead; 967 had chosen to take their own lives rather than be sold as slaves by the Romans. Two women and a small number of children survived, and they related the events at Masada to the historian Josephus, who recorded them for posterity in his book, *The Jewish War*.

Elazar Ben-Yair was the Sicarii commander at Masada and, as such, commander of the entire settlement. His final speech to the residents, before the fall of Masada, was:

> Since we, long ago, my generous friends, resolved never to be servants to the Romans, nor to any other than to God himself, who alone is the true and just Lord of mankind, the time is now come that obliges us to make that resolution true in practice....We were the very first that revolted from them, and we are the last that fight against them; and I cannot but esteem it as a favor that God hath granted us, that it is still in our power to die bravely, and in a state of freedom, which hath not been the case of others, who were conquered unexpectedly. It is very plain that we shall be taken within a day's time; but it is still an eligible thing to die after a glorious manner, together with our dearest friends. This is what our enemies themselves cannot by any means hinder, although they be very desirous to take us alive. Nor can we propose to ourselves any more to fight them, and beat them...Let our wives die before they are abused, and our children before they have tasted of slavery; and after we have slain them, let us bestow that glorious

benefit upon one another mutually, and preserve ourselves in freedom, as an excellent funeral monument for
us. But first let us destroy our money and the fortress by
fire; for I am well assured that this will be a great grief
to the Romans, that they shall not be able to seize upon
our bodies, and shall fail of our wealth also; and let us
spare nothing but our provisions; for they will be a tes-
timonial when we are dead that we were not subdued for
want of necessaries, but that, according to our original
resolution, we have preferred death before slavery.

...And as for those that are already dead in the war,
it is reasonable we should esteem them blessed, for they
are dead in defending, and not in betraying their liberty;
but as to the multitude of those that are now under the
Romans, who would not pity their condition? and who
would not make haste to die, before he would suffer the
same miseries with them? Some of them have been put
upon the rack, and tortured with fire and whippings, and
so died. Some have been half devoured by wild beasts,
and yet have been reserved alive to be devoured by them
a second time, in order to afford laughter and sport to our
enemies; and such of those as are alive still are to be
looked on as the most miserable, who, being so desirous
of death, could not come at it. And where is now that
great city, the metropolis of the Jewish nation, which was
fortified by so many walls round about, which had so
many fortresses and large towers to defend it, which
could hardly contain the instruments prepared for the
war, and which had so many ten thousands of men to
fight for it? Where is this city that was believed to have
God himself inhabiting therein? It is now demolished to
the very foundations, and hath nothing but that monument of it preserved, I mean the camp of those that hath
destroyed it, which still dwells upon its ruins; some
unfortunate old men also lie upon the ashes of the
temple, and a few women are there preserved alive by the
enemy, for our bitter shame and reproach. Now who is
there that revolves these things in his mind, and yet is
able to bear the sight of the sun, though he might live
out of danger? Who is there so much his country's en-

emy, or so unmanly, and so desirous of living, as not to
repent that he is still alive? And I cannot but wish that
we had all died before we had seen that holy city demolished by the hands of our enemies, or the foundations
of our holy temple dug up after so profane a manner. But
since we had a generous hope that deluded us, as if we
might perhaps have been able to avenge ourselves on our
enemies on that account, though it be now become vanity, and hath left us alone in this distress, let us make
haste to die bravely....[O]ur hands are still at liberty, and
have a sword in them; let them then be subservient to
us in our glorious design; let us die before we become
slaves under our enemies, and let us go out of the world,
together with our children and our wives, in a state of
freedom....Let us therefore make haste, and instead of
affording [the Romans] so much pleasure, as they hope
for in getting us under their power, let us leave them an
example which shall at once cause their astonishment
at our death, and their admiration of our hardiness
therein.[1]

Some years ago, an article appeared in a Jewish newspaper at a New
York City university entitled, "On Shabbos and Other Junk," telling the
story of a chance encounter between a synagogue's guest lecturer and a ten-
year-old boy named Brian who was playing there with an electric gun on
the Jewish Sabbath.

I called Brian over...."That's a gun," I said, "and *Shabbos*
is a time for peace and love—" I got no further. Brian
interrupted, declaring he had "heard all that junk before." He walked away. And I followed him. I asked what
he thought about his being Jewish. "It's boring."
    ...I asked if he were proud to be Jewish, positive I
would at least get an encouraging answer this time. I was
instead floored. "No, I'm proud to be an American.
That's enough." It took me time to recover. "What's
boring about Judaism?" I ventured. "You know," he said,
"the services, school, Hebrew, history." That about cov-
ers it, I thought.
    I decided to agree with him about the
services...."But history boring?" I asked. "What have you

been learning?" He told me had learned of Abraham, Joseph, Moses. I found an opening. My eyes lit up, my voice rose as I demanded to know if he'd ever heard of Menachem Begin and the Irgun. Of course, he hadn't. "Did you know that Jews blew up buildings, fought the British army, freed prisoners and even died for the land of Israel a few years ago?" No, he did not. But he was interested. And now he was asking me the questions.

What kind of buildings? How many prisoners? Why were the Jews in jail? Wasn't there always an Israel? Who is Begin?

...When I finished the story of the Irgun, I asked if *this* was exciting. "Yeah!"

...It is natural for young boys and girls to find the services they attend boring.

...It is not natural, however, for ten year olds to find Jewish history boring, yet they do.[2]

(The upshot of the story is that when the lecturer rose to speak, Brian and a young friend of his sat on the floor in front him and stayed for the evening's program.)

Brian was bored by Jewish history because he had never learned about people like the Irgun commander Menachem Begin. Stern and his fighters, and the ninety thousand members of Jabotinsky's Betar youth movement in Poland, were not bored by Jewish history. They faced persecution and death in the 1930s, but they lived simultaneously on Masada with Elazar Ben-Yair and in Modi'in with the Hasmoneans and Maccabees who began there the revolt against the Greeks that culminated in the holiday of Hanukah.

Israel Eldad, Stern's successor as ideologue of Lehi, wrote in the notebook commentary he gave Stern,

> Healthy is our stock...and it will shake off the dust by the power of its flowing, boiling blood. And with the crumbling of the walls of European and American civilization, the fortress of modern idolatry, the Hebrew nation's stock will stand firm and strong, untouched by worms of rot. The race's fortune was set in the days when Abraham, Isaac, Jacob, and Moses blessed it; the race's destiny was set in the days of Isaiah, Amos, and Jeremiah; the race's heroism stems from the days of

Shimon and Levy and David and the Hasmoneans and
the Zealots; the race's culture stems from the days of the
sages in Yavneh and those in Tzippori and Usha, the days
of Yochanan Ben Zakai and Rabbi Akiba and Shimon Bar
Yochai and Judah the President; the race's song began in
the days of the Psalms and the prayers of Kalir, the poems of Halevy and Ibn Gvirol, and the prayers of the
Kabbalists and the Hasidim. The bearers of the culture
of these generations will march proudly and scornfully
over the ruins of Slavic, German, and Anglo-Saxon culture as they marched over the ruins of ancient cultures.
They will march toward their destiny....[3]

Beyond Persecution

The roots of the Hebrew war for liberation were not, contrary to what
many well-intentioned friends of Israel and even many Zionists believe,
based in a history of persecution. The Abraham that Eldad and Stern knew
is not the 100-year-old Abraham afraid he will be killed by neighboring
kings who desire his wife, he is the young Abraham as Destroyer, wreak-
ing havoc on ancient idol-worshipping civilizations and marching against
the current of the ancient world's greatest river toward his destiny. In this
history the sons of Jacob, Shimon and Levy, are vigilante brothers aveng-
ing the rape of a young Jewish girl. The Talmud's Rabbi Akiva is seen slip-
ping between cities to coordinate military operations and organizing tens
of thousands of freedom fighters in a revolt against imperialist Rome. The
generation of the freedom fighters was weaned on the love songs of Judah
Halevy, the fervent prayer-poems of Elazar the Kalir, and the spiritual energy of the Kabbalists trying to bring redemption from the Galilean city of
Safed in the sixteenth century. Lehi's Judaism is alive and drunk with the
knowledge of its own destiny.

Though Abraham is more often portrayed today as a spiritual man than
the warrior who fought and defeated four kings (a war he fought because
one man, his nephew, was being held captive by them), his story is available and occasionally read, given its inclusion in the Bible. Rabbi Akiva is
studied more for his talmudic arguments than his heroism, but the story
of his death is also familiar, given that he was murdered at the stake in 135
by the Romans who crushed the free Jewish state he helped found. That
which comes next, however, is a black hole in Jewish history. Most Jewish
day schools, in the Diaspora and in Israel, fly through the centuries, set-

ting down only on an occasional poet or persecution: the Temple was destroyed, the Jews resigned themselves to their sad fate for two thousand years and became sheep.

To understand Stern one must follow him to Masada. To understand his successor as operations chief of Lehi, Yitzhak Shamir, one must know he said he left Europe and moved to Eretz Israel because he was inspired by the heroes of the Bible and specifically, the personality of King David.[4]

The freedom fighters were inspired by a Jewish history that went beyond persecution. "The main and decisive points," they wrote, are not to be found in the history books everyone reads, "perhaps they were deliberately omitted….Thus we do not yet have a history with a national foundation."[5] They felt that "the true Hebrew history…has not yet been written."[6]

An article in the second issue of Lehi's underground paper, *Bamachteret*, tells of some of the heroes and would-be heroes of the Jewish people and concludes,

> In all the diasporas of the Exile, the Hebrew people tried in every generation to restore its independence by means of arms. The attempt to paint the life of the Hebrew people in Exile as one huge effort to explain every letter and jot of the Torah, with the most interesting events being arguments between rabbis and Karaites, Medieval linguistic disputes and the different opinions of Hasidim and their opponents—is a great falsification….A ridiculous theory….[7]

War and Independence in the Middle East, 70-1200

As the fighters saw Jewish history, it went something like this:

The Jews were committed to national liberation before the destruction of the Temple and their state in the year 70 and remained so afterward. This commitment was most easily and naturally expressed by those Jews who were forcibly relocated to countries adjacent to their native land when it was "cleansed" of Jews by the victorious Romans, while, according to Yalin-Mor, the rebels who survived the Roman massacre of the Jewish forces "fled not to save themselves, but dispersed to all parts of the Roman Empire to every place a Hebrew heart beat and organized the continuation of the war, on foreign soil."[8]

So when Rome moved to invade Armenia in 114, the leader of the Jewish community in the Middle East (known as an Exilarch), Shlomo Ben-

Hunya, resisted the local Parthian government's plans to abandon the region to Rome. Instead, he raised a militia to harass the Roman troops threatening Parthia. He called on the Jews throughout the empire to revolt, and rallied them and also the Parthian forces. The Jews were anxious to throw off the yoke of Rome, so they fought for their freedom in Egypt, Cyprus, and today's Libya. This was in effect a second revolt against Rome, following upon the Great Revolt, which had essentially ended with the fall of Jerusalem in the year 70. It took the Emperor Trajan about a year to subdue the fighting Jews of this second revolt. He slaughtered as many as he could, and Jews were entirely barred from Cyprus afterward.[9]

A Roman procurator, Lucius Quietus, erected an idol in the ruins of the Temple in Jerusalem and ignited what became known as the Kitos War. He conquered other areas with large Jewish populations, who naturally sided with the local populace against him. Though Quietus was successful in battle, the wars took their toll on Rome. When Trajan died, his successor, Hadrian, had Quietus executed and abandoned the disputed faraway areas. Rome's enemy, the Parthians, rewarded the Jews for their military prowess, which helped prevent a permanent Roman takeover of their regions, by recognizing the Jewish Exilarchs in Babylon as princes.[10]

Hadrian proved no friend of the Jews. As Rome had done before the Great Revolt, it attempted once again to impose a foreign culture and values on Judea. In 131, Hadrian changed the name of Judea's capital, from the Jewish "Jerusalem" to the Roman "Aelia Capitolina." He forbade the practice of circumcision and began to reconsecrate the Jewish temple on Mount Moriah in Jerusalem as a Roman temple honoring a Roman god, Jupiter. Shimon Bar-Kochba led a war of independence (in Lehi's words, he "once again raised the banner of revolt in an underground"[11]), which has come to be known as the Third Jewish-Roman War. For almost three years, Bar-Kochba led an independent Jewish state. The coins his government minted were imprinted with images of the Temple and other Jewish national-religious symbols, as well as the name Shimon and slogans such as "Year one [or two] of the redemption of Israel," or "For the freedom of Jerusalem." The Romans defeated the Jews in 135, executing the revolt's rabbinic leadership, including the leading talmudic scholar, Rabbi Akiva, and wiping out Bar-Kochba's last stronghold, the city of Betar. Hadrian marked the destruction of the Jewish state by changing the land's name, from "Judea" to "Syria Palaestina," after an ancient people, the Philistines, who had lived along the coast and fought the Israelites in biblical times but who no longer existed. He hoped to erase the Jewish tie to the land that had until then been known either as Judea or as Israel, but was henceforth known as Palaestina, or Palestine.

In 1932, Abba Ahimeir, a writer and historian who influenced and worked with Stern and the underground fighters, wrote that the three revolts against Rome were "stages in one event: the great Israeli revolution.... The Israeli revolution was a revolution of grand proportions, the likes of which we find in every great historical nation."[12]

The Jewish yearning for independence did not end there. In 351 a revolt broke out in Tzippori in the Galilee, apparently when the Jews recognized their leader as a sovereign king. The revolt spread to Tiberias and was crushed the following year by the Romans.[13]

In 512, a Persian king denied a teenaged Exilarch in Babylon named Mar Zutra II the right to organize Jewish self-defense. Mar Zutra did so anyway, and did not stop there; he raised an army and declared Jewish independence from Persia. He led this army and maintained Jewish independence for seven years. Thus in 513 the Jews had an independent state and a victorious army, four centuries after the destruction of the Temple and after the Bar-Kochba revolt was crushed. In 520 Mar Zutra, then in his early twenties, and his father Mar Hanina were defeated in battle and were crucified in the city of Mehoza (in today's Iraq).[14]

The struggle for freedom did not end with Mar Zutra. In 517 Joseph Du Nuwas, Mar Zutra's cousin and a grandson of the Exilarch Huna (the fifth Exilarch so named), whose daughter had married the king of Himyar, crowned himself ruler of this kingdom in the area of today's Medina in Arabia. The Himyar king Abu Karib had earlier converted to Judaism when he married Huna's daughter; upon the king's death, a pagan usurped the crown. Du Nuwas now dispatched him and retook the crown for himself. The local Christians revolted and seized a town; in what Lehi's paper called "the great war of the Hebrew king Joseph Du Nuwas,"[15] Du Nuwas defeated them and was now in revolt against Rome. The Roman Emperor Justin I arranged for his allies the Ethiopians to attack Himyar. Du Nuwas defeated them, too. Christians in the northern town of Najrab took up arms against him. When his peace offer was refused, he laid siege to Najrab and eventually executed all the rebels. He then insisted that all Christians in his kingdom pay a tribute as financial compensation for the persecution of Jews in Christian areas.[16]

Du Nuwas' natural ally in the war against Rome would have been Persia, but the Persian king had already crucified Mar Zutra and did not care to support an armed Jewish fighting force anywhere. In 525 the Romans joined with their allies the Ethiopians and attacked by sea; Du Nuwas laid chains across the landing sites but was unable to prevent the armies' landing. With the Romans and Ethiopians attacking by sea and local Christians attacking on land, he was greatly outnumbered. Rather than surrender, he rode his stallion off a cliff into the sea.[17]

Mar Zutra and Du Nuwas lived relatively near their ancestral land, and they were imbued with a commitment to liberty as well as the more well-known Jewish commitment to the God of Israel. They were also imbued with the fighting spirit and skills of their ancestors. This same spirit soon animated another scion of the Exilarch's family, Nehemiah.

In 602 or 603 a Roman rebel named Phocas overthrew and killed the Emperor Maurice, and then fought a war with the Persian king, Khosrau. Khosrau wished to enlist the Jews as an ally. He gave them civil and religious rights, reopened the great rabbinical academies, and appointed Nehemiah, son of the Exilarch Husha, as Commander in Chief of his Persian armies. Nehemiah raised an army of twenty thousand troops. A Jewish prince was now leading a Jewish-Persian army against Rome, over five hundred years after the destruction of the Jewish state.[18]

Some time later, as the battles continued, Phocas was overthrown and the new emperor decided to counteract the Exilarch's influence by appointing a priest as head of his own army. The Persian-Jewish-Roman war then became a Zoroastrian-Jewish-Christian war.[19]

A wealthy Jewish leader, Benjamin of Tiberias, took the opportunity to raise an army of his own to fight for Jewish independence in the Holy Land.[20] The Jews of Tiberias, Nazareth, and the entire Galilee marched on Jerusalem with a Persian division supporting them. The Jews of southern Eretz Israel joined, as did some Arabs. In 614, the Jewish-Persian army conquered Jerusalem. Nehemiah was made ruler of the Holy City. He began preparing to rebuild the Temple. Some months later, before he could do so, he was killed, along with his ruling council and many other Jews, by Christians. The rest of the Jews fled to Caesaria.[21]

From there they launched another attack on Jerusalem and once again took the city. They attacked Tyre and other cities. They besieged Tiberias, conquering it 20 days later. In 625, the city was retaken by Byzantium. The Byzantines killed many of the Jewish rebels, but amnestied Benjamin in 628. Nonetheless, for 14 years the Jews had been free from Christian domination. The sad ending to this story is that Khosrau betrayed the Jews, allowing the Romans to kill thousands outside Jerusalem. The Jews realigned themselves with Rome, but to no avail; the Romans, too, betrayed them.

The ironic outcome was that Nehemiah's brother was sold as a slave; he accepted the leadership of a newcomer to local politics, Mohammed, and became Mohammed's top military man, renamed Solomon Farsi, in which role he led an army of Jews and Arabs against Byzantium in the part of Palestine that is today the Hashemite Kingdom of Jordan.[22]

In about the year 700, another relative of the Exilarchs, Isaac Ovadia, known to Persians as Abu Issa el Isfahani (and nicknamed Abu Issi) defeated the Persians in battle—according to one report, when surrounded he drew a circle around his troops and the enemy amazingly retreated—and announced he would play a messianic role in history. Shortly afterward he himself fell in the war he initiated.[23]

In 720 Jews from as far away as Spain flocked to Syria in response to the call of Serenus the son of Jacob the son of Isaac (this latter being an Exilarch), who was on his way to try to conquer the Jewish homeland. Though fighting for the Land of Israel, he himself did not abide by Jewish law and probably rejected much Jewish doctrine as well. He was defeated by Khalif Yazid II.[24]

David Alroy was born in 1160 in Kurdistan. He also claimed to be a descendent of an Exilarch. He announced that he would free the Jews from foreign control and liberate Jerusalem. He took up arms against the Arab rulers of what is today Iraq, won a major battle in Mosul, was joined by Jewish fighters from Azerbeijan and Baghdad, and won a series of battles before meeting his own death on the battlefield.

Clearly, the Jews expelled from their native land not only longed to restore their country but made real efforts to do so. Sometimes they succeeded and returned to the Jerusalem they loved, other times they died on battlefields from which their city could only be seen with an inner eye. Such attempts to return home were most common in the first millennium of the Common Era, in areas bordering Eretz Israel. As time passed, the Jews were dispersed further afield. In these countries, too, they were not the passive persecuted they are often imagined.

Raising Flags and Armies in Europe, 1500-1666

One of the more infamous Christian persecutions of Jews is the Inquisition, during which Jews were forced to convert to Christianity. Some Jews continued to worship the Jewish God in secret (those who did were called Marranos). But not all Jews were reduced to worshiping in rooms with the curtains drawn.

Juan de Abadia, for example, organized a team of six other men that assassinated the chief inquisitor of Saragossa. The torturer always wore armor around his torso and head; the conspirators followed him into church and when he knelt they stabbed him in the neck. Juan killed himself in prison. Most of his comrades were tortured and died at the stake.[25]

Emanuel Da Costa posted a placard on the door of the Cathedral of Lisbon in February 1539. In defiance of the Christian authorities then burning Jews and at the risk of his life, Da Costa wrote: "The messiah has not yet appeared," and attacked Christian deceit. The king and the pope offered rewards of thousands of ducats for information leading to his arrest. When arrested, he confessed and was tortured on the rack and burned at the stake.[26]

"Caesar's Rome could not subdue [the Jews'] faith and loyalty and neither could papal Rome's Inquisition. When heroes are presented as educational examples and paragons, the fighter will learn to walk in their paths and not the paths of betrayal,"[27] wrote Yalin-Mor in a Lehi newspaper.

Into the cauldron of misery and torture in Europe, a messenger from the Jewish past and future emerged: David Hareubeni (David of the Tribe of Reuben) had traveled from Arabia, he explained, where he was brother to a Jewish king. He said he had been sent to win European Christian assistance for his hundreds-of-thousands-strong Jewish army so that it could expel the Turks from the Jewish homeland. He rode into Rome on a white horse, was received by Pope Clement VII, and won his support. Hareubeni next journeyed to Portugal to win King John III's support; here, too, he arrived royally, with flags flying and a royal retinue. John, desiring to have Hareubeni and the Jews as an ally, promised Hareubeni eight ships and thousands of guns, and apparently delayed for a time the planned persecution of his own Jews. Hareubeni did not have an easy time of it, though, in such desperate times. He was arrested in Spain, released by the intervention of the Emperor Charles, traveled to areas under papal jurisdiction, and ended up back in Rome. He negotiated with the Venetian senate. In Ratisbon he asked the emperor to allow Marranos to arm themselves and join the Jewish army in order to free the Jewish homeland from the Turks. This was too much for the emperor, and the plans for an army of liberation in 1532 amounted to naught. Hareubeni was put in prison and probably died there.[28] "Hareubeni saw himself in the role of a liberation movement, an irredentist movement, a movement to restore the homeland to its owners," wrote Lehi.[29]

One young man inspired by Hareubeni was Shlomo Molcho. Molcho dropped his family's pretense of Christianity and returned to the fold. He circumcised himself and fled the Inquisition, finding safety in Turkey. He became a Kabbalist and studied with one of its masters, Joseph Taytasak, and he himself inspired Joseph Karo, author of the *Shulchan Aruch* (Code of Jewish Law), to become an adept of Kabbala. Molcho journeyed to Rome, lived in rags as a beggar, had several visions, and proclaimed that a great flood would strike the city and an earthquake, Portugal. These indeed came to pass, in 1530 and 1531, respectively. Molcho spoke publicly in synagogues and created his own flag, under which he and thousands of Jews marched, expecting redemption. Early in 1531, when the Inquisition insisted on laying its hands on him, the pope helped him escape from Rome. Hareubeni had been imprisoned for trying to convince the emperor to arm Jews; when Molcho was finally caught he could not claim the diplomatic immunity of Hareubeni. Molcho was condemned to burn at the stake. Afraid he would sway the crowds come to watch, the Inquisition led him to his death gagged. But at the last minute, a messenger arrived with a message from the emperor: if Molcho would return to the Church he would be spared. The gag was removed. Molcho replied that he had always desired to die a martyr's death.[30] His flag can still be viewed today, in the Jewish Museum of Prague.

Two Jewish leaders widely remembered today are Donna Gracia Nasi and her nephew and son-in-law, Don Joseph Nasi (Joseph the Prince). She was born in 1510 to a Marrano family. She and her husband ran banking and shipping companies; when he died, she took over. When her brother died, she took over his banking operations, too. She became one of the wealthiest people in Europe; her bribes to the pope delayed the introduction of the Inquisition into Portugal for some time. She herself had to flee several cities in order to remain alive. In 1553 she moved to Istanbul. There, her daughter married Don Joseph Nasi.

He was born in Spain after the expulsion of its Jews, also to a Marrano family. He fled ahead of the enmity of local rulers or the Inquisition; first to Portugal, then Antwerp, France, Venice, and, finally, Istanbul. There he was a sort of foreign minister, negotiating peace between the Ottomans and Poland and heavily involved in the wars with Venice and between the Netherlands and Spain. The Ottoman Sultan Selim appointed him Duke of Naxos.

In 1558, just under one thousand years after Benjamin of Tiberias and his Jewish forces lost the city, Donna Gracia leased Tiberias from the Sultan. In 1561, Don Joseph attempted to realize his dream of rebuilding his homeland: the sultan gave him permission to resettle Tiberias. Don Joseph rebuilt the city and its walls and spent a small fortune trying to turn it into a self-supporting town. Eventually another war intervened and plans for Jewish resettlement there had to be abandoned.

The next major attempt to restore the Jews to their homeland had an even more unfortunate conclusion. Shabtai Zvi proclaimed himself messiah in 1665. The entire Jewish world and much of the Christian followed his every step with great enthusiasm. Jews sold their homes and property in order to prepare for the journey to Eretz Israel. For reasons still unknown, during a conversation with the sultan the next year he converted to Islam. He is known as the mystical messiah, who thought to bring redemption not by means of arms but by use of the Kabbala. Because of the debacle resulting from this failure, the Lehi's Eldad believed that Shabtai Zvi made a contribution to actualizing Jewish sovereignty: the Jewish people learned that if they wanted to be redeemed, they would need to do more than pray and rely on Heaven. Stern's fellow-poet Uri Zvi Greenberg, another father of the underground, mentions Shabtai Zvi in several of his poems. In World War I, as a soldier, he even troubled himself to visit Shabtai Zvi's grave when it was within range and banged with his rifle butt on the tomb, calling a greeting to the would-be redeemer.[31] Greenberg and many of the fighters saw all those who dreamed and worked for redemption as kindred spirits. In an underground newspaper published in 1943, Lehi wrote, "Shabtai Zvi intended to realize the messianic longings of Israel. David Hareubeni planned to liberate Eretz Israel. Both were born of the deep, vital internal roots of the nation. Of course, their failure is no yardstick, just as the failure of the Polish rebellions of 1831 and 1863 are no yardsticks...."[32] (In the 1970s Eldad gave a course entitled "Zionism As a Messianic Movement That Is a Continuation of Previous Messianic Movements.")

Flags and Armies from the Galilee to Jerusalem, 1697-1938

Thirty years after Shabtai Zvi and exactly two hundred before Theodor Herzl, Jews from the Diaspora began returning to their land, to the Jewish communities of Hebron, Jerusalem, Safed, Tiberias, and other cities in which Jews had continued to live since biblical times. Rabbi Judah Hasid organized and led a march of fifteen hundred Jews to Eretz Israel in 1697. It took them three years and only one thousand survived the journey. Rabbi Judah Hasid himself died about a week after their arrival in Jerusalem; he was 41 years old. The freedom fighters did not see Theodor Herzl, whose 1896 book *The Jewish State* sparked modern political Zionism, and who created the Zionist movement by staging the First Zionist Congress in 1897, as a quirk in Jewish history. They saw him as another Hareubeni, another Molcho. They said so explicitly:

> Herzl spoke in the name of the Hebrew people, though in reality the people did not yet exist in terms of a body ready to act, rise, make aliya, conquer, and settle; in actuality there were only individuals....[Hareubeni's] "fib" about being a messenger from a Hebrew army is no more a "fib" than Herzl's saying he represented the Hebrew people. And Hareubeni undoubtedly saw the tribes of Hebrew fighters, which still existed in his time, and they gave him the idea. Potentially, a Jewish army could have been established in Europe; in reality things were different; in reality, David Hareubeni had only a handful of "pioneers," to use our word.[33]

Like Hareubeni and Molcho, Herzl had the gall to negotiate with a pope and with an emperor (in his case, the German Kaiser). The fighters saw themselves heir to this tradition. And, since many newcomers to Lehi were encountering for the first time the opposition of their families and the leaders of establishment Zionism, Lehi emphasized that Hareubeni, Molcho, and Herzl had met with opposition from the establishment Jews of their times: "Anyone who carefully reads the story of David Hareubeni and his diaries from Italy, Spain, and Portugal, will find in them much to compare with the tragic parts of Herzl's diary. The internal front each faced was much tougher than the external."[34]

Herzl's greatness was in overcoming or circumventing the opposition of assimilationist well-to-do Jews and turning the desire of the Jewish masses into a political movement. He turned the existing settlement movement and the "redemption" of parcels of land into tools harnessed to create a state. Like Molcho before him, he raised a flag and knew the Jewish people would follow him home to Zion. Once, he replied to a taunt that he would fail as Molcho had by noting that Molcho did not have trains.[35]

Herzl was the first in a line of modern heroes emulated by the underground fighters. They admired the scope of his vision and his political genius. Herzl died in 1904, at the age of 44, sure his vision would become reality. The next big step toward this vision was made by a group of Jews in Palestine during World War I, a time when the Ottoman Empire still ruled the country. These included Aharon Aaronsohn, an agronomist who had won worldwide fame when he discovered wild wheat, the prototype for cultivated wheat (he made the discovery in the north of Eretz Israel); Aharon's sister, Sarah, who had seen the Turkish massacre of the Armenian people as she traveled from Constantinople back to the Galilee; Absalom Feinberg, a poet engaged to the Aaronsohn sibling Rivka, and perhaps in love with Sarah; Joseph Lishansky, a champion horse rider and shootist respected by local Arabs as one of their own; and several others based around the Aaronsohn agricultural center in Zichron Yaacov. They combined to form a group they called NILI, which is the Hebrew acronym for "The Eternal One of Israel Will Not Lie" (meaning, Heaven will help free their land).

NILI became a spy network operating for the British behind Ottoman lines. They believed the Turks would just as soon kill the Jews as they had the Armenians, and that only a British victory would allow the Jews to attain independence in Eretz Israel. They risked their lives to gather data about Axis troop movements, which they sent to British headquarters in Egypt. Members of NILI were arrested and escaped from jail, were hunted by the Turks and by Jews afraid they were endangering the community, crossed the Sinai Desert by camel and foot to ensure the British would get their reports, swam to and from British boats idling miles offshore, and were eventually undone by a carrier pigeon that landed among the Turks with NILI's coded reports. Feinberg had already been killed in a skirmish with Beduin in Sinai. Sarah Aaronsohn committed suicide while being tortured by the Turks. Lishansky and Naaman Belkind were hanged. Aharon was out of the country when the ring was discovered. At war's end he headed to the Peace Conference to press his claims for Jewish statehood. His plane went down over the English Channel, for reasons unexplained.[36] According to the man in charge of Near East Intelligence in the British War Office during the war, General Edmund Allenby's successful conquest of Palestine was "largely owing" to NILI's work.[37]

Joseph Trumpeldor was another World War I figure who established a fighting unit to assist the British. He—with Jabotinsky, and as Aaronsohn—knew that if the Jews were to have a place at the peace negotiations after the war, they would need to earn it by their deeds during the war, the same as any of the Allies. He—as Jabotinsky and Aaronsohn—knew that an Allied victory was a necessary step in the direction of Jewish statehood. Trumpeldor was born in 1880. He was the only Jewish officer in the Russian army before the Russian Revolution. He lost an arm in the Russo-Japanese War, in the Battle of Port Arthur. He moved to Palestine and was among the many Jews deported to Egypt by the Turks during World War I. In Alexandria he met Jabotinsky and the pair agitated for the establishment of a Jewish Legion within the British army, dedicated to the liberation of Palestine. The British offered a corps to fight the Turks elsewhere; Jabotinsky went to London to continue pressing for a Legion, while Trumpeldor accepted the proposal.

Raphael Abulafia, who served in the corps (and, after he was wounded, in NILI), recalled that the Jewish troops who enlisted in Egypt "expected to leave for Gaza to take Eretz Israel from the Turks." As their boats readied to set sail, they and their families and the others who had come to see them off sang *Hatikva*. "But later we didn't see Gaza, only water and sky. So we expected to land at Tel Aviv. But we saw only water and sky. We hoped we were heading for Haifa. But—only water and sky. Finally we saw the Greek Isles and on April 25 landed with British forces from many other countries in Gallipoli."[38]

Trumpeldor led the seven hundred Jews who had volunteered. They fought at Gallipoli in 1915 as a transport unit known as the Zion Mule Corps. After the British defeat in Gallipoli, the unit was disbanded.

The British still refused to create the Legion Jabotinsky was lobbying for, so, following the Russian Revolution, Trumpeldor headed to Russia to see if he could talk the Russians into establishing a Legion. He knew the new liberal and socialist Russian government viewed Zionism favorably and hoped to win its permission to recruit Jewish volunteers to fight Turkey. After receiving encouragement from Deputy Minister of War Boris Savinkov, he submitted a detailed plan to the government to raise an army of one hundred thousand Jews.[39] Before anything could be done, the Bolsheviks overthrew the government.

At the same time, England had invaded Palestine and issued the Balfour Declaration supporting the right of the Jewish people to the country. Trumpeldor decided he no longer needed an army. Since, in any case, he could no longer expect the support of the Russian government, he instead promoted an "army" of one hundred thousand pioneers who would march from Russia to Eretz Israel to build the country. He spent a year and a half organizing tens of thousands of these pioneers, then returned to his home in Eretz Israel to get the country ready for their arrival.

By the time the chaos of the revolution had subsided and they could travel, the Russian government had decided they should not be allowed to do so and sealed the borders. Until then Trumpeldor had imagined massive marches and sailing; now only a trickle of pioneers managed to escape. Meanwhile, Eretz Israel had also devolved into chaos. The border areas were contested by the British and French, and local Arabs were pillaging and battling. Trumpeldor took command of a fort in the Galilee called Tel Hai and met his death there, shot in the stomach by Arabs.[40] His dying words, recorded by his doctor, were, "It does not matter, it is good to die for one's country."[41]

Trumpeldor's stoic death inspired the youth and he became a national hero. Trumpeldor's name was incorporated by Jabotinsky in the name of his youth movement, which he called Brit Trumpeldor (usually called by its Hebrew acronym, Betar). The Lehi underground, which was created two decades after Trumpeldor's death, and which included many members of Betar, both admired and differentiated itself from Trumpeldor. The Lehi fighters believed that goals and methods needed to change with the times, and Trumpeldor's image was too "defensive" for the underground. Nonetheless, they compared him to Stern: Both wanted to raise an army of tens of thousands in the Diaspora and bring it to Eretz Israel; Trumpeldor acted alone, with only Jabotinsky at his side, to establish the fighting legions, as Stern acted against the wishes of the establishment Zionists in order to create the underground; both Trumpeldor and Stern had the courage to stand alone, under-armed and outnumbered by the enemy; and both faced their end alone, at the head of a small group with no home front behind them.[42]

In London after Trumpeldor had left the Zion Mule Corps, Jabotinsky succeeded in organizing the Jewish Legion. He enlisted in it as a soldier and fought in the battle to liberate Palestine. Jabotinsky had hoped the Legion would become the nucleus of a Jewish army that would remain there after the war, but the British balked at this idea. After Trumpeldor's death in 1920, Jabotinsky recruited some Legion veterans and many Jerusalem youth and created a self-defense unit called the Hagana. He planned to protect Jerusalem's Jews from an attack similar to the one in the Galilee that killed his friend. This the Hagana did—six Jews were murdered in the Old City where the British forbade the Hagana to operate, but Jabotinsky's Jewish forces protected Jerusalem's newer neighborhoods. Jabotinsky was arrested for this, charged with possession of weapons and inciting segments of the population against each other, and sentenced to 15 years hard labor. On appeal the verdict was quashed and he and his 19 codefendants were exonerated.[43] By 1929, Jabotinsky had been barred by the British from entering Eretz Israel and the Hagana had atrophied. When Arabs attacked Jews, scores were killed throughout the country. The activist elements of the Hagana left and created the Irgun, making Jabotinsky its "supreme commander."

When Arabs began murdering Jews again in the mid-1930s, the Irgun commanders, Jabotinsky included, did not know how to respond. Some advocated reprisal attacks; others opposed this in principle or in practice. So, Jabotinsky, too, was both admired and yet left behind by the Sternists. In 1938, Irgunist Shlomo Ben-Yosef was hanged by the British for a reprisal attack on Arabs near Rosh Pina, and his name entered the pantheon of Jewish martyrs stretching back to Molcho and Rabbi Akiva.

Jabotinsky had chosen as a slogan for the Betar movement the name of Trumpeldor's fort, and Betar members greeted and parted from each other not with *shalom* (hello) but with "Tel Hai." After the British hanged Ben-Yosef in the Acco Fortress Prison and a would-be Jewish immigrant drowned near Gaza trying to get past British patrols, Uri Zvi Greenberg suggested adopting a new slogan, "Gaza-Acco," symbolizing a move from the defensive position implied by "Tel Hai" to a readiness to do whatever is necessary to free the homeland.

This was the history Stern knew and taught. One attempt after another through the centuries, the millennia, to liberate the homeland from foreign rule, whoever the foreigner: Romans, Persians, Byzantines, Christians, Moslems, Turks, British. Bar-Kochba passed the baton to myriads of dreamers, and the members of Lehi saw themselves as part of the chain, the only legitimate link left. In a 1943 memorial article, Lehi wrote, "Ben-Yosef! The Fighters for the Freedom of Israel do not hold ceremonies at your grave. This is not a time for the people of Israel to hold ceremonies. The Fighters for the Freedom of Israel are faithful to you, faithful to your path. Only we few."[44]

3

How is This Zionism Different from All Other Zionisms?

On the one hand, the Lehi fighters' belief that they were the few proponents of Jewish goals in Zion—and their self image as a select few—may seem absurd, given the existence of, in their own time, almost fifty years of Zionist congresses, the Jewish Agency for Palestine, the World Zionist Organization, the National Council of the Jews of Eretz Israel, Zionist youth movements stretching from Jabotinsky's Betar to the socialist Hashomer Hatzair, and hundreds of thousands, if not millions, of Jews who either lived in Eretz Israel or sought to move to there.

On the other hand, the fact cannot be denied that they were few. Only about one thousand of the hundreds of thousands of Jews in Eretz Israel joined Stern or Lehi, and another five thousand joined the Irgun, which during Stern's stint at the helm in the 1930s, and again in the late 1940s, propounded the same kind of Zionism as Lehi.

At the time there were (and today, there still are) several forms or schools of Zionism: Practical Zionism, which emphasized creating facts on the ground; Political Zionism, which belittled the value of such facts (farms and homesteads) and sought political recognition and broad political solutions; socialist-Zionism, which sought to create an egalitarian society run by a socialist party; and Revisionist Zionism, which hoped to revise the minimal Zionist goals of the 1920s and 1930s and return to Zionism's original goals, which it deemed a Jewish state on both sides of the Jordan

River, to which endangered Jews from Europe and elsewhere would be evacuated en masse.

Most Zionists were in one way or another either Practical or Political. The Irgun usually derided the former; Lehi derided both and preached revolution. Six thousand fighters out of a population of six hundred thousand—one percent of the Jews in Zion—were Revolutionary Zionists.

Practical Zionism emerged from the Hibat Zion (Love of Zion) movement of the late nineteenth century, which sought to afford Jews from Eretz Israel and from the Exile an opportunity to till and settle the land. The Lovers of Zion, as they were called, purchased land in faraway areas of the country, trained settlers to farm, and its members relocated to these new farmlands. Many died of hunger or malaria and no one, Lehi included, questioned their sacrifices and devotion. Some of the immigrant settlers emerged from the European Enlightenment and from a semi-socialist desire to make Jews "productive" members of society (i.e., farmers) as opposed to middleclass tradesmen. Because these goals could not be achieved in the lands of Exile, such enlightened socialists sought to return to Zion. This last fact allowed them to join Herzl's political movement, though in most respects they were far from his Political Zionism.

Before Herzl, as Lehi saw things, the Love of Zion had not been focused on a Jewish state. For its members and followers, settlement had become an end in itself. In the years that followed, as they were building towns and farms, they needed a legal framework in which to operate; they also needed to defend their settlements. They saw themselves as a vanguard reclaiming the land but statehood, an army, and other Zionist goals were an afterthought. Herzl refocused the movement on a political goal to be achieved by political means: a state to be won by grand diplomacy.[1]

Political Zionism, too, emerged from European culture, with its roots in the Emancipation of the Jews from the ghettos. The Emancipation had failed; the Jews remained either discriminated against or in danger. Famously, Herzl became a "Zionist" when he witnessed crowds of "enlightened" French citizens calling for death to all Jews when a French Jewish soldier, Alfred Dreyfus, was falsely accused of treason. Political Zionists did not demand that one particular nation recognize the rights of its Jews but that, internationally, the rights of the Jewish nation be recognized. This essentially meant that the right of the Jewish people to a state in its homeland be recognized. While the tools of the Practical Zionists were agricultural, those of the Political Zionists were legal and diplomatic, and they included Zionist congresses, rallies, and petitions to foreign governments.[2]

Implied by the tools adopted by Political Zionism was faith in the world's conscience. The Lehi fighters were critical of the hopes pinned by Political Zionists on international conferences held to consider the plight of the Jews and find solutions for Jewish refugees. At a Betar conference in Warsaw in 1938, Menachem Begin spoke about taking up arms to liberate the homeland and was chastised by Jabotinsky, who compared him to a squeaky door serving no purpose. Future Lehi leader Eldad spoke shortly afterward and reminded Jabotinsky that sometimes a squeaky door alerts one to the presence of thieves. Jabotinsky told Begin that if he did not believe in the world's conscience he had no option but to drown himself in a local river. Begin and Eldad did not have any faith in the world's conscience; the British appeasement of Germany, the world's acquiescence to the dismemberment of Czechoslovakia, and the shipping of Jewish refugees back into the Holocaust would soon prove them right, but they had no wish to drown themselves. Instead they chose Revolutionary Zionism.

Revolutionary Zionism differs from Practical and Political Zionism in its ends as well as its means. Both Practical and Political Zionism had within them different ideas about their end goals. In addition to farmers and socialists, Practical Zionism also included "Cultural Zionists." They were led by Usher Ginzburg (known by his pen name, Ahad Haam), who thought it obvious that even were a Jewish state to be established, Eretz Israel could never absorb a million refugees in a short period. Thus, he reasoned, pursuing mass emigration from the Diaspora was pointless just as was pursuing a Jewish state. He felt that an elite should move to Eretz Israel, there to develop the cultural aspects of Judaism, so that when a Jewish state would be formed in the distant future, it would have a truly "Jewish" character.

Within Political Zionism, some based their commitment to a Jewish state on the catastrophe awaiting the Jews of the Diaspora. Anti-Semitism was the major factor in the thinking of these Zionists. Max Nordau was Herzl's deputy in the days of the First Zionist Congress. In 1920 he called for evacuating half a million Jews to Eretz Israel; he was ignored by the Practical Zionists who had taken over the movement after Herzl's death. Nordau was not the only one concerned about a catastrophe on the immediate horizon; for many Zionists, Zionism existed solely to provide a "safe haven" for persecuted Jews. The French public's behavior toward Dreyfus proved to Herzl that even in a civilized country such as France, anti-Semitism can still sway the masses. Jabotinsky played on this theme when he wrote of different kinds of anti-Semitism ("of people" and "of things"), one of which would destroy Polish Jewry. Throughout the 1920s and 1930s the *New York Times* was full of reports of pogroms, economic persecution and hardship, hunger, and other plights affecting millions of Jews. In Russia and the East, the Jews had suffered from pogroms and social discrimination for generations. Some Jews responded by fighting for their rights in these countries. Other Jews believed that if socialism would triumph, the workers' governments would no longer persecute Jews. Zionists believed the solution to the Jewish problem was to leave the countries in which Jews were a minority and establish a Jewish state.

Revolutionary Zionism rejected all these goals. Its proponents did not want to be on the international agenda as a refugee problem; they wanted to be a player in the international arena.[3] To ask others for recognition meant to consider the Jews objects, not subjects. The Revolutionary Zionists did not focus on the Jews as objects of anything, including persecution. Lehi had not come, the fighters wrote, for individual Jews, but for the Jewish people as a unit, a political subject. They cared not whether a Jew escaped from one country in the Diaspora to another; to them this would be a temporary haven, because the fate of Jews in any Diaspora is sealed in advance. In the 1940s, Lehi claimed to speak not for victims of European or German persecution but in the name of all the victims of all the Exiles as well as those Jews who would be persecuted in Eretz Israel, too, in the future, if they did not succeed in establishing the Hebrew kingdom they sought.[4]

They did not see the Jewish people as an object with a problem but a subject with desires. They described what they wanted as redemption.[5]

In one newspaper article, they wrote that Zionists until then regarded "redeeming the land" as an economic project with a philanthropic aim (to provide land for Jews in trouble). But, they said, no other nation purchased its own land in order to solve a social problem.[6] They asked, "What are the Poles, the French, and the Greeks fighting for? To solve a Polish, French, or Greek problem?...Can one imagine a French person convincing someone that he is fighting for a free France because he has no other place to live?"[7] For the Sternists, the homeland was not a solution to the Jewish problem. It was not a safe haven or an "orphanage," not even a place to be settled or defended; it was the object of national desire, and its purpose was to be liberated. After that, an ingathering of the Exiles would be possible and then it would be settled.[8]

The Lehi leaders explained that a belief that Zionist goals would be achieved by settling the land acre by acre and seeking international recognition was a "foolish superstition."[9] A belief that petitions or protests would bring results or that anti-Semites would be moved by cogent arguments was a "fantasy."[10] They rejected these tenets of establishment Zionism as unrealistic, just as they rejected the socialist-Zionists' claim that making Jews "productive" would lead to redemption; instead, they argued, redemption would lead to the Jews becoming as productive as necessary.[11] They mocked the claim of the Practical Zionists that each new settlement or factory was a step toward sovereignty; new settlements and factories found favor in Lehi's eyes only because they could be used as springboards for liberating more territory. Nonetheless, Lehi warned that this benefit came at a great cost: it blinded Jews to the fact that their enemies were growing stronger while they were engaged in building an individual settlement or factory. Political Zionists thought that they could turn to the world to prevent the enemy from attacking. Lehi believed that the world had no conscience, and the duty of Zionism was not to pressure others but to act on one's own behalf; and Jewish arms were not for defending Jews but for crushing an enemy.[12]

For Lehi, sovereignty was not a solution but a goal, an expression of Jewish culture, as any nation-state is the expression of a people's culture.[13] The few hundred Lehi fighters of 1943 declared themselves determined to fight a war to liberate the homeland from the foreigner; it mattered not to them whether this foreigner was Turk, as it had been, British as it was then, or someone else in the future. They wished to "establish the Hebrew kingdom based on our historical rights, on our national desire as expressed in all the messianic longings and attempts."[14] "We have within us Shlomo Molcho, Joseph Nasi, and Mordecai M. Noah, but our stock is that of David Hareubeni," they wrote.[15]

This obviously incomplete gene pool includes one man who united Jews under his flag (Molcho), two diplomats (Nasi and Noah, an American consul and journalist who tried to establish a Jewish state on Grand Island in New York in 1825), and primarily Hareubeni, who operated during an age of persecution but who hailed from lands not feeling the whip, and whose goal was not to save unfortunate Jews but to exploit international politics to liberate the homeland by force. The Sternists were not Zionists because they were fleeing something, they were running toward their goal; they were not moved by fear but by love.

For them, then, Zionism was not to be justified by the Holocaust. That they, and the Irgun and Hagana, fought to create a Jewish state in the 1940s during and after the Holocaust is a coincidence made lamentable by two facts: First, one of their goals, the creation of a Jewish state, was realized too late to save the Jews of Europe; secondly, the Jews of Europe were trapped and unable to participate in the war of liberation, then murdered and unable to assist the Jewish state in the making. Had they been able to participate, the Jews of Eretz Israel would have had a much greater numerical and qualitative advantage over their enemies. The small size of the state in 1948 directly reflects the missing millions of brothers and sisters, hundreds of thousands of whom would have come to Eretz Israel;[16] many of these wanted to join the underground, many others would have served in the army, built factories and towns, and contributed their material and spiritual talents to the efforts to create and later preserve the state.

That the war to liberate the homeland had nothing to do with the Holocaust was stated by Lehi; the evidence for this claim is found in the dates. "Practical Zionism" (it was not yet called "Zionism") began as mass immigration long before German anti-Semitism became dangerous. Rabbi Judah Hasid sought to hasten redemption by bringing more than a thousand Jews to Eretz Israel in 1700. Three hundred students and followers of the Baal Shem Tov, the founder of modern Hasidism, moved to Safed in 1777, some of them later moving to Tiberias. Five hundred students of Rabbi Elijah of Vilna (known as "the Vilna Gaon") made aliya in 1809; they moved first to Tiberias, then to Safed. By the time this wave of immigration had ended, over five thousand Jews from Eastern Europe and North Africa had come.[17] Throughout the nineteenth and early twentieth centuries, Jews continued to return to the homeland.

"Political Zionism" also began long before the Holocaust (though it, too, had yet to be called "Zionism"). The Sternists generally looked to NILI as their first modern predecessor. NILI sprang from the mountains and shores of Eretz Israel and its political and military actions were based on local geopolitical considerations. NILI's Sarah Aaronsohn had been born in the country, in Zichron Yaacov; and Feinberg and Belkind also, in Gadera. Aharon Aaronsohn and Joseph Lishansky had been brought to the country as six year olds.[18] Their goal was not to save refugees but to liberate the homeland, during World War I or immediately thereafter. At the same time, Trumpeldor tried to form an army of one hundred thousand Jews to take the country. The soldiers of the Jewish Legion crossed the Jordan River in British uniform with the same intent, and intended to remain here as a Jewish army afterward. The Hagana was formed in 1920; the Irgun, in 1931. The justification for Zionism was the desire of the Jewish people to be free in its native land, not the Holocaust.

The League of Birionim, the First Freedom Fighters

The flag bearers, soldiers, diplomats, natives, immigrants, and finally NILI were the forerunners of the Lehi underground, but the 1930s saw Lehi's actual conception. Three men who later cooperated with Stern and often wrote for Lehi publications were Abba Ahimeir, Joshua Yevin and Uri Zvi Greenberg. They formed a "maximalist" group within Jabotinsky's movement in Eretz Israel. Their political platform was the most extreme and their means were the most activist in an extreme, activist movement. When it came time to name the group, the name selected by its members was League of Revolutionary Zionists. Greenberg, who by virtue of his fame as a poet, his inspiring verses, and his near-prophetic gift was regarded by all with a bit of awe, ordered a name change to Brit Habirionim, the League of Birionim. *Birionim* is Hebrew for thugs or bullies, but the name meant more than proudly asserting their toughness; it was the name of one of the freedom-fighting organizations in the Great Revolt against Rome in the year 70. Greenberg wanted to be sure the youth would see itself as a link in a chain going back at least that far, and wanted to make clear their goal: a revolt against the foreign occupier of their homeland.

These new Birionim engaged in what one member, Haim Dviri, called "learning the alphabet of revolution,"[19] as any people about to declare a revolution must learn for itself how to do so. They taught their members about the revolutions of the Young Turks and the Irish but, in Ahimeir's words, the jails of Eretz Israel became their real schools.

Their operations were much condemned by the establishment, though in hindsight they appear rather tame. In 1930, Moshe Segal blew the shofar at the Western Wall in defiance of British regulations limiting the Jews' right to pray there. A week later they rallied in Tel Aviv against the British deputy colonial minister, Drummond Schiels; when attacked by the Tel Aviv police they refused to disperse and ended up where they wanted to be— in jail, the first Jews to go to prison as Zionists in Eretz Israel in the struggle for a state. In 1933 they set fire to the gate of the German consulate in Jerusalem and tore down the Nazi flags from German consulates in Jerusalem and Jaffa (this did not stop the establishment from trying to paint them as friends of the Nazis and Fascists abroad). At about the same time, they succeeded in propagandizing against a British census of the population in Palestine that was intended to set the stage for an administrative government to British liking, and they thwarted census takers' movements, to the point that the census was deemed useless for British purposes. In essence they engaged in civil disobedience, which was the first step in the movement for liberation, and their willingness to go to jail lit the way for those who took the next steps. One of Stern's poems from that period begins, "Do you know where the messiah will be born? In a prison...on the floor."[20]

The terms that appeared in Stern's own writings or those of the Lehi underground after his murder were not coined by Lehi. Terms like *Malkhut Israel* (the Kingdom of Israel; meaning, sovereignty), "foreign occupier," and "Revolutionary Zionism" make their first appearance in the writings of Ahimeir, Yevin, and Greenberg, as do a readiness to sit in prison and ascend a gallows.

In 1928 Ahimeir wrote:

> The politics of the Exile is a politics of lobbying in order to attain, at the most, rights, which are accepted as gifts. But politics that is statecraft and that knows how to create does not accept, it takes. It gives when it wishes to give, but takes when it has the strength to do so. We need to develop in the youth a "will to power," to use Nietzsche's phrase.
>
> These things are understood by us, the citizens of this land, more than they are understood by you, who are geographically distant....An army is prepared during peacetime. The outbreak of a war is not the time to begin to prepare an army. Decades before their lands were liberated, the Czechs, Poles, and Italians worked on the concept of legions....When another international crisis occurs, the legions of our "national guard" will appear naturally.[21]

In 1930, at the time of his rally in Tel Aviv, for which he, Moshe Segal and three others were sent to jail, Ahimeir wrote:

> [T]he road to Zion, to the Kingdom of Israel, is not paved with roses. The public that wants, truly and completely, to redeem itself, must pay dearly for its redemption. No people received its state as a gift....
>
> In a liberation movement the majority is not decisive, the herd is not decisive, only the minority is decisive, the activists, the youth....[22]

In a similar vein, he wrote in 1932:

> The Zionist youth was not taught that sacrifices

would be necessary, therefore the creators of Revolutionary Zionism were so few. Therefore the voices of Trumpeldor, Aharon and Sarah Aaronsohn, and Jabotinsky were lone voices calling in a desert. Few followed them....

Let Revolutionary Zionism come...the road to the Kingdom of Israel passes through torture and persecution....Our youth will find the content of its life in Zionism. Let the lives and deaths of the heroic Joseph Trumpeldor, Aharon and Sarah Aaronsohn be our symbols. They are the innovators of Zionism....[23]

Joshua Yevin recalled in the 1960s that Ahimeir's operations were characterized by a commitment to nonviolence and by his personal participation. They were the first notice given the British regime and the local Jewish community that the relationship between the two was not a romance. In 1932, Yevin wrote a book about local politics. Tellingly, he named a character who was based on Ahimeir, Kochba. Yevin ensured that his readers would see Ahimeir and his followers as modern incarnations of the second-century rebel against the foreign Roman occupation of their homeland. One passage opens with a poetic description of

that first Eretz-Israeli rainfall coming at the end of the month of Tishrei or the beginning of Heshvan, from an almost clear sky, lasting only a few minutes, and then the sky is clear again, for another month or two; this first rain that comes after seven dry months, this rain that barely wets the ground, just washes the dust off the trees and deposits drops trembling like tears on the leaves— yet it would seem that in this rain were contained all the desires, all the soul's yearning, all the sadness in the world, and after it falls, the entire world is satiated....[24]

Given that Yevin's text moves from the rain to an organizational meeting and lecture by Kochba, the intended metaphor is as clear as the sky of which Yevin writes. Yevin goes on to describe the Birionim movement:

News reports come from everywhere, from Eretz Israel and abroad, that a new camp is being called together and rising, that youth are gathering in masses under the new flag being raised, preparing themselves for the day to come, when they will ascend the mountains of Judah and Gilead to plant there the Jewish flag....

Kochba tells the small group gathered in the cabin, the kernel of the new Brit Habirionim:

"We have lost almost all. But we begin with a and b, just as David Hareubeni began, just as Herzl began. For redemption will come...."[25]

Elsewhere, Yevin wrote of the third man in the Birionim leadership, Greenberg. In the late 1930s, he published an analysis of Greenberg's poetry entitled "The Lawgiving Poet." Yevin writes,

> The pairing of messianism with cement and iron is the basis of our liberation movement....Cement and iron without messianism means giving up on the idea, giving up on the political conditions, and instead building for the sake of building, without giving thought to whether it helps the people of Israel or simply prepares booty for England or Abdullah. Cement and iron without messianism would be capable of giving up Jerusalem, and bargaining over pieces of Eretz Israel....
>
> [But Greenberg] maintains the optimism of the Vision....Not that sort of optimism that bends and always surrenders while lying to itself that surrender is a victory....but the optimistic faith in a revolution to be generated....He never prophecies that liberation will come of its own, but that the liberator will come.[26]

Greenberg's poems, according to Israel Eldad, helped create the underground.[27] They brought young men and women into the struggle, inspired them to risk all they had, and instructed them in the course the struggle was to take.

Greenberg was a well-known Yiddish expressionist poet in Europe before he moved to Eretz Israel. There, in the 1920s, he sang the praises of the pioneers who drained swamps and built cities, who left "Londons, Parises, New Yorks! Hey, good, we left Europe and all the grandeur" in order to join "the cult of the feverish barefoot, whispering its love to the dunes and rocks of Canaan."[28] He gloried in the privations they endured on behalf of the homeland being reborn under their feet:

> Tell, bones, of fever-filled nights
> There is a hunger that knows how to shine, Yes! It
> shines on and on—Sing of it!

I say to you—Behold the very soil of the Land of Israel!
　　Poets say it is sweet even to lick these clumps of earth;
Stand, young man, I say, stand even when the sand
　　dunes and vast plazas of blazing rocks seem devoid
　　of any growth.
Thus the camel, most brilliant beast of our land, stands:
　　stands and stares.
Stare at the heavens, you, too, and declare: How
　　wonderful!
Are there in other lands skies such as these?
And the end of this wonder: like the camel, hold your
　　head high.

Sing, stomach, of hunger in the prophets' land; in the
　　wadi there is no water. Eucalyptus trees have seized
　　the ravines.
And branches do not bear pastries.
The scarlet evening is like the slice after a decapitation;
　　there is the same scent, too...
And the evening, like the camel, falls with appalling
　　thirst and seeps with its deadly desires into our blood.
Tables are set in festive white, across the world
And young men are invited to feast, across the world
By the light of chandeliers,
Far across the world.
Take comfort, stomach, a eucalyptus tree in the Land of
　　Israel is dearer than any forest of honey in Europe
And dearer than all their storerooms of fresh fruit
Here is the classic state in which fever becomes Glory,
　　tuberculosis—a Vision.
And therefore, yes! Therefore it was here that young
　　men and women planted these eucalypti; trees that
　　lust—lust for swamps.
Stomach, would you think it good if pastries grew on
　　trees and milk flowed from stones like a spring?
Shhh, stomach, peace and quiet, my dear one. Now I will
　　leave for the city, walking by the curbs of these
　　Hebrew streets,
Collecting cigarette butts and raising a sort of incense—
Tonight, by the light of the moon, I have already become
　　a tailor (Ah, I've mended my tattered clothes, out of

respect for the light of dawn
So that people should not suffer the sight of my skin...)
And if I find no cigarette butts in my Hebrew city, I will
  keep walking, as if I were road planner
For a government existing only in dreams
Whose bills have yet to be printed.

My thoughts have no choice, but must reveal
  themselves—for my flesh has shriveled and between
  my bones and me there's barely a layer of silk—
A layer that is nonetheless lit by the light of that hunger
  that shines and shines and shines
And my long fingers shine even they, and there is no
  lust, not in the blood nor the brain
Only in the shrinking stomach: for bread, for soup.
(The pain weakens after many days, a most mysterious
  kind of needle.)
I feel the shining brightness tearing through my 30 years
As if from my body rather than the sun light filters to
  the dunes
(Dunes among which this body will one day find its rest).

Tables are set in festive white, across the world
And young men are invited to feast, across the world
By the light of chandeliers,
Far across the world...

I just—don't—care, Mother!
I just—don't—care, Father!
Even if I am becoming like the dry ravines, even if this
  be my last day.
I stand now, in the sunshine, already strangely beyond
  the thinness of my skin, and the first signs of
  morning
Penetrate my every phrase.

And there are those signs in my ribs,
And there are those signs in my sunken cheeks, the
  measure, I know, of the storm.

Sing, stomach, of how we shrivel. Sing!![29]

In this poem, "Hunger in the Land of Israel," Greenberg recalls a midrash that predicts that when the messiah comes, the trees in Eretz Israel will bear ready-made cakes. He seems to prefer that the Jews earn their baked goods through the work of their own hands, though this preference may be a case of a wistful adjustment to reality. Similarly, Greenberg's glorification of the pioneer's spirit is not simple or superficial, it is spiced with melancholy and an awareness of the different layers in the feelings of the pioneers: their pride in their hunger along with their longing for those tables "set in festive white" in other lands.

Yet this longing was not naive. Greenberg knew what awaited those tables in the lands of the Exile. In 1923 he wrote, "But I will prophesy— the black prophecy: \ .... \ And you will not be able to see the horror in corpses. \ ...When the poison gas penetrates the shrines...." He said one Jew in ten would survive, and people would remember that once, Jews lived in Europe.[30] In 1925 he published, "We had to leave. The ground screamed under our feet, the beds shook \ .... \ We had to leave the towns sadly and look back through burning tears, one last time, at the homes— \ Knowing, they would one day burn."[31]

Greenberg parted ways with the pioneers and the Labor movement when he saw the pogroms and dangers facing the Diaspora reappearing in Palestine, and the leadership in the homeland adopting the attitude of the Jews in Exile: asking the non-Jewish government to protect them and preferring to die rather than take action. He saw the pogrom of 1929 coming and afterward castigated the establishment Jews for eating their dinners and continuing with their paperwork while the ancient Jewish community of Hebron was wiped out, and Jews were dismembered in Safed.[32] He described their deaths in his poems, as in the 1940s he would detail the deaths inflicted on Europe's Jews even before he had heard the details. Now he seemed angrier at the establishment Jews who had mocked his warnings and chosen to do nothing than he was at the Arabs who had done the murdering. Stern and his followers understood Greenberg's point, though as far as their own activities were concerned, they focused on the enemy and not on the establishment.

But Stern, and the young Irgunists and many in the Hagana, did follow Greenberg to his next conclusion. Abroad, Christians were or would be murdering Jews. In Eretz Israel, Moslems were and would be murdering Jews. The official Zionist leadership was acting exilic; the Zionist leaders were dependent on the goodwill of the foreign ruler and claimed to be proud of their refusal to counterattack. Greenberg predicted (correctly) more attacks on Jews throughout the 1930s and predicted the response of the Jewish youth. Perhaps this prediction was self-fulfilling, given that many such youth took the path Greenberg predicted because they were inspired by his poems. Greenberg wrote—in 1929—that "Bar-Kochba's way is true even though Betar fell" and proclaimed that "In our sheep's flesh the blood of the Sicarii has awoken."[33] In another poem, he wrote that he sees the young Jews of Eretz Israel "ascending the gallows, and the dawn of Jerusalem in the luster of their faces."[34]

The Songs of Abraham Stern

Stern did not care for Greenberg's poetic style—long lines with few rhymes—but he was obviously influenced by Greenberg's poems and their content, as he had been influenced by Ahimeir, Yevin, and the Birionim's activities. He put a line from a Greenberg poem at the top of one of his own poems: Greenberg had written, "A Jewish soldier prays with his rifle." But Stern went a step further; in his poem Stern writes, "We'll pray with a rifle, a machine gun, a land mine."[35]

Stern called this poem "To the Gangs of Crazies," referring to the pejoratives cast at him and at his soldiers by the British and the establishment Zionists. In this poem he embraces the epithets and writes, "We are possessed with a craziness for the Kingdom, we fighters for freedom in the homeland...." He lists the curses hurled at him: "The rebel—is insane, and the avenger of Hebrew blood—is a criminal." "To battle, Zealots!" he calls, and echoes Greenberg's prediction: "Every neck—to the hangman."

Stern took the political terms first used by the Birionim and drew organizational conclusions. Greenberg's parched pioneers became Stern's stalwart soldiers:

> In the summer—our bones steam in the heat.
> In the winter—our blood freezes in the cold.
> Always, every step and inch of our beat
> Dark danger's wings enfold.
>
> In a basement's stifling heat
> Tongues cleave to palates and shirts cling to skin.
> A palm and a gun handle meet,
> Freeze together, and lips grin.
>
> Or, in a dirty alley, with rain pouring,
> So cold our swollen hands ache,

> While musty Mazkeret Moshe is snoring,
> At midnight we'll be outside, awake....[36]

Stern goes on to promise that he and his unit are willing to sleep on a filthy floor, subsist on olives and dry bread, continue to guard, and if necessary die for their brothers. In this untitled poem, written in 1934, Stern expresses his love for his brothers—though not without an ironical jab at the residents of the Jerusalem neighborhood, Mazkeret Moshe, who sleep while he and his friends endure hardships to protect them—but more than that, he expresses his love for danger and his awareness of death.

Most of Stern's poems were written in the early 1930s. Many were written during his studies in Florence. His march-like anthem, "Anonymous Soldiers," describing life underground fighting the British Empire in order to establish a Jewish state, was written in 1932, eight years before Stern founded his underground, when even the Irgun, which he joined before founding Lehi, was far from an urban underground. Like Greenberg, Stern's poems commanded and created more than they described.

Verses like "We live underground!" gathered to Stern those who were prepared to live underground. His poems to Jewish mothers gave teenagers the means to keep going despite the pain their absences from home and the risks they took with their lives caused their parents. He encouraged the young women who would join him,

> You are mothers of life, mothers of death
> You love and you hate, too.
> In days of battle and nights of stealth
> Our danger is shared with you.
> You are Judith, Yael and Sarah....[37]

He encouraged them, as he encouraged those who would sit in prison:

> My brother, do you know where the messiah will be
>   born?
> In a prison will he be born, on the floor,
> On which a whore has thrown up and a thief responded
>   to nature's call
> And a bandit and an aged murderer, who raped his little
>   girl.
> He'll be greeted by the warm knees of the Diaspora
> His mother, who was raped by the Arabs from Hebron,
>   drunk with

Blood and murder
(seed of horses is their seed and flesh of mules their
    flesh).
And she will nurse her pale child on milk bitter as
    wormwood.

Between four damp walls, on a floor of moist filth
In a cell whose window has witnessed the passage of gray
    days,
Burdensome and worry-laden.
Before him a network of iron, on which has been latticed
    tens of
Times the shining skies of the homeland—the fine, the
    soft, the pure.
And beyond this—caravans, caravans of gray days,
Burdensome and submissively bent.

He does not know the meaning of time, hours and
    minutes,
Like the pendulum of a clock the guard walks the halls
Back and forth, back and forth, back and forth.
And the messiah knows, for this will be the hour of
    Redemption
When the echoing steps of the guard will cease and be
    heard no more.

The shadows, which crawl the walls as an assembly of
    spiders
Mournful, who have woven there a web of despair to
    hunt
The golden bee, the Hope, that brings
The honey of comfort to the beehive heart of the
    messiah.

The orphaned silence trembles in a corner and cries
But suddenly—a ray of light, a silver sword slices the
    window's bars
And banishes the spidery shadows to a corner, ashen and
    outcast.
And the messiah knows, for the path to Redemption is
    the sword.

> Or, in the morning the light of dawn drips into the cellar
>   and fills
> The floor with a pool of red blood.
> And the messiah knows, for two paths are there to
>   Redemption:
> Blood and sword.[38]

As his poems and writings made clear, Stern's goal was nothing less than redemption. Thus it was fitting that his poems included discussions of the messiah. As Greenberg focused his writings not on the role of heavenly intervention but on the role of the liberator himself, Stern concluded the messiah would be born in a prison. This is both metaphor and consolation: A metaphor to help those readers asking whether the road to something as good and pure as redemption leads through the heretofore disdained and feared prisons; and a consolation for those readers sitting in prison, or soon to enter them, where they would spend years in subhuman conditions. Stern wanted them to know they were each fulfilling a messianic role.

Stern's poems spelled out the means to redemption: guns, landmines, loneliness, danger, and death. In 1934 he wrote that underground, in a solitary confinement cell, or at the front,

> I pledge allegiance
> To homeland, people and liberty.
> I'll sacrifice my conscience
> And life; obey, fight and die.[39]

Stern's poems spelled out the end, too: the nature of the redemption that was being sought. He asked God, "Master of Jerusalem and Zion," to place "the royal crown on the head of the doleful city."[40] He predicted a day when, the struggle successfully resolved,

> The heavens above like God's hand
> Will rest on our heads.
> And we'll kiss our country's sand
> And weep with joy like children.[41]

He described this day:

> Be happy and sing, Zion,

Sing. Despair has ceased and sadness fled.

The nightingale sings, the pomegranate blossoms,
The fields are plowed throughout Zion.

From east and west, from south and north
Those redeemed by God return to Zion.

And God will turn their mourning to joy,
Slaves abroad—masters in Zion.

The women and children will dance for joy,
Lebanon and Mount Hermon will dance like little lambs.

From Tel Hai in the Galilee to Ein Hai in the Sharon
From Yarkon River's ripples, from the Sinai to Hermon,

From the Nile to the Euphrates and the Mediterranean,
The trumpet will be heard, the victory call;

Be happy and sing, Zion,
Your children are joyously returning.

And the Galilee will celebrate, the Sharon be full of glee
Judah shine with gladness, and the Negev sing.

Be happy and sing, Zion.[42]

As noted above, most of Stern's "Zionist" or revolutionary poems were written as a university student in the early 1930s. But he continued polishing them over the next ten years, and most of his poems survive in many drafts. Often he marked lines with the number of syllables, and many of his poems have a standard ABAB rhyme scheme. His chosen academic field was Latin and Greek literature, and he preferred a classic style of poetry to Greenberg's long expressionist sentences bursting with enthusiasm and unpoetic words, just as he preferred to write prose in a succinct, clear style rather than in the emotional, mystic language that Eldad used in his 46-page commentary to Stern's own political platform, the "Principles of Rebirth."

Stern's "Principles of Rebirth"

The "Principles of Rebirth" were written for the second issue of the Lehi underground newspaper in late 1940. Stern had already created the underground and needed to define its goals for people who considered joining. He also needed to clarify its goals for those who had joined but who were not yet knowledgeable about the details. The platform of the Fighters for the Freedom of Israel had to be clear enough for those outside the movement to understand and powerful enough for those inside to commit themselves to. They had to obligate the fighters of that specific year and yet be true for generations. Thus the language is different from Stern's poetry.

The principles became Lehi's platform and as far as the Sternists were concerned, the platform for all future Zionists. Distinct from Practical and Political Zionism, these are the principles of Revolutionary Zionism. The 18 theses Stern posted onto the gates of Zionist thought and action in 1940 were:

> 1. THE NATION—The nation of Israel is the chosen nation; creator of monotheism; legislator of the prophetic morality; bearer of age-old civilization; great in tradition and in dedication; in the will to live and the ability to endure suffering; in the light of its spirit and in its certitude of redemption.
>
> 2. THE HOMELAND—The homeland is Eretz Israel in its biblical boundaries ("To your seed have I given this land from the River of Egypt to the great river, the River Euphrates," Genesis 15:18), it is the land of life in which the entire Hebrew nation will live securely.
>
> 3. THE NATION AND THE HOMELAND—Israel conquered Eretz Israel by the sword. In it, Israel became a nation and only in it will Israel be reborn. Therefore Israel and only Israel has right of ownership to Eretz Israel. This right is absolute: it has not been and can never be abrogated.
>
> 4. DESTINY—(1) Redemption of the land (2) Establishment of sovereignty (3) Revival of the nation. Sovereignty cannot be established without the redemption of the land, and the nation cannot be revived without sovereignty being established.

And these are the roles of the organization regarding war and conquest:

> 5. EDUCATION—Educating the nation to love liberty and develop a zealous loyalty to its eternal heritage. Inculcat-

ing the idea that the fate of the nation is in its own hands. Renewing the understanding that the "book and sword descended together from heaven" (Midrash Vayikra Raba 35:8).

6. UNITY—Uniting the entire nation around the flag of the Hebrew liberation movement. Using the genius, status, and strengths of individuals for channeling the energy, dedication, and revolutionary fervor of the masses into the war of liberation.

7. ALLIANCES—Forming alliances with all those interested in the organization's war who are prepared to offer direct assistance.

8. STRENGTH—Glorifying and forging the power of the fighter in the homeland and in the Diaspora, in the underground and in army barracks, into a Hebrew army of redemption with its own flag, arms, and commanders.

9. WAR—Never-ending war against anyone standing in the way of realizing our destiny.

10. CONQUEST—Conquering the homeland by force from the foreigners, to be our land forever.

And these are the roles of the movement regarding mastery and redemption:

11. MASTERY—Renewing Hebrew mastery over the redeemed land.

12. A JUST RULE—Establishing a social polity based on Israel's morality and prophetic justice. Within it, no one will be hungry or unemployed. Within it, all members of the nation will, as such, live lives of harmony, respect, and brotherhood, a light and example to the Gentiles.

13. REVIVING THE WILDERNESS—Rebuilding the ruins and reviving the wastelands for immigrants who will come by the millions and be fruitful and multiply.

14. FOREIGNERS—Solving the problem of foreigners through population exchanges.

15. INGATHERING OF THE EXILES—A complete ingathering of the Exiles in the Kingdom of Israel.

16. RULE—Bolstering the Hebrew nation and turning it into the top military, political, cultural, and economic factor in the East and along the Mediterranean coast.

17. REBIRTH—Reviving the Hebrew language among the

entire nation, renewing the historical and spiritual independence of Israel. Refining the national character in
the process of rebirth.
18. THE TEMPLE—Building the Third Temple as a symbol
of the time of complete redemption.[43]

Stern's readers' reactions to the principles were not uniform. Three
months after their publication, the fourth issue of the underground paper
included the text of a speech; if the speech was delivered before an audience and transcribed, or prepared specifically for the paper in the form of
a lecture, is unclear. The introduction claims it was commissioned by the
organization's command, and in any case, Stern was involved in editing the
paper, so the speech was either prepared or approved by him. Its stated
purpose was to disperse the strategic and ideological fog among many Irgun
and Sternist fighters and provide a conceptual base for an independent
underground. To this end it references the principles. Toward the end of the
speech, the "speaker" says they were written to ensure no external political entity would be able to curb or direct the underground's actions, and
to detail for the underground's members the goals for which the command
would be asking them to make great sacrifices. "Each and every one of us
must carefully review the principles and determine for himself once and
forever, and without any doubts, if these principles are 100 percent the same
as those for which he is willing to fight. He who cannot do so, should leave
now. But those who stay must know that these principles are set and nothing can change them."[44]

Apparently not all the readers could make that commitment. The next
month Stern introduced a "Letters to the Editor" column in the paper. Its
letter was published anonymously, given that this was an underground
paper, but today we know it was written by Eliahu Lankin, an Irgunist who
in 1948 commanded the *Altalena* arms ship.[45] Lankin argued that the
movement's goals until then had been limited to creating a Jewish state in
the entire homeland by force of arms. He felt that mention of the Jewish
people's "chosenness" was unnecessary, as was including among the aims
a just regime and a Third Temple. Regarding these points, Lankin argued
that: Any nation should fight for its independence; the type of government
and social order should be determined after independence, and until then
the single goal should be independence; and as a nonreligious Jew he felt
no sympathy for a temple.[46]

Stern wrote the editor's reply (also anonymously). He explained that
establishing a Jewish state by force was indeed the goal as it always had

been, but the organization was now independent of the Revisionist party and expected to become the liberation movement for all Israel. Its struggle would go on forever. "We want to plan the way to mastery and authority, to a life of liberty and honor, first for the freedom fighters and then for the entire nation." The underground sought to be a "chosen sect within a chosen people...a sect of people who seek freedom and fight for it, who seek the complete material and spiritual redemption of the entire nation." Stern added that the goals set in the "Principles of Rebirth" are not for the moment: "The great Hebrew nation needs to follow the path of mastery and power till the end of time." He ruled, "The conquest of the homeland and the establishment of sovereignty are the first stage."[47]

Stern then expounded on the principles questioned by Lankin. He agreed with Lankin that a nation's right to its land is not dependent on its chosenness. But, he wrote, the Hebrew people are the chosen people, and its detractors from without or even from within cannot change its glorious, heroic past, its success in Exile, and the divine Hebrew sparks that shine for the whole world.

Stern also acknowledged Lankin's point about the sole aim of Zionism as it was propounded by Betar and the Irgun. "But," he wrote, "we are not Political Zionism." If he and his movement were, he said, they would not have become an independent underground. They made the choice to be a "new movement, a Hebrew liberation movement," which wants to establish an Israel based on brotherhood and mutual respect, in which no one goes hungry or without employ. Stern stressed that such desires say nothing about the type of government or regime that should be formed.[48]

Finally, Stern took umbrage at Lankin's remark that Lankin was not religious and therefore had no sentimental feeling for a temple. Stern wrote, "The Temple is not specifically religious, and even someone not religiously observant can have positive feelings about the Temple, which has always been a symbol of Hebrew independence."[49] Stern noted that in the past, the Jews' wars and their struggles for freedom had centered on their religion. The Hasmoneans, Zealots, and Bar-Kochba all fought when foreigners desecrated the nation's sacred grounds. In Exile, the Jewish religion kept the nation alive and provided "citizenship" and a "constitution." The Jewish religion thus provided the ground for Zionism and the Hebrew liberation movement. The blood of the Maccabees flows in the veins of the modern fighters. Even nonobservant Jews should therefore respect the Jewish religion, Stern concluded.

As for the Temple, it symbolized the nation's spirit. When the Temple fell, the state fell. The state was reconstituted after the Hasmoneans cleansed the Temple. Later, the Second Temple fell, and destroyed with it were the Jewish state and homeland. "In the war of the Zealots," wrote Stern, "the Temple became a fortress and it remained the fortress of zealots throughout the ages." The entire nation prayed and continues to pray for its renewal. Thus they will indeed see in its renewal a symbol of the complete redemption.[50]

In 1983, Yitzhak Shamir, then Speaker of Israel's Knesset (parliament), was asked if he felt himself still committed to the "Principles of Rebirth." He replied, "They were not divinely revealed at Sinai. They had a general force."[51]

Eldad viewed them differently. For the rest of his life, Eldad attached near divine importance to each phrase of the principles.

In the 1940s, Eldad and Lehi co-leader Nathan Yalin-Mor breathed fire and life into the principles of Revolutionary Zionism in the pages of the Lehi newspapers and wall-posters, educating hundreds of fighters, inspiring thousands of supporters, and striking fear in the hearts of tens of thousands of enemy troops; and Shamir, Eldad, Yalin-Mor, and some 950 Fighters for the Freedom of Israel brought the phrases to life in deeds that shook the country and the world.

4

Principles in Practice:
Lehi's War

The morning Stern was shot to death, Israel Tevuah was meeting in Tel Aviv with some friends from Lehi. He described their reaction to the day's events:

> The British did not intend to kill Yair, the man. They wanted to kill "Yair" the thinker, the founder of the true liberation movement, who defined the British as a foreign force in Eretz Israel. The British believed that this murder would end the underground and the national aspirations of the nation of Israel.
>
> We heard the news about Yair's murder sitting with Nehemiah Torenberg in a café on King George Street in Tel Aviv. It is hard to describe our feelings. We held back to avoid crying...we sat in shock and shortly afterward parted, determined to prepare a plan of attack.[1]

In the first two months of 1942, the British decimated Stern's outfit. Most of the trained fighters and experienced commanders were arrested or shot. The British assault reached its denouement with Stern's elimination on February 12. After that, most of the Sternists who remained free were in disarray. Several more were arrested or turned themselves in. One or two tried to avenge Stern's death but failed. Tuvia Chenzion, a 21-year-

old truck driver doubling as a Sternist radio announcer, rejected this ad-
hoc approach to revenge, telling his associates that "Our mission is to wage
a war of liberation. Achieving our goal will be the best revenge." Afraid that
a British provocateur might have had a hand in the Sternists' recent set-
backs, Chenzion and some thirty people who trusted him broke off contact with the larger movement and regrouped in underground cells of no
more than three or four fighters each.[2] On February 17, the High Commissioner asked the British government to deport to Jamaica or Trinidad
80 detainees whom he assumed he could not convict in a court of law, but
whom he suspected of being involved with the Sternists. The government
turned him down, but in April the Acting High Commissioner made the
same proposal, again unsuccessfully, this time noting he had 150 people
he wanted to send to Jamaica.[3]

One Teenager at Large

With all those in charge of the movement now in jails or cemeteries,
the rank and file had no one to turn to, no address to approach with their
questions or their readiness to act. Joshua Cohen, 19 years old, kept the
movement alive.

Cohen was born in Tel Aviv, grew up in an agricultural environment
in Kfar Saba, joined the Nationalist Hagana when in high school, and by
the age of 15 was in the Irgun. In 1938 he participated in reprisal attacks
against Arabs. When the Irgun split, he went with Stern. He was on the
rooftop across the street from 8 Yael Street when Lehi's bombs went off.
His finger was poised to press a switch that would set off a third bomb,
down below, designed to eliminate more policemen. Cohen saw that inter-
spersed with the underground's archenemies below were several civilians
and chose to walk away, leaving the bomb undetonated and the policemen
whole.[4]

The teenager met Stern once, at a lecture. The Hagana had just stolen Lehi's arms cache in Kfar Saba and Lehi's young members there wanted
to be armed so they could teach the local Hagana members a lesson. Stern
said the time was not right to fight the Hagana. Cohen challenged him and
asked if he expected those present to tell their charges to remain passive;
Stern replied in his standard quiet voice that this is exactly what they
should say. Cohen thought to himself that this is a man who knows what
he wants and is not afraid to say so, and Cohen was ready to follow him
anywhere.[5] After his speech, Stern asked each person present if he had a
place to sleep. Cohen replied that he did. After the crowd dispersed, Cohen

went to sleep on a nearby park bench. He had not wanted to worry Stern.[6]

Now that Stern was gone and all the members of the organization hunted, Cohen left home to hide in the orchards that surrounded Kfar Saba and Raanana. He and his girlfriend (later, his wife) Nehama Srulovitz subsisted for several months on oranges and sometimes bread that she was able to bring. Cohen carried a gun at all times, determined not to be taken alive, or at least not without a fight. Word made its way around the country that Lehi had not died with Stern, that one fighter remained free.[7]

In May, the British put a price of 1,000 pounds on Cohen's head—the same reward they had offered for Stern. An informer had told the British back in March that Cohen was in charge of the Stern Group in Kfar Saba and was "the most dangerous terrorist in the Group." By May the British knew he had planted a mine under Morton's car; by August they knew he was lecturing others on how to assemble bombs.[8]

One by one, Stern's soldiers found their way to Cohen, who kept track of them and called on them for whatever attacks he mounted against the British police. One midnight, for example, Nehama brought Anshel Spielman, a new immigrant from Poland—therefore unknown to the police—to the orchards. She led the way through the dark growth without hesitation as he struggled over every step. Finally she whistled a bar of *The Marseillaise* (actually it was a Hebrew song, "Masada Fell and Masada Will Rise," with the same melody[9]), and Cohen appeared. He said he feared the owner of the orchard was suspicious and they needed to move out. The three walked briskly to a nearby wood, where Nehama handed Cohen a sandwich and left them to talk. Spielman noticed Cohen's appearance: an unkempt beard, damp worn-out clothes, he was barefoot as they walked, and carried torn sandals in his hands. The next time they met, Cohen came to see Spielman in Tel Aviv; this time he was riding a bicycle and wearing a policeman's uniform.[10]

Even Eldad found Cohen in the orchards. Other fighters Eldad had met with wanted to discuss who would run the movement. Cohen opened with a discussion of how the underground should forge diplomatic ties with India, which was also seeking freedom from imperialist England.[11] Eldad later wrote that the young man exuded authority and his eyes were like machine guns.[12]

A Tunnel to Freedom

At the end of the summer Cohen had another special visitor. On August 31, Yitzhak Shamir escaped from the Mizra Detention Camp. He and

a friend, Elihau Giladi, left their barrack in the southern wing of the camp
and hid under a stack of mattresses in a warehouse at the camp's northern perimeter. At 9 P.M. the other inmates sang an agreed-upon song to signal that Shamir and Giladi's absence had not been noticed and they were
free to continue. They cut their way through the camp's thick barbed wire
fence and walked hours to Haifa. Nehama and Spielman gave Shamir a
Polish army uniform to wear and a pistol to bear and he was taken to
Cohen.[13] Cohen turned the movement over to him. (Giladi proved coura-
geous and dedicated but an uncontrollable live wire; his comrades decided
they would not survive his behavior. One, Pesach Levy, Giladi's contact,
had been insulted and struck by him and had committed suicide, and Giladi
had already ordered his soldiers to throw bombs at British soldiers during
Jewish rallies in order to cause bloody clashes between the public and the
police. This last plan had been averted at the last minute when Spielman
collected the explosives and ordered the Lehi members to disperse. Giladi
threatened to kill Shamir in retaliation. The Lehi leadership killed him
first.[14])

Shamir took his time reorganizing the remnants of Lehi and incorpo-
rating new blood. He reintegrated Chenzion's thirty or forty fighters. He
moved slowly and insisted on meeting every soldier. He never considered
an operation unless he knew all the details. Therefore, there were not many
military operations in those days. Just as Shamir had hearkened to Stern's
missive, sent shortly before Stern's death, stating that the movement would
be doomed unless he and others escaped, Shamir now banked on the other
forces still behind bars.

On November 1, 1943, the investment paid off: twenty Lehi fighters
escaped from the Latrun Detention Camp just off what was then the main
Jerusalem-Tel Aviv road. Nine months earlier they had begun digging their
way out. The camp commanders encouraged the detainees to beautify the
grounds and gave them tools to tend gardens. The detainees used the tools
in the gardens but also in the barracks. They commandeered other items
from an Arab repairman brought to the camp to fix windows and floors they
asked to have fixed. The repairman agreed not to complain about the missing tools, knowing that if he did the inmates would stop reporting broken
windows. The residents of the barrack chosen by Lehi for the tunnel turned
one corner of their barrack into a closet, into which they put all their clothing, blankets, one or two suitcases, and whatever else they could find loose
in the cabin. After the camp guards grew accustomed to the inmates' neat-
ness and the new closet, the stone floor under the closet was broken into

pieces and a six-foot-deep hole dug. Rings and ropes were fastened to the floor stones for easy removal and replacement and they became the tunnel's door. White flour and blackened coals from the kitchen were cooked into a gray paste that resembled the cement ordinarily holding the floor stones in place.[15] During one of the British searches of the camp, this barrack's prisoners again displayed their obsession with cleanliness by emptying the entire barrack of all they owned and washing the now-bare floor. The guards searched the insides and contents of all the other barracks, but had an easy time with the personal possessions on display outside this barrack, and could examine the floor without even stepping on it, so as not to muddy the sparkling and still-wet stones. Thus the tunnel went undiscovered.[16]

At night the prisoners would sneak out of their barrack and remove the flowers they had planted during the day, put down another layer of sand that they had taken from the tunnel, and replant the flowers.[17]

When the gardens were getting too high, sand from the tunnel was carried out by the inmates in small bags under their coats. The bags' openings were loosened as they circled the camp so the soil would slowly disperse over the camp grounds. The rains washed much of it away and covered the traces of the rest. When the rainy season ended, one prisoner, known for his temper, went on a rampage and destroyed all the seedlings and gardens that had been prepared. Afterward, they had to be repaired and replanted, affording another opportunity to disperse massive amounts of sand and rock.

The prisoners had estimated they would need to dig approximately 120 feet. After a few dozen, the ceiling began collapsing. The diggers dismantled an empty barrack across the way to provide lumber for beams to support the tunnel's wall and ceiling. They took the barrack apart from the inside, piece by piece, and hoped it would not blow away in the wind. It held up.

As the tunnel got longer, it also got darker and danker. Candles burned for light but also burned up any oxygen. An electric wire was run from the lavatory where a bulb was always on, and the constant flow of electricity allowed for light. The lack of air was a bigger problem; diggers could work no more than ten minutes before being pulled out, breathless and in pain. Eventually the prisoners solved their problem: they stole a raincoat that became a bellows and turned some cloth into a pipe, and were thus able to pump air into the depths of the tunnel.

When they thought they had dug enough, they poked a rod upward and, from above, scanned the terrain for a sign of it. Where they expected to see it, they did not; they finally spotted it directly under a guard tower inside the camp. The digging resumed. By the time they finished, the Lehi members in Latrun had dug a tunnel approximately 250 feet long under the camp's electrified and regular fences.[18]

The night they escaped, Joshua Cohen stationed fighters in the fields around the camp, several miles away in every direction, in case the escapees lost their way. A bus was hired to pick them up. The driver was told en route who his passengers would be. The passengers were three hours late; from midnight to three in the morning the bus drove back and forth trying not to attract attention. In the course of the night a tire burst, which the driver did not report. His company fined him two lira, which Lehi offered to pay, but the driver refused to take the money, saying the honor of helping the prisoners escape was worth a fine ten times as high.[19]

One of the fugitives from Latrun—the electrician who had run the wires for the tunnel—was killed a few days later by police; the other 19 were a major boon to Shamir. One of them was Nathan Yalin-Mor. From then, Shamir, Eldad, and Yalin-Mor ran Lehi: the brawn, the brain, and the tongue, respectively, though responsibility for everything was shared.

The First Shots

While still behind barbed wire, Yalin-Mor had sent the underground paper an article entitled "Liquidate the Prisons." The idea was that prison was destroying the movement; Lehi members were called upon to avoid imprisonment. Lehi then adopted Joshua Cohen's attitude: all members were to be armed at all times and to prefer a shootout to an arrest, regardless of the results.

Yalin-Mor's exhortation brought results. On February 14, 1944, Lehi's Haifa representative, Yaacov Banai, and one of his best fighters, David Shomron, were walking home. Banai was one month short of 24 years old. He was born in Poland, left with a group of friends in 1940 for Eretz Israel, and in 1943 had been given charge of Lehi in Haifa. Shomron was 19, a native of Istanbul who had moved with his family to Haifa in 1934. He and his two brothers had joined Betar; at 14 he joined the Irgun and since the split had been with Lehi.[20] Banai and Shomron were carrying stenciled underground pamphlets publicizing the story of the shooting of Amper and Jack at 30 Dizengoff Street two years before.

At about 11 P.M., when the two young men stopped at an olive grove to relieve themselves, Banai noticed they were being followed. In order to be sure, they stopped again at a billboard on Ben-Yehuda Street in the Hadar Hacarmel neighborhood, pretending to relieve themselves again. Before

Banai could turn around, his arm was pinned behind his back and a British voice demanded to know what was in his package. Banai answered "papers" and was glad when the man took it from him, instead of searching his pockets, where he had a gun. The man's companion shined a flashlight on the package as the first man opened it. "Illegal papers!" he declared and demanded Banai's and Shomron's identifications.

Banai reached into his pocket for his identity card but pulled out his gun. He shot the man holding the package. The second man ran across the street and Banai shot after him into the dark. He saw the man with the package, now on the ground, reaching for a gun and shot him again. The second man was now crouching. Banai was unsure whether he was wounded or taking aim and shot at him again, too. Shomron, who was unarmed, fled. He and Banai met up later in their safe house. The men they shot turned out to be plainclothes detectives Inspector Robert Green and Constable Harold Ewer, who died the next morning. Banai quickly transferred to Tel Aviv; Shomron, to Jerusalem.[21]

Sometimes the armed-at-all-times policy did not work so well for the Sternists. On March 19, Yerachmiel Aaronsohn (code name: Elisha) was ordered by British detectives in Tel Aviv to halt and identify himself. Though he was not a wanted man, he could not afford to be searched because of the gun in his pocket. He ran, the detectives shot at him, he returned fire, and he was finally cornered in the stairwell of 33 Mazeh Street, where the British killed him.[22] According to one of the detectives who pursued him, Daniel Day, Aaronsohn "was a very brave boy, for he came down the stairs and attacked us after he found he could not get out to the roof." Recollecting the incident years later, Day added, "I do not think I would have stopped the patrol and gone after him, only he started to run as soon as we came near him! Just a little more nerve and he would have got away with it."[23]

Three weeks later, Joseph Rosenbaum was bending over a Lehi copy machine in an auto repair shop in Haifa, getting ready to print a memorial broadside for Aaronsohn, when his gun fell from his belt and fired, hitting him in the stomach. Rosenbaum ordered his partner, David Hooliansky, nicknamed "Hooligan," to save himself and run. Hooligan ran to get help, but when he returned with two other Lehi fighters, Moshe Bar-Giora and Shabtai Drucker, his wounded friend was gone. By questioning the children playing outside they found the house to which Rosenbaum had limped, but before they could move him out, two British officers and a Jewish policeman arrived.

Bar-Giora and Hooligan made it to the porch; Drucker was jumped by the officers, who tried to disarm him. The two fighters on the porch shot the two British officers, and all three fighters fled. The Jewish policeman stood on the porch and shot at them. The mortally wounded Rosenbaum yelled at him, "You're Jewish, stop shooting, I beg of you—stop!" The policeman continued shooting and wounded Drucker. Rosenbaum pulled out a grenade and blew up the apartment. The policeman was killed but Rosenbaum managed to get outside and fell, dying a week or so later while being questioned in a hospital room.

Meanwhile, the three fugitives sought to get as far away as possible and also to get medical treatment for Drucker. They delivered Drucker to the home of Menachem Luntz in Yavniel, across the Galilee, leaving him there to heal. The British found him before he had recovered and opened fire on the house without warning. Drucker and Luntz shot back, but when their ammunition ran out they used their last bullets on themselves.[24]

While the Lehi was shooting it out with the police in these and other instances, and as Shamir, Eldad, and Yalin-Mor planned bigger operations, the Irgun was also changing. Its new Commander in Chief was Menachem Begin, who had challenged Jabotinsky to adopt a more activist and militarist policy at the 1938 Betar Conference in Warsaw. Begin had continued to lead Polish Betar until after Germany invaded Poland. He and as much of his youth group and political party as was able escaped to Vilna. Hiding outside the city, Begin was playing chess with Eldad when the Soviet secret police arrested him. Eldad made it to Eretz Israel by land and ship while Begin remained in Soviet prisons and camps. Begin was released by the Soviets, with tens of thousands of other Polish prisoners, only after the Germans invaded Russia. One of these prisoners, Władysław Anders, was supposed to lead the others in fighting the Germans. "Anders' Army" made its way through Iran and Iraq to Eretz Israel. Many Jewish members of the unit deserted when they arrived in their own country, but Begin refused to do so and waited for his discharge. In late 1943, Begin was given command of the Irgun, and he quickly ended the doldrums it had been in since the split with Stern in 1940.

Stern and what became Lehi had been the first to target the British and first to fight them. Lehi's great political achievement was analytical. Its leaders took a cold look at global politics and were convinced that England's opposition to Jewish independence was not accidental; it was based, they said, on British interests. Lehi expressed this insight by declaring the Jewish national liberation movement opposed to "British imperialism." They were opposed not to this or that British government or policy but to Britain's interests in the region. A British-Jewish war was thus not one option among many; it was, from both the British and the Jewish perspectives, a necessity. Lehi's political achievement led to its first military one; it drew the practical conclusions from its analysis and initiated the war.

Begin adopted the Sternists' political attitude, which was that the war in Europe was not a reason to pretend the British were friends of the Jews or to hope they would aid Jewish national aspirations. In February 1944, Begin's Irgun declared what it called a "revolt" against England. Some time later Begin adopted the Sternists' terminology and called the British presence in Eretz Israel imperialist. Because at any given time the Irgun had about ten times as many fighters as Lehi, it did not need to adopt the Sternists' military tactics, which were based on individual attacks on British policemen or soldiers. The Irgun could mount major military operations against British installations. In any case, by the mid-1940s the Irgun and Lehi were in the fight together, and they were sometimes joined by the Hagana in a United Resistance Movement, though at other times the Hagana cooperated with the British and "hunted" (the Hagana's word, and their leaders referred to such times as hunting "season") Irgun and Lehi fighters, to be tortured and turned over to the British. For the next few years, the Irgun and Lehi discussed merging and though this never happened, they did coordinate their operations so neither organization would be caught politically or militarily off guard by an operation of the other, or caught in the other's crossfire. Early on, Begin argued vociferously against the Lehi policy of arming all its foot soldiers and Lehi soon changed this policy, realizing that while its dead were perhaps useful examples of heroism for the youth, their deaths might have been avoidable.

Arrests

One man who was unarmed and who was captured alive was Begin's chess partner, now Lehi's ideologue, Eldad. His day job was teacher in a Tel Aviv high school. He was warned the British were on to him; Shamir asked him to stay away from home and work, but Eldad committed what he later called a "war crime," that is, a crime against the war, by refusing to abandon his seventh-grade class. "How could I not finish teaching the book of Job? Could I…omit the mighty conclusion with God's speech from out of the whirlwind?" he asks in his memoirs.[25]

Eldad was writing on the blackboard when the principal called to him that the police had come. Eldad left his class, crossed the hall to another classroom, walked past the students and teacher and climbed out the window. Outside he saw no police, assumed he had time, returned to his own class, and arranged for a student to take his briefcase full of underground papers to his wife. Then he walked out of the school. But as he passed the office on his way, he saw police inside and imagined he had been spotted; he began running, which actually alerted the police to his exit. He was caught in a student's apartment several blocks away; Eldad left through a bathroom window, holding on to a drain pipe, from which he slipped. He awoke in Hadassah Hospital, with an injured spine; the next day his body was put in a cast.[26]

As soon as he could be moved, Eldad was taken to the Jerusalem Central Prison (today a Museum of Underground Fighters, off Jaffa Road, near City Hall). He was incarcerated, body cast and all, in the prison infirmary. Describing this time, he writes:

> As for my spirit, those first months in the Jerusalem Central Prison:
>
> A concentration of all my spiritual energies on the will to war and its joy. A soaring of emotion and imagination and logic and memory and 24 internal forces to counter the 24 physical breaks. Final diagnosis: strength from Heaven. Perhaps the same strength Jacob possessed as he dreamed of the ladder. He, the dreamer, a wretched pauper, sleeping on a stone, hunted and persecuted. Dreaming of a ladder set in the ground, its top in heaven, angels climbing and descending, and the Promise, the fabulous promise of the land that will be, that already is, his.
>
> I lay on a parcel of land no wider than his, though he enjoyed freedom of movement while I was chained. But I, too, had my good angels with me. The boys of cell 18, the "Sternist Room" to which I was only later transferred, came and went by means of various reasons and ruses. And what were Jacob's angels compared to these?
>
> The boys of Israel, already "sitting" twenty, thirty, forty months in prison....Strong boys, eating hummus (ground chickpeas) three times a day and disgusting lentil soup, boys brimming with unreleased energy, while the whistling of other boys walking in the street outside wafts in from beyond the barred windows. And voices of

women…light and merry. And Joshua, Joshua Zetler, the most macho of them all, suffers most when he hears the sounds of young children, little kids crying, laughing, talking. And Eliahu Amikam sits, too. He speaks ten European languages but prefers Bengali. He is being yelled at by a British officer who does not understand when he, Eliahu, in a playful mood, speaks English with a Scottish or Welsh accent. And now Eliahu intends to study Sanskrit. Nor is he equaled in his use of obscenities. Eliahu's obscenities could stand in the Holy Sanctuary itself. Some men speak simple words which sound obscene; Eliahu speaks in obscenities which sound like melodic, soft, silky music. I detest obscenity, but his never sounds discordant, not once. And Joshua Becker sits—only generations of breeding and modesty could bring forth one so tender and gentle. And Moshe Svorai, who stole the birthright from me, to be the first teacher of Israel and rebel and prisoner….

So they sit, men of great spirit, in this suffocating cell; and so they will sit for years. And they are the most powerful room in the prison, and perhaps there is not a room more powerful in the entire land….

In all my life I was never as free and strong as during those first months of prison. My bones were shattered, my body in a cast, my entire self in a prison basement under heavy guard. And just one week after my arrival I [was] already able to dictate to Anshel Spielman or Becker or someone else the articles for *Hehazit* [The Front, an underground newspaper].[27]

Of the men mentioned by Eldad above, Zetler, Amikam, and Becker had been arrested for various bank robberies. Zetler was 27 years old; he had joined the Hagana at the age of 14, moved to the Nationalist Hagana-Irgun, and gone with Stern to the new underground. He had been arrested once and escaped, then been arrested again after organizing a bank robbery in Tel Aviv. Amikam was 28; he had joined Betar in Poland at 13, immigrated to Eretz Israel with a student visa in 1935, and joined the Irgun in 1936. He took and passed a pilot's course sponsored by the Irgun, becoming one of the first licensed pilots in the country. He was arrested dressed as a British officer during a foiled attempt to rob a bank in Jerusalem. After sitting in the Jerusalem prison with Eldad, he was transferred to hard labor in rock quarries. Joshua Becker was 22 years old and also from Poland, where he had been a member of Betar. He reached Eretz Israel in April 1939 and worked in agriculture, then joined Stern's new organization upon its formation. He was captured after the January 1942 attempt to rob a bank clerk in Tel Aviv, which had resulted in the shooting deaths of two innocent passers-by. Svorai, in whose apartment Stern had been shot, was 30 years old. As a teenaged member of the League of Birionim he had removed the Nazi flag from the German consulate in Jerusalem. In 1935, after the Birionim disbanded, Svorai went to Poland and established a network of "national cells" within Betar that formed the basis for Stern's Irgun cells. When the Irgun split, Stern appointed him head of Lehi's intelligence unit and later the Tel Aviv area. He was arrested in May 1941 and escaped in November. After he and Yaacov Eliav recovered from wounds sustained in the British attack at 30 Dizengoff Street in January 1942, they were transferred to the Jerusalem prison (Eliav escaped from the prison in December 1943). Anshel Spielman, who after his encounters with Joshua Cohen in the orchards had been put in charge of activities in Tel Aviv by Shamir, had been convicted on a weapons charge and sentenced to ten years.

Spielman had been arrested with Hisia Shapiro, who had been Stern's contact and had taken his last letter the morning he was shot. She was 19 at the time. She, too, had been born in Poland, had joined Betar at 13, and then joined an Irgun cell. When the Germans invaded, she fled to Vilna, as had Eldad and Begin and so many others. When the Soviets clamped down on Jews there, she and her friends used forged transit documents to get to Eretz Israel. As soon as she arrived, she joined Lehi; after Stern was killed, she continued.[28]

Two years later she lived in an apartment at 68 Rothschild Boulevard in Tel Aviv. Spielman walked her home one night; inside the apartment he sat down to read a newspaper but the proverbial knock on the door was immediate. Apparently the landlord had become suspicious of Shapiro's activities and informed the police. Ten detectives rushed in and grabbed the pair.[29] In her purse were a loaded gun and a matchbox wired to explode.[30]

Around the same time, several others were arrested: Zvi Tavori, in an apartment in Bat Yam, for possession of a gun; David Hameiri-Begin, one of Lehi's first intelligence operatives, who had helped build the unit by striking up conversations with waiters at restaurants and hotels, government clerks, taxi drivers, and policemen, in order to find people who would prove useful and who they would one day ask for favors.[31] He was arrested while looking for Shapiro's landlord. The British caught him in a nearby alley and tortured him to force him to reveal his address, which he did not do. His apartment was full of Lehi material, which his friends were, thanks to his silence, able to move to safer quarters; and Matityahu Shmuelevitz, who was spotted on a Tel Aviv street, ordered to stop, and shot in the leg when he pulled a gun and began to shoot.[32]

These five fighters all faced the charge of weapons possession—which the British in Eretz Israel had just made a capital offense. Their trials were held in May and June of 1944.

The Five Trials

Until then underground defendants had pled their innocence or extenuating circumstances and tried to wriggle out of harsh sentences.

Had the British read Lehi's recent underground literature, or had they been more astute in their reading of it, they might have known that their judicial system in Palestine would never be the same. In the December 1943 edition of *Hehazit*, Eldad had called the line of defense adopted by kibbutz members charged with possessing weapons, in the aftermath of a violent British search of Kibbutz Hulda in October, "an embarrassment." Eldad castigated the defendants who, in their search for justifications for hiding arms, went so far as to attempt to move British hearts with stories of kibbutz members who had been killed by Arabs. He wrote that the defendants were seemingly unaware that the British disarming of the Jews was deliberate. Eldad wondered what the British judges thought of such defendants, "in the middle of this terrible World War, in the middle of this terrible massacre of Jews, while the gates of immigration are terribly closed, while the Arabs are openly planning and preparing—these defendants are bringing character witnesses to prove they are men committed to 'labor and peace.'" He asked, "Doesn't this bring to mind the abject constant apologetics of the Jew in Exile standing before the devilish, mocking goyim who are spitting in his face? 'Forgive us for breathing the air; forgive us for drinking the water; forgive us for living.'" The defendants, Eldad wrote, should have stood tall and offered to be sentenced to ten years instead of seven, rather than shaming the Jewish community by trying to win sympathy by invoking the names of the dead, humbling themselves, and begging for mercy from those who despise them.[33]

The Lehi leadership believed that the British were at this point determined to convict regardless of the evidence. The Lehi leaders also knew that until now, Lehi's propaganda was not well distributed. The public had little

sympathy for Lehi because it had little knowledge of Lehi. Now, the fighters and higher ups in Lehi decided to use the courtroom as a platform to
attack the legitimacy of the British occupation of Eretz Israel and to appear
in the newspapers as freedom fighters. They would turn the tables on the
British and put the British in the dock.

Zvi Tavori was first. Asked whether he was guilty, Tavori replied:

> The charge against me reads that I am accused of
> possessing a gun and bullets without permission and
> without reasonable justification. I admit possessing the
> gun and bullets; I deny that I held them without legal
> authority or reasonable justification. I received permis-
> sion to carry the gun from the one regime I recognize in
> Eretz Israel. This is the Hebrew freedom fighters' move-
> ment, which wishes to return the nation of Israel to its
> proper place among the nations, which means a Hebrew
> state in this land.[34]

The judges threatened that such talk would bring him a harsher sentence, to which Tavori answered that he did not care if they went hard on
him, nor if they added to his charge sheet, adding after a few more volleys
with the judge, "I declare that this whole trial is of no interest to me, your
verdict is of no interest to me, and I will not answer any more questions."
On this basis he, who was acting as his own attorney, refused to cross examine prosecution witnesses. In a summation allowed him by the judges,
he repeated that he rejected their right to put him on trial. Further, he said,
he thought it quite reasonable that he should carry a gun, given that for
years the British had been murdering Jews whose hands were raised or already cuffed, in their homes and in the streets; deporting refugees from
Nazism; and inciting Arabs to attack Jews.[35]

Tavori was sentenced to seven years in jail.

The second trial was that of David Hameiri-Begin. The judges this time
forbade the defendant from speaking at the opening of the trial. Hameiri-
Begin said he would save the court's time by not cross examining any of
the witnesses against him. After the evidence had been lodged against him,
he explained why he had dismissed his attorney:

> When we met to discuss the defense, we found no com-
> mon ground. In accordance with my conscience, I asked

him to inform the court of my political stance, that I am a soldier in the Hebrew underground movement. To my regret, the lawyer refused to accept the defense under those circumstances. I do not wish to blame him personally....The conditions created by the police and regime in this country, which supposedly enjoys all the rights of the much-praised English democracy, these conditions have created an atmosphere endangering lawyers who might wish to appear in a clearly political trial and defend a person arguing that his weapon is earmarked for a war with the English.[36]

Hameiri-Begin admitted having a cartridge but noted that a gun found nearby with a bomb took different bullets:

I have no intention of denying that the cartridge was on me. I emphasize that even if the gun and bomb were on me, I would not deny it. Mostly because I would have proved it by drawing the gun and using it as soon as I saw the gentlemen, the police, jumping me and shooting at me....I am very sorry I did not have a gun and did not have a bomb; I could not defend myself as I should have and escaped....In any case, facts are not relevant to the verdict, which is entirely dependent on political considerations.[37]

He noted that England was pretending to implement laws and the Mandate, and most of the Jews in Eretz Israel were law abiding, but the underground saw that England was perverting the law and Mandate for its own ends. He also referred to the recent liberation of Rome, in which Jewish soldiers from Eretz Israel serving with the British army had taken part: "When the Hebrew soldiers return to Eretz Israel, the radio in Jerusalem will be forbidden to play the national anthem....I belong to the Hebrew soldiers who do not want to march in Rome under Britain's flag, as long as they cannot march in a free Jerusalem under a Hebrew flag."[38]

Hameiri-Begin was sentenced to 12 years.

The third speech was given a week later by Hisia Shapiro. She refused counsel and told the court that she was "sorry the police entered my room deceitfully, thus robbing me of the opportunity to defend myself with my gun." She declared that the British government should know she "belongs to the Fighters for the Freedom of Israel, which opposes it and fights to liberate this country from its imperialism."[39]

The court translated a French document that was found in Shapiro's purse and had it read into the record. In part, it stated:

> The Fighters for the Freedom of Israel…is a secret organization whose members are armed and obedient. They are spread throughout the Hebrew community in Eretz Israel. The Hebrew liberation movement seeks to immediately free the Hebrew nation and establish its sovereignty in all of Eretz Israel. This desire is based on our historical rights as the heirs of our forefathers, who lived in this country until their state was destroyed and their liberty taken from them by the armed forces of foreign occupiers. We, the natives of this land, see it as our homeland and our heritage, in the past, present, and future.…
>
> [The British] are trying to abrogate our right to this country by inciting a nationalist Arab movement that they created in various parts of the Moslem population, by means of propaganda.…[40]

As the trial drew to a close, Shapiro stated that this document had already communicated her views to the court, leaving her with nothing to add other than, "The thing that not only legally and morally allows, but also obligates, me and every Hebrew here to bear arms, is the fact that the Hebrew nation is being oppressed in its own land and its strong desire to be free of such oppression.…"[41]

Shapiro was sentenced to four years in prison.

One day later, Anshel Spielman addressed the judges at his trial.

> If you appear as representatives of justice, I appear as the representative of righteous demands. If you appear as representatives of the British people, I appear as the representative of the Hebrew people. From the moment I joined the Fighters for the Freedom of Israel, the person Anshel Spielman disappeared from the horizon.
>
> …I am a Jew, scion of one of the oldest nations in the world, which you must think should have ended its existence when the Temple was destroyed.…

...I do not want to deny your right to judge....I would never think of denying your right to judge me as a Jew on English soil in England....But only there, in England, and I definitely deny the right of English foreigners on the soil of the people of Israel in Eretz Israel to judge a son of the Hebrew nation.

...Had Eretz Israel been conquered by the Japanese, I might have to explain to them about Jerusalem. But Eretz Israel was conquered by a nation of the Bible for whom this is not necessary....When you dare stand in this Jerusalem of David, Isaiah, and the Maccabees to judge me, it would be best for you to know that you are not standing on the graves of the dead, but that from these graves the children of Joshua, Yiftah, Samson, David, and all the heroes are rising to life, these children you so love to read about when they are dead, but get so angry with when you see them alive.[42]

Spielman said that he would neither deny having a gun nor claim that it was meant to be used defensively, "unless Tito's arms are also to be called defensive." David is not a dead hero to him, he said, but he is alive. "I am not Shylock," he concluded, "nor a merchant. I am a fighter. I am not in Venice but in Jerusalem. I am in the ranks of the Hebrew underground of the Fighters for the Freedom of Israel, fighting to allow the grandchildren of David to govern in his Jerusalem...."[43]

Spielman was sentenced to ten years.

The fifth trial that month was of Matityahu Shmuelevitz. Shmuelevitz was 24 years old. He was born in Poland, where he had been a member of Betar. In 1938 he immigrated to Eretz Israel on one of the "illegal" refugee boats. His parents and brother were murdered in the Holocaust. Shmuelevitz had been arrested in 1940 and was one of the 20 Lehi prisoners who dug their way out of Latrun in 1943. The police who shot and arrested him in Tel Aviv did not know his real name or background.[44]

When the trial opened he admitted carrying a gun and a bomb and shooting a British policeman. He asked to call as defense witnesses the British High Commissioner, to prove that the British had betrayed the terms of the Mandate and betrayed the Jewish people; David Ben-Gurion, to prove that the entire Jewish people saw England as partner to the Nazi murder of the Jews; and Colonel Harrington of the police, to prove the police regularly tortured and shot prisoners. The court ruled it could not summon the High Commissioner, so Shmuelevitz passed on Ben-Gurion and Harrington as well.[45]

The final day of the trial, when Shmuelevitz was taken from the Jerusalem prison, as Joshua Zetler records, the Lehi members in cell 18 were tense, worried he would be given the death penalty. He passed by the cell and the inmates tussled at the door to shake his hand, wondering if they would ever have another opportunity. Zetler jumped onto the window sill as Shmuelevitz was led to a police van and yelled after him, "Matti, Matti, be strong!"[46]

Shmuelevitz surprised the court by announcing he would confess to more crimes than he had been charged with; the judges warned him that he was under no duress to do so, but he continued,

> According to the British legal code I am an illegal alien in this country. And it is too bad that hundreds of thousands of Jews did not manage to break the law as I did, this law that bans Jewish immigration to Eretz Israel. They would have been saved from the disaster that came upon them and would not need your mercy. And my fate would have been bitter had I decided to obey this British law. But I want to mention someone who has violated the trust put in him, allowing him to be in this country. There is someone who received an immigration certificate from 52 countries and a license to be here, in order to establish it as a Hebrew state. And he who got this certificate—betrayed it and betrayed this document in full view of the entire world. Were the League of Nations an institution of international justice, as it should have been, it would put you in the defendant's chair and accuse you: Britain, you betrayed the trust put in you, based on which we let you be in this country.[47]

Shmuelevitz related the plot of a novel by John Steinbeck, *The Moon is Down*, which he had found in the prison library; in this book, the people of a village subjugated by an occupying force (by implication, a European village under German occupation) stubbornly refuse to act as slaves. The oppressor holds military trials to provide its rule with the image of legality and tries "based on the law to convince the weaker population to be slaves, and that their desire to change the situation is a crime." Shmuelevitz read part of the book aloud, then stopped and asked the judges, "Why are you trying me? Why don't you just shoot me right away?"[48]

Shmuelevitz concluded by reciting the entire text of Psalm 144 ("Blessed be the Lord who readies my hand for battle..."), then he kissed his Bible and sat down. He was found guilty on all counts and that afternoon was sentenced to hang. The headline on page 3 of the *New York Times* was "Sings at Death Sentence: Palestine Terrorist Renders Anthem in Court Room." The audience in court stood as Shmuelevitz sang *Hatikva* and sang with him. On his return to the prison, he informed Zetler, who had jumped back onto the window sill when he heard the approaching van, of the verdict by pointing to his neck. When he passed the cell, he bantered with his friends, "Don't worry, guys. You only die once."[49]

Shmuelevitz sat on death row, adjacent to the prison's gallows. His sentence was commuted to life imprisonment.

The Lehi strategy of turning the courts into extensions of the battlefields and standing on the moral high ground of refusing to recognize the right of the British to operate courts in Eretz Israel was soon adopted by the Irgun, whose soldiers took the same tack. When sentenced to death, these soldiers even refused to beg for mercy by requesting clemency.

Attempted Assassination: MacMichael

Outside the courtrooms the war itself continued. In March, Lehi had tried to assassinate the commander of the British police in Tel Aviv. In July, the fighters planned to kill the British High Commissioner in Palestine, Harold MacMichael. MacMichael was a symbol of British oppression; he had been in charge of British policy in the country for years and had presided over the discriminatory White Paper regulations as well as the ban on Jewish immigration.

Joshua Cohen arrived in Jerusalem wearing a blue shirt with a red string and a dunce cap, the unofficial uniform of Labor movement youth. Shomron recalls, "He looked like a kibbutznik and slept on the floor. Every morning I brought him every newspaper published, which he read in order to keep track of the High Commissioner."[50] Cohen was now in charge of operations in Jerusalem and he directed the attempts on MacMichael's life. His fighters tried to get MacMichael in church, at a concert, in a movie theater, and on the street. Six times they tried and six times MacMichael evaded the traps. On August 8, 1944, the fighters made their seventh attempt.

The High Commissioner was due to leave Jerusalem for a farewell party in Jaffa, marking the end of his tenure in Palestine. Cohen set an ambush on the road leaving Jerusalem, at a sharp turn opposite the village of Lifta. Three groups were posted: Cohen and Yaacov Bentov waited with the guns and grenades for the attack; closest the road were Yaacov Granek, Moshe-David Eichenbaum and Abraham Liberman, their job being to roll boulders onto the road when given a signal that MacMichael's entourage was approaching; and near Givat Shaul, Yaacov Banai, Eliahu Hakim and Baruch Kotlicki waited, in case MacMichael tried to escape in that direction. The Lehi fighters were disguised as government-employed surveyors. They took their positions at 7 A.M., since they had no idea when MacMichael would pass by.

In the course of the day, an Arab sanitation worker happened upon the boulders and, cursing, rolled them away from the road into a gulch. Cohen ordered smoke-bombs be used to stop the British cars in place of the missing boulders.

At 4 P.M., David Shomron, sitting on a nearby hilltop, gave the signal; excited after so many hours of waiting, and determined that his friends not miss MacMichael, he also jumped and waved his arms. Cohen ordered everyone to position. At the motorcade's approach, the smoke-bomb was set off. The lead motorcycle stopped first, a petrol bomb going off ten yards ahead. The other cars stopped behind it. As flames spread over the road, all the Lehi fighters opened fire, some at the High Commissioner's car, others with the intention of preventing the police from coming to his aid. The driver of MacMichael's car was wounded in the neck. The constable sitting next to him was returning fire, but after a few seconds or moments he grabbed the wheel and swung the car around, disappearing into a bank behind a cliff, where Lehi's bullets could not follow. Cohen ordered a retreat and the fighters returned to the city, sure that this time they had accomplished the task. They were wrong. MacMichael was only hit in the hand and thigh.[51]

The British pursued Cohen's men as far as the village of Givat Shaul but failed to capture them, so they imposed a 500 pound fine on the Jewish community of Givat Shaul, which they "found guilty of failure to render all assistance in their power to discover the persons who committed the crime" while admitting to London that the population being punished had "offered no opposition to the Police."[52]

The fighters continued with their underground work. One night, Shomron and Eichenbaum were pasting Lehi posters on walls and shop windows on Ben-Yehuda Street in Jerusalem when a supposedly drunk man ordered them to surrender and pulled a gun; he fired as they ran. Shomron got away; looking back, he saw Eichenbaum being felled and beaten by a group of British police.[53]

Assassination: Wilkin

A month after the attack on MacMichael, Banai and Shomron acted again, more successfully. This time the target was Assistant Superintendent Thomas J. Wilkin, the British officer in charge of investigating the underground, who had been present at the shootings of Jack and Amper and Stern.

Shomron had spotted Wilkin, wearing large sunglasses, leaving the King David Hotel in Jerusalem. A Hagana operative leaked Wilkin's address: a Romanian church hostel for police officers, on St. George Street. A Sternist dressed as an Arab selling bread and olives waited near the hostel and was soon able to confirm that Wilkin left the hostel for the nearby Jerusalem prison at 8 A.M. every morning, in one hand a briefcase and the other hand in his pocket, probably holding a gun.

Shamir called Banai to Tel Aviv to discuss a plan for the assassination and ordered him not to waste time on taking aim when the time came, just to shoot all he had at Wilkin.

Banai and Shomron disguised themselves as well-dressed Englishmen. Their suit jackets concealed holsters and pistols under their arms, as well as automatics under their belts, for extra protection. At 7:45 they were on St. George Street. Cohen waited with a getaway car at a gas station near the Romanian church. A Sternist sitting at the corner of Mea Shearim and St. George Streets saw Wilkin leave the hostel; the Sternist tossed his hat in the air. The getaway car drove along St. George, passed by Banai and Shomron (Cohen nodded from the car to acknowledge all was set), turned left to today's Helena Hamalka Street, and idled near an Armenian church.

Banai asked Shomron, who had seen Wilkin at the King David, if he could make positive identification. Shomron did. But as they and Wilkin walked toward each other, they realized they would meet him too far away from the getaway car. They turned around and retraced their steps, then once again turned to face Wilkin and walked forward. Banai asked to be the one to open fire, and Shomron agreed to his superior's request. Banai saw Wilkin's right hand twitch inside his pocket and wondered whether Wilkin suspected anything; he suggested letting Wilkin pass so he would not be able to draw first. As soon as Wilkin passed them, they turned around and fired simultaneously. Wilkin twisted toward them and tried to draw his gun

but died before he could. The two assassins fired 14 bullets, 11 of which
hit Wilkin.[54]

A few blocks away, the gunfire was clearly heard in the Jerusalem Central Prison. Obviously no one inside knew who was "hit" or who performed the deed. Every inmate speculated as to the nature of the operation and each underground movement claimed credit for whatever it was. Finally the warden himself revealed the secret, perhaps unintentionally; in an offhand remark to Eliahu Amikam, whose prison labor was to cut gravestones in a yard opposite the main prison building, Warden Charleton said, "You know, you in the Stern Gang, you do a job from start to finish." Amikam asked him what he meant, and he explained, "Your friends outside are killing our officers. Anshel Spielman, the [prison] carpenter, prepares the coffin, Eliezer Ben-Ami [the prison sign maker] writes the information on the crosses and you do the gravestone. So you do the job from start to finish."[55]

Across from the prison in the Government Hospital, Tova Svorai and another underground prisoner were undergoing medical examinations. A nurse told them a seriously wounded Englishman had been brought in. A little later Svorai heard the British guards at the door talking about how "He didn't want a bodyguard...he was walking alone...." Finally Miriam Shuchman, who was being treated elsewhere in the hospital, came and told them in Yiddish that Wilkin had been killed. When the policewomen standing watch over them went to see what was happening, Svorai and her friend went, too, and watched Wilkin's body being carried out.[56]

After they had shot Wilkin, Shomron and Banai ran toward the car. Cohen had planned to throw a smoke-bomb to conceal their escape but did not have time. They piled into the car and drove through the Mamilla neighborhood and up Aza Street to Rehavia. Banai changed clothes, hid the guns, and took a bus to the main bus station where he boarded a bus out of the city. The bus was stopped five times at roadblocks, but he was not identified. The getaway car also stopped at the bus station; the driver offered several British officers a lift to Tel Aviv. He took their bus tickets in exchange for the ride. Because of these passengers, the car was waved past the roadblocks.[57]

Shomron almost immediately began consulting on plans to eliminate John Shaw, the Acting High Commissioner. This did not work out. But meanwhile the Lehi leadership had other high-level plans.

Assassination: Lord Moyne

Lord Walter Edward Guinness Moyne was the British Resident Minister of State for the Middle East, based in Cairo. On June 9, 1942, in a debate in the House of Lords on whether to recruit Jews from Palestine to fight in the British army, he referred to Zionism as "racial domination by these newcomers over the original inhabitants" of the country and told the House of Lords that "it is very often loosely said that Jews are Semites," but anthropologists know that "the Jewish race has been much mixed with Gentiles since the beginning of the Diaspora. During the Babylonian captivity they acquired a strong Hittite admixture, and it is obvious that the Armenoid features which are still found among the Sephardim have been bred out of the Ashkenazim by an admixture of Slav blood." He claimed that Palestine was already overcrowded, "all the fertile soil is not only occupied but very closely cultivated," and allowing large numbers of Jewish refugees to immigrate would be "a disastrous mistake." He hinted that the Jews would do well to consider resettlement in Poland and Germany after the war, or in Madagascar. (He also suggested the British explore with Arab rulers the possibility of settling Jews in Lebanon, Syria, and Trans-Jordan, areas he called connected to "historic Syria.") Moyne accused the British of "having broken faith" by not ensuring that the rights and position of local Arabs were not impaired. He argued that the Zionists should have been happy with the British offer to allow only 75,000 more Jews to immigrate after 1939, and said those who wish to impose an "imported" regime on local Arabs are "guilty of the spirit of aggression and domination" displayed by the Nazis.[58] According to Joel Brand's testimony at the trial of Adolf Eichmann, after Brand left Hungary he was arrested by the British and taken to Moyne. Brand relayed a Nazi offer to free a million Jews in exchange for 10,000 trucks. Moyne shrugged and said, "But what should I do with a million Jews?"[59]

Lehi chose to assassinate Lord Moyne without knowing of Brand's mission and without caring much about Moyne's anti-Semitic views. He was chosen because he was the highest ranking British official in the Middle East and directly responsible for backing up the anti-Jewish laws that barred immigration and sent refugee boats back to sea to sink.[60] (The day of the assassination, the Secretary of State for the Colonies mistakenly assumed the act was related to the dispatch of 251 suspected underground sympathizers to Africa two weeks earlier. He reported to the War Cabinet that "the attack on Lord Moyne might be connected with the action approved by the War Cabinet in deporting certain detainees to locations outside Palestine."[61])

Eliahu Hakim, 20, was born in Beirut and had lived in Haifa since he was 7. At 12 he marched in mourning over the hanging of Shlomo Ben-Yosef. He later said the hanging of Ben-Yosef was one of the events that convinced him to fight for Israel's freedom. He joined the Irgun at 15 and went with Stern during the split. At 17 he recorded an attack of despair in his diary: he had read so many attacks by different Jewish parties on each other, he began to wonder whether "it might not always have been thus in our nation, arguing and fighting over the sacred goal," and after reading through old newspapers that proved the point, he "came to despair completely" of the prospect of redemption. He found solace in the "noble" writing of Max Nordau and, realizing he was not alone, began to believe again in his ideals.[62]

That same year, on a camping trip with his class, he wrote of reclining on sacks of wheat and "looking around at the mountains; the mountains of this country on which the Prophet Elijah had walked, and the kings of Israel....How great to remember our nation's past and to dream of days to come, when the country will be restored."[63]

After Stern's slaying, when the underground was paralyzed, he joined the British army. When Shamir and Giladi escaped from Mizra, he offered them hiding places in Haifa, and as the underground reorganized he disseminated its literature and smuggled arms from abroad. He requested Lehi's permission to go AWOL from the British army and when his request was granted, he went underground. He quickly proved one of Lehi's best marksmen and was chosen for the mission in Cairo.[64]

Hakim's partner in this operation was Eliahu Bet-Zuri. Bet-Zuri was 22. He was born in Tel Aviv. He joined the Irgun in 1936 and was expelled from high school because of his many Irgun-related absences; nonetheless, he studied on his own and received a diploma. Like Hakim, he was moved by the hanging of Ben-Yosef and wore a black armband at the time. He enrolled at Hebrew University. When the Irgun split, he remained neutral. He peppered Irgun Commander in Chief Yaacov Meridor with requests to assassinate the High Commissioner and was repeatedly rebuffed, leading him to join Lehi after Shamir's escape and Lehi's renewal of activity.[65]

On November 6, 1944, Moyne's car pulled up in front of his mansion, where he intended to eat lunch, as was his routine. Hakim opened the car door and shot Moyne three times. The chauffer jumped out. Bet-Zuri ordered him to the ground but he rushed for Hakim. Bet-Zuri shot him. Hakim and Bet-Zuri took off on bicycles. Moyne's assistant alerted the police, and a traffic cop who happened to be on the spot, also with a bicycle, gave chase. As Bet-Zuri cycled, he shot at his pursuer's bicycle tires. A police bullet hit him and he fell. Hakim stopped and stayed with him. A mob surrounded them and the policeman caught up and disarmed them, without their resisting.[66] At their trial, Bet-Zuri insisted they had not wanted to hit the policeman when they shot, only the bicycle, because their argument was with the British, not the Egyptians.[67] Eldad wrote that "We viewed Egypt in its struggle to liberate herself from the British yoke as a possible ally."[68] Indeed, the Egyptian students and public supported the Jewish freedom fighters, since the Egyptians, too, opposed the British occupation of their homeland, and Egypt's best lawyers defended Hakim and Bet-Zuri.

The two fighters were tried, admitted their deeds, and were convicted. A Jewish lawyer sent from Eretz Israel tried to convince them to use various legal ruses to avoid the gallows. Bet-Zuri replied, "Some people live short lives in which nothing meaningful happens. That's a tragedy. But to live a short life and do something for the homeland—that's a victory."[69] Hakim wrote his parents from jail, "I was sent as a soldier to the front and was captured. It is necessary to know not only how to fight but also how to fall." He wrote that ultimately truth would prevail, and one day a Hebrew flag would fly over the Jerusalem mountains as mothers and fathers played freely with their children.[70] When he was put in the red robes of the condemned, Hakim, whose family was well-to-do and who had been a good dresser, declared, "This is the finest suit I have ever worn."[71]

The night before they were to be hanged, the Egyptian prison warden called a rabbi to be with them and commiserated with the rabbi over the fate of the young men. Hakim recited *Vidui* (confession), wrote a last letter to his parents, and was led to the gallows. The guards moved to handcuff him; he interrupted and said, "Why cuff me when I am going with you willingly?" Informed it was the law and they had no choice, he consented. On the gallows he sang *Hatikva*.

Bet-Zuri did not speak on the way to the gallows. He, too, sang *Hatikva*.

The rabbi, watching, broke down and was comforted with kindly pats on the back from the warden.[72]

The "two Eliahus," as they came to be known in Israeli history, were vilified at the time by the establishment organizations, who fretted over London's possible reaction to the assassination of its highest-ranking official in the region, a personal friend of Prime Minister Winston Churchill. The Fighters for the Freedom of Israel was castigated in the Jewish press. Thirty years later, following the Yom Kippur War, Egypt returned Hakim's and Bet-Zuri's bodies to Israel as part of a prisoner exchange. Prime Minister Yitzhak Rabin attended the funeral ceremony, which was held in the former Jerusalem Central Prison's Hall of Heroism. They were interred in the military cemetery on Mt. Herzl with full honors.

After their arrest the Lehi cell in Egypt was broken up. Benjamin Gepner, its organizer, eventually made his way to New York, where he worked for Lehi.

Two weeks before the assassination of Lord Moyne, and without trial, Joshua Cohen was deported with 250 other detained Jewish suspects to exile in Africa. He had been spotted in a Jerusalem café in October and, after a scuffle, taken into custody. Once in Africa, Cohen did not hide his views; British authorities almost immediately intercepted a letter he sent to Hisia Shapiro, then incarcerated in the Bethlehem Women's Prison, in which he wrote that he approved of Moyne's murder and felt "every Jew must be prepared to sacrifice his life in continuing the fight."[73]

Lehi slowed its operations in the months following the operation in Cairo. Yalin-Mor had promised the Hagana that Lehi would do so. On the assumption Eldad would oppose such a cessation of activity, Eldad was not informed of this agreement. For most of the next year, Hagana members hunted down Irgunists and turned them in. The next summer, Lehi joined with the Irgun to blow up a railroad bridge. In September 1945, Shomron tried to rob a Discount Bank; it was a Wednesday afternoon and the bank was closed. The bank's owner and several dozen associates were meeting there and they interrupted their board meeting to investigate the goings-on. Shomron pretended to be a British policeman and herded them upstairs. Since the safe was locked for the siesta and the manager absent, the robbery could go no further. Lehi came back a month later and made away with 26,000 pounds.[74] During the coming months there were several more robberies of money and of weapons.

Major Operations

The attitude of the Hagana was beginning to change. Its leaders had pinned their hopes on a Labor party victory in that summer's British elections, but following their electoral win the British Laborites proved just as antipathetic to Zionist aims as their Conservative predecessors had been, as Lehi had predicted would happen. The Hagana's rank and file, especially in the Palmach, began to envy the Irgunists and Lehi fighters whom they were supposed to hinder and to lobby for their own anti-British activity. In November 1945 Lehi again joined with the Irgun, this time to sabotage the rail line at Lod with the approval of the Hagana, which was sabotaging the rails in almost two hundred spots that same night.

Just before the end of the year, Lehi resumed full-scale operations. These, too, were initiated by a joint operation with the Irgun. On December 27, the Irgun and Lehi blew up the headquarters of the CID in Jaffa and Jerusalem.

Just as the Irgun learned from Lehi how to use the courtroom, Lehi was learning from the Irgun how to mount major operations. Seventeen fighters from the two undergrounds participated in the attack in Jaffa. The fighters blew their way into the CID building, planted explosives, and three minutes later the second floor was gone. In line with Irgun policy to minimize loss of life, four of the fighters whose task was to mine the road to prevent access were also assigned to post warning signs, so innocent people, or even British soldiers, would not be injured by these mines.

In both cities the operation was commanded by an Irgunist with a Sternist as deputy. In Jerusalem the deputy commander was Yaacov Granek. He headed the attack force with the explosives. He led the way, throwing grenades with one hand and shooting with the other. The bombs brought down the four-storey CID headquarters. One Lehi fighter was killed by British gunfire during the retreat.[75]

By now all three undergrounds were cooperating fully. In February 1946, while the Irgun was attacking an airfield in Kastina, Lehi attacked an airfield in Kfar Sirkin, near Petach Tikva. Granek commanded the Lehi operation. Shomron and his brother were also on the team. When the fighters were in position, the airfield's fence was cut and they entered. Nine saboteurs headed for each of the air force's planes. They placed the explosives between the wing and body. A patrol passed and did not notice them. The fighters left as they had come. The planes blew up on schedule.[76]

Over the next few months, Lehi managed to steal arms from several army bases, blew up a bridge, attempted to blow up a battleship, and attacked a military parking lot in central Tel Aviv. In June, Lehi engaged in its biggest operation to date: it destroyed the British rail works near Haifa.

The Railway Works

The rail works attack was Lehi's portion of a triple action in which, over the course of one week, the Irgun stopped three trains, evacuated the passengers, blew up the engine cars, and burned the trains, and the Hagana blew up ten bridges along the country's borders. Fourteen Hagana members were killed in one of the bridge attacks.

The night after the Hagana's action, Lehi sent over forty soldiers to the rail works, which they blew up. During the retreat, a truck carrying the fighters ran a British roadblock and was subjected to heavy fire. Eleven fighters were killed in the truck or as they jumped out. Twenty-two fighters were caught and put on trial. They decided to make a mockery of the trial. Haim Applebaum made a brief statement on behalf of the group demanding to be treated as prisoners of war. The next time a judge spoke the group stood and sang "Anonymous Soldiers." When the charges were read, they sang again; again after a recess; and again the following day, and the day after that. They continued singing so often and loudly that they did not hear the sentences being pronounced: four women were sentenced to life imprisonment and eighteen men to death.

Malka Granewitz (later, Hepner) was one of the women. She was 15 when the impending Holocaust abroad and the occupation at home caused, in her words, "my blood to churn; I wanted to do, to liberate, to act."[77] At the time, Malka may not have expected to face life in prison, but by the time she was 17 she had joined Lehi, was beseeching Yaacov Banai to send her on military operations, and knew that prison and worse were possibilities. At the rail works two years later, Malka's task was to plant mines and warning signs across an access road, the former to hamper British pursuit of the fighters and the latter to avoid civilian casualties. She was in the truck when the British opened fire and was soon bathed in her own blood and that of her friends, her back and legs full of bullets and shrapnel and her spine an open wound. At first paralyzed from the waist down, she could move only her arms and shared a hospital room with a fighter whose arms were in casts and could use only her legs. This patient managed to get the food trays close enough to Malka, who then fed the both of them.[78]

Of the defendants' behavior in court, Malka later wrote, "our families called out to be careful but...we answered: 'One cannot get two death sentences....' We became a Hebrew military choir in a British military court." Malka writes that when the court recessed and the prisoners were removed, their hearts went out to their worried relatives who were waiting for them, but "we could not show emotion. Self-pity and weakness were luxuries the few members of the underground could not afford. Our strength was in our courage." Malka admitted that some of her courage was a façade: "Inside, feelings for our families welled up, but we put up a front of quiet apathy." Similarly, Malka admitted that when the verdict was read to the four women—by three British officials in the back of a police van—she wanted to hear what was being said but the words were drowned out by her own singing and that of her friends. When the sentence was passed—in a room inside Acco prison that had been converted into a courtroom for the occasion—she was able to discern the gravity of the situation only by the pale faces of the journalists present.[79]

Since the night of the attack, Haim Applebaum had kept a diary, which he smuggled out of Acco prison to his wife, Hannah. Hannah, like Malka, had been mining roads during the attack, but her unit had been further away and, because it was not picked up by Lehi's truck, had escaped. Hannah, who in addition to blowing up bridges and mining roads for Lehi was also an underground instructor and typist, transcribed the diary, and Lehi added it to its list of must reading for new recruits.

Under the threat of unparalleled bloodshed in the event the convicted men were hanged, the British commuted the death sentences.[80]

Prison Escapes

Despite the Sternists' strategy of turning the courts into theaters of operation from which to attack the British and challenge their legal and moral right to be in the Hebrew homeland, those fighters in court and those in prison had but one desire: to rejoin their comrades on "the outside" where battles were being fought with weapons of steel and not only with words. Since the famous escape of the 20 from Latrun, a steady stream of fighters had escaped: Yaacov Eliav and a partner escaped from the Jerusalem prison while doing electrical work for the warden in his home; Joshua Cohen's brother, Menachem, escaped from Latrun; three fighters escaped from the camp they were exiled to in the Sudan; one escaped from a train on his way to Egypt. In June 1946, the Sternists were finally able to realize a dream and free Eldad.

Eldad had been moved to Latrun from cell 18 in Jerusalem, but he was occasionally brought to Jerusalem for medical treatment by a Dr. Treu. Once a plan had been formulated to free him during one of these visits, the only question was when that would be. One Lehi youth sat at a street corner facing the doctor's office for 21 days waiting for Eldad.[81] Every day Lehi sent a taxi from Tel Aviv in case he showed up and would need to be driven away.[82]

When Eldad was notified by the camp authorities that a doctor's visit had been set, he knew he would soon be in the true underground and his whereabouts would be kept secret from friends as well as foes. He writes of those last days in Latrun:

I am privileged to enjoy one last family visit. Those
precious moments when my eyes cannot see enough of
my daughter and when I have so many things to tell
them. We barely speak. Batya takes a letter for Nathan.
She has a contact. By now, the underground is already
able to help support families (again, thanks to that same
bank!). A fair sum has also gone to treat my daughter
who has been ill....She, of course, does not know what
is in the letter; perhaps if she knew she were helping me
escape, she would have hesitations about delivering it.
Still, she senses something and asks that I promise not
to escape, it is best for me to sit a while longer, she is
trying to have me freed in ordinary ways....And what is
she afraid of? The risk, life underground, the fear that
begins after the escape. When someone is under detention there is no danger he will be arrested, but when he
is outside, and especially when the situation worsens
and curfew is imposed, with searches day after day and
night after night, then no moment is ever free from fear.
She is of course right. "But deliver the letter immediately,
immediately! It's very urgent! It's about an informer who
was discovered in the camp!" I do not know whether she
believes me. I see her leaving, running down the road
dragging our poor, tiny girl, quickly, quickly....[83]

Seventeen-year-old Chaya Brandwyn, known in Lehi circles then and
since as "Yael" (after the biblical heroine who, the Book of Judges records,
killed Sisera, a general attacking Israel, thus saving her country) was born
in Jerusalem to a family descended from Rabbi Israel Baal Shem Tov, the
founder of Hasidism. As a child she had joined the religiously oriented Brit
Hashmonaim, the League of Hasmoneans, and by 15 she was a Fighter for
the Freedom of Israel. Like other members of the underground, as long as
she was not wanted by the police she continued with a daily routine "above
ground." Yael lived in a basement apartment on David Yellin Street, down
the block from Eldad's doctor. She was a natural choice for lookout duty.

Yael worked as a nanny across the street and three houses down from
the doctor. She spent almost all her time watching not only the children
but also the doctor's office. Opposite Dr. Treu's office was an electric store
Yael frequented with the children, and as the workers played with them she
continued to watch the office. Lehi sent another woman from Tel Aviv to

help watch; but Yona Frank was apparently too pretty and therefore too noticeable on the street. So Yael introduced Frank to the electric shop employees; they watched her, and Yael was free to watch Treu's gate. In principle one of the men in the Lehi cab was also a lookout. If he spotted Eldad arriving he was to go to a nearby apartment and alert the rest of the unit.

One day Yaacov Banai told Yael to be ready, and she assumed he knew the time was coming. Yael relates:

> I saw a big British vehicle pulling up, with one short man inside and two British. I had not seen Eldad till then. I ran excitedly to the cab. When the unit in the apartment saw me running they understood without being called. I told "Dov" [Yaacov Granek], "You don't need all the men from the apartment, there are only two British." Dov asked, "Who's commanding here?"[84]

After going to the cab, Yael escorted the unit from the apartment and pointed across the street to show them which clinic was Treu's. The fighters had poured tomato paste on one of their own to make him look injured.[85] He was carried into the clinic on a stretcher by two fighters wearing white gowns. These jumped the armed British guards. Granek threatened the guards with a pistol and quickly disarmed them.[86] Eldad, further inside, heard a ruckus and thought the sergeant guarding him would certainly intervene and all would be lost. But the sergeant was engrossed in a newspaper. When the fighters found Eldad, he ran past the sergeant, who apparently reached for his gun and was lightly wounded by one of the Lehi men. Eldad later expressed relief, noting, "Our instructions were not to hurt anyone unless necessary....The goy was wounded but recovered completely; I had not wanted him to die."[87]

In the courtyard, on the way to the car, Eldad was handed a gun, which he politely declined, remembering that since a course with Abraham Amper in Vilna he had not held one, and, "I am simply afraid that I might hold it the wrong way and cause trouble." Eldad ran. "It seems to me dozens of lads are around me, because for the tens of yards I run they are on either side of me, as if forming two chains. This was afterward revealed, of course, to be an illusion, there were only seven or eight, but two guarded me from the sides and showed me the way."[88]

The group jumped in, carrying the guns confiscated from the guards: two Tommy guns and several pistols, and several more taken from passing soldiers. Granek yelled to the driver, "Fly!" and the car took off dodging British bullets, at least one of which entered the car through the roof.

The car made several turns and pulled into an alley where Granek and Eldad switched to another vehicle. A few minutes later they were driving through fields outside the city.[89]

The owner of a café across from Treu's clinic called the police and reported that a woman who had been frequenting the area of late was in charge of the operation; he had seen Yael point to the clinic and had drawn the wrong conclusion. But that was enough to make Yael a wanted woman, and she had to leave her family and go completely underground.[90]

The leadership of Lehi was now reunited. But Eldad, Yalin-Mor, and Shamir were not to enjoy much time together. The last Saturday in June became known as the "Black Sabbath," when the British arrested the leaders of the Jewish Agency and imposed a country-wide curfew on Jewish areas. Over a thousand people were arrested immediately. Within days almost three thousand had been arrested, four killed and eighty injured.[91] In Tel Aviv, thousands of Jewish men were corralled and forced to appear before the police. Sergeant T. G. Martin recognized Shamir's bushy eyebrows and arrested him. Shamir was sent to exile in Eritrea, in Africa. Martin was killed by Lehi a few months after he identified Shamir.

Shamir escaped by digging a two-hundred-plus-foot tunnel out of the detention camp. He and four Irgunists, including former Irgun chief Yaacov Meridor, escaped together. They made their way to Asmara. One went ahead to Addis Ababa to prepare a safe house there. Shamir and the others bought an oil truck and added a small box between the driver's compartment and the oil tank. They lived inside this box for three days as the truck was driven across the border to French Somalia. They were arrested in Djibouti by the French. The British demanded their extradition but the French, apparently sympathizing with the Jewish goal of independence, first sentenced them to jail to prevent their extradition, then allowed them passage to France on an aircraft carrier, and once there granted them political asylum.[92]

Foreign Policy: A Neutral Middle East

As Shamir was profiting from French regional interests, Eldad and Yalin-Mor were coincidentally addressing the same issue of foreign regional interests, but on a broader scale. The two developed and began propounding an independent Zionist foreign policy. It was doubly independent: Lehi pursued it without consulting and in opposition to the pro-British Zionist establishment, and the policy advocated was for a Jewish state and the entire Middle East to sever military ties with all the world's major powers.

This became the major foreign policy innovation made by Lehi.

Yalin-Mor authored the September 1946 article in which the proposed "neutralization of the Middle East" first appeared in print, Eldad authored its major exposition in a full political platform in February 1947, and in between both held forth on it in the pages of the underground press. They argued that England saw Eretz Israel as one piece of its Middle Eastern puzzle, the purpose of which was to preserve British domination of the entire region, maintaining it as a primitive area supplying natural resources for the empire. To this end, Lehi claimed, England needed to oppose all movements for economic, cultural, or political independence. As long as "British imperialism rules throughout the Middle East" and its forces "are based from Haifa to Persia and from the sources of the Nile to the Turkish border, as long as a geopolitical ministry in Britain sets the policies of peoples and countries,"[93] Lehi stated, neither the Jews nor these other nations would ever gain liberty. Lehi declared,

> In opposition to Britain, bearer of oppression, must stand the Hebrew nation, bearer of freedom. Without a doubt, the oppressed will march toward freedom. Not just the Kurds, the Druse, and the Azerbaijanis; even the Arabs. A mass movement will shake the foundations of oppression and force the oppressor to retreat.[94]

Lehi argued for a neutral Middle East, whose people would be completely independent of foreign powers. Eldad and Yalin-Mor believed that keeping the region neutral in the coming Cold War would help its peoples live with each other, on a local level, and help prevent a third world war, on a global level.

This led Lehi to oppose any Jewish agreement to host British bases (or anyone else's) in a Jewish state.[95] According to Lehi, England wanted these bases as a bulwark against "Soviet political interests, French cultural interests, and American economic interests," but none of these were as dangerous to the cause of Jewish independence as British rule.[96] Indeed, Lehi advocated accommodating the Soviet desire to be free of a British threat in the Middle East, as well as the American desire to invest in the region— provided this was done with no political or military strings attached. Lehi seemed to believe that the Soviets did not seek political hegemony in the region and the United States did not seek to replicate the British imposition of feudal lords on the Arab populations. They also suggested that Arabs and Jews join forces to fight imperialism.[97] Unsurprisingly, given the length and nature of its war for independence from England, the neutrality sought by Lehi was focused mainly on getting the British out of the area.

The leaders' diplomatic initiatives did not diminish their military efforts. By now the Sternists were attacking daily and usually several times a day, all over the country. British bases were invaded and relieved of arms, others were blown up; British armored vehicles, jeeps, police cars, and trains were hit by road mines or gunfire; government tax collection was disrupted, oil and transportation offices were destroyed; high-level policemen were attacked. The Irgun was also attacking in force, and the British were forced to relocate to their own compounds or ghettoes for fear of being seen on the streets. (The Hagana had backed out of its cooperation with the Irgun and Lehi in July following the Irgun's bombing of British military and civilian headquarters in Jerusalem's King David Hotel, an operation the Hagana had okayed but later condemned because of the large number of civilian deaths.)

While Shamir was digging his way out of his African exile, his fighters were striking in Haifa. On January 12, 1947, a car belonging to the Royal Air Force was "confiscated" and painted to look like a car belonging to the CID. One ton of explosives was also added to the inside of the vehicle, then covered with oranges. A Sternist dressed as a British policeman drove into the parking lot of the CID's Haifa station without being checked. The plan went slightly awry when he found his expected parking spot taken; he moved a bit further away to another, only to incur the wrath of another driver. The Sternist ignited the explosives, shot the driver, and escaped, though by now a large number of policemen were shooting at him. A wing of the building was destroyed and six policemen were killed.

In early 1947 the British launched operations against the Jews both outside and inside Palestine. The Colonial Office, Foreign Office, and army accepted a Secret Intelligence Service proposal to deter potential Jewish immigrants by attacking their boats. The plan was called Operation Embarrass and the idea was to blow up refugee boats and ensure that blame was laid on a nonexistent group they called the "Defenders of Arab Palestine." In addition to slowing immigration, this would, they expected, create more friction between Arabs and Jews. The British sought to score more points by having any agent caught during the operation claim he was working for Western capitalists frightened by what he was to portray as a Soviet attempt to plant Jewish Communists in Palestine. Yet, not satisfied with stirring up mutual Arab and Jewish enmity and Western fears of Soviet expansionism, the British also leaked to the Soviets forged data alleging that the British were themselves responsible for smuggling the Jews out

of Eastern Europe, in the hope that this would goad the Soviets into taking action against Jewish refugees. With these rather incredible orders,
teams of saboteurs were sent out and boats were indeed blown up over the
next year. The British took pride in this operation's stopping the emigration of Jewish refugees from Italy.[98]

On March 28, London announced it was going to "get tough" on the
Jews inside Palestine with more police patrols, surveillance of people sus-
pected of sympathizing with the fighters, and plans to execute captured
Irgunists. No change would be made in Jewish immigration quotas or in
regulations preventing Jews from purchasing land in most of the country.
High Commissioner Alan Cunningham and other officials were sure "forces
already on hand can cope with developments."[99] The next day, Golda
Myerson (later, Meir) told a gathering in Tel Aviv that the actions of the
Irgun and Lehi were assisting the British, and if not for the fighters, the
establishment Zionists could have achieved more politically. She threatened to "finish with the terrorists" if need be,[100] apparently referring to a
Hagana-Jewish Agency plan to kidnap and execute several hundred leaders of the Irgun and Lehi in one night (this plan was never implemented).[101]
On March 30, a Lehi unit snuck into the oil depository of the British-Iraqi
oil company in Haifa and blew up 11 oil tanks. The Associated Press reported that "All Haifa was lighted by the fires that followed. Flames raged
along a quarter-mile waterfront area near oil refinery installations." Reuters
called it "the biggest fire in Haifa's history."[102] Several days later, with four
tanks still burning, the British government stated in an official release that
the effects on the country's oil supply and the economic damage would be
measured "not in days, weeks or months, but possibly in years." The British called the attack by the Sternists a blow to the largest single commer-
cial and strategic interest of the British Empire in the Middle East, while
Ben-Gurion condemned and threatened to take action against the Jewish
terrorists.[103] Bulgarian Premier Georgi Dimitrov, when he met with representatives of Palestine's Communist party, ridiculed their anti-imperialist
stance by asking sardonically whether it was they who had blown up the
Haifa oil tanks.[104]

At the same time that Lehi was expanding its operations in Eretz Israel with such major attacks, the Sternists were also expanding internationally. Benjamin Gepner, who had organized the Lehi cell in Egypt that
supported the Moyne-assassination team, naturally had to find other fields
to plow afterwards. He eventually left Eretz Israel for New York on a boat
with Shoshana Gartenhaus. Gartenhaus (later, Hilkiyahu) was a 20-year-

old former New Yorker, whose parents had moved to Eretz Israel with her when she was 7. She joined Lehi at 15 and spent her teen years carrying weapons to caches, transporting them to safe houses for instructional courses, and pasting Lehi broadsides on walls at night. Gartenhaus' father suspected she was a member of the underground and, hoping to get her away from local politics, encouraged her to visit New York. His arguments did not move her but they provided a good cover story when Lehi asked her to accompany Gepner to the United States. On arrival in New York the pair went to City Hall, married in name though not in spirit, and thus paved Gepner's way to stay as long as he liked in the United States. Gartenhaus went to target practice with Lehi youth, met with other Lehi agents in New York, and tried to enlist people she met for the cause. Mostly she longed to return to Eretz Israel.[105] Gepner organized a Lehi cell in New York, where he and others did public relations and fundraising for Lehi. Gepner sent funds, plans, and sometimes explosives to Lehi's European agents to be used for attacks there.

Gepner worked out of New York's Greenwich Village trying to influence public opinion and held meetings around the country when the goal was to influence politics. He managed to be received by former U.S. vice president Henry Wallace, who had served under Franklin D. Roosevelt from 1940-1945 and had just recently retired as secretary of commerce. Wallace paced the room silently as Gepner sat and spoke. Gepner kept talking, Wallace kept walking, so Gepner cut short his explanation of how the British were stirring up hatred between Jew and Arab, whose mutual enmity was not a fact of nature, in order to remain in the country and govern. Despite his lack of response, Wallace had been paying close attention and asked Gepner to continue. Gepner explained Lehi's foreign policy, the neutralization of the Middle East. Lehi wanted a Jewish state and the entire Middle East to be unaligned in the developing Cold War, he told Wallace, so the region would be free of British, Soviet, or American imperialism. Gepner had no idea whether he had made an impression on the taciturn Wallace, who said only that he opposed terrorism. Wallace did invite Gepner to a public lecture and party that night; much to Gepner's surprise, in the course of his speech Wallace called for the neutralization of the Middle East.[106]

Operations in Europe

Yaacov Eliav had created a letter bomb used to blow up a Jerusalem post office in the late 1930s, been arrested with the Irgun High Command in

1939, been shot with Svorai, Amper, and Jack at 30 Dizengoff Street in 1942, and escaped from the Jerusalem prison in 1943. He went to Paris and represented Lehi in talks with the French government. France wanted a foothold in the Middle East, and Lehi wanted a base in Europe. The French viewed Lehi's war favorably—witness, their assistance to Shamir when he escaped—and Eliav negotiated with the militant socialist André Blumel, former Chief of Cabinet in socialist Leon Blum's pre-war government and now an emissary for the post-Vichy regime. Blumel said the French government wished to assist Lehi, though because of British pressure, and financial constrictions, this would not necessarily be easy. The French did supply arms for the Zionist undergrounds in Eretz Israel. However, Eliav was occasionally asked by French authorities to leave Paris and "vacation" elsewhere—when the British monarch visited, for instance.[107]

On one such occasion, Eliav had to continue respecting France's official neutrality when the anti-Semitic British foreign secretary, Ernest Bevin, was in Paris for a peace conference. Unable to blow up the hotel, which he claimed to be able to do, Eliav nevertheless found a method of scoring points for Lehi: he set a meeting with a *New York Herald Tribune* journalist in the hotel and, indeed, Lehi's top bomber was able to get past all the security posts and hold an interview there. The resulting publicity took no lives and damaged no buildings but embarrassed the British and caused their dignitaries no little anxiety as they traveled around the world.[108]

Eliav focused his attention on London. He was assisted greatly by Betty Knout; she was the daughter of Ariane Scriabin, herself the daughter of the Russian pianist and composer Alexander Scriabin. Ariane had converted to Judaism and married a French resistance fighter. In 1944, at the age of 38, she was killed carrying arms and messages to the resistance fighters around Toulouse. Betty, her daughter, carried on the family tradition and took one of Eliav's bombs into a cloakroom in the highly guarded Colonial Office in London, where it was discovered and defused, again to much publicity. A man named Jack Martinsky, a former fighter with the Maquis guerillas opposed to the Vichy government and German occupation, and later with the Free French Forces, smuggled a time bomb into the Ministry of War. The bomb exploded the next morning, causing damage and injuries. Robert Mizrachi, a Sorbonne student who worked with French philosopher Jean Paul Sartre, carried a coat lined with explosives into the "Colonial Club" frequented by Colonial Office VIPs; the club was wrecked and three men injured. Agents were dispatched to Italy—so as not to compromise French neutrality—with sixty letter bombs, which were mailed to

Bevin and other prominent British politicians; again, the results caused little damage but great stir. Luck ran out for Eliav and Knout when they crossed into Belgium with enough explosives to sink a British battleship docked in a Belgian harbor. The explosives and a stack of letter bombs were discovered and the pair arrested.[109]

Lehi's Yaacov Heruti left Eretz Israel to study in England and take over. He and his team followed Bevin for quite some time with hopes of assassinating him.

Avner Gruschow may have succeeded in placing a bomb under Bevin's seat in Parliament. In a memoir, Gruschow claimed that he and a partner hollowed out two books and turned Shakespeare into a time bomb. They walked to Parliament, stopping at shop windows as if out for a stroll, and all the while Gruschow thinking,

> If our hearts beat a little faster than usual, it was because we were at the most difficult period of our task: the crisis which precedes the moment of danger, as experienced by men waiting in line for an injection when they see the needle pierce the arm of the man in front of them.
>
> If one surmounts this crisis, if one does not go home under the pretext of some good old ideological reason fished out of the dustbin for the purpose, the game is won. Once the action has begun, it gives out an invigorating odor which can turn a bank clerk into a national hero.[110]

As they approached Parliament, Gruschow writes, he grasped his partner's hand and urged him to walk slowly so as not to arouse suspicion. They joined a group of tourists being led into the parliamentary chamber. At an opportune moment when the guards were looking elsewhere, Gruschow bent down as if to tie a shoelace and attached the book with a fish-hook under Bevin's seat. They walked out and waited in Paris for Bevin to take his seat the next Tuesday. The day and hour passed and there were no news reports of a bomb in Parliament.

Gruschow writes that he went back to London and sent two other Lehi operatives to test the air. They entered Parliament with books under their arms on the assumption that had the bomb been discovered, any tourist carrying a book would be stopped and questioned; they were not. The next week Gruschow went to remove the bomb, if it were still there. "I approached the seat and threw it a timid but longing glance." He felt there were too many people around him, but with an accomplice's help he would be able to take it. "But now I was frightened, like an assassin who is afraid to look at the body of his victim, and, above all, of touching it." So he left. His partner was so worried that he may have left his own fingerprints on the bomb that he returned with his girlfriend, also on Lehi's London team, and he showed her where it was. She stooped down and pulled it out. This was three months after he and Gruschow had originally placed the bomb in Parliament.[111]

More Prison Escapes—and Deaths

In Eretz Israel the underground's war continued apace with bombs and bullets, on the streets and on army bases. But much was going on in the prisons, too.

Many female members of Lehi were incarcerated in the Bethlehem Women's Prison. Some, like Tova Svorai, had been let out after years, only to be picked up again after their release and held under "detention," given that they had already served their time. These rearrested women were released at the discretion of the authorities, weeks or months later. One of the women in Bethlehem did not wait for the British to free her: Geula Cohen was the voice of Lehi, the "anchorwoman" of the underground radio station. She had been arrested during a broadcast and wanted to return to the microphone, as a symbol that Lehi could not be silenced. In April 1947 she was taken to the Government Hospital in Jerusalem's Russian Compound, near the Central Prison. An Arab member of Lehi, Yousuf Abu Ghosh, pretended to visit an old woman in the same hospital. A Lehi member pretending to be his wife left an Arab woman's dress in the bathroom for Cohen. Cohen used the lavatory, and while she changed clothes two members of Abu Ghosh's family held a fistfight in the hallway to distract the guard's attention. Cohen climbed out the lavatory window and was driven away to resume her broadcasts.[112]

Also that April, four members of the Irgun were transferred from the Jerusalem prison to the Acco prison and hanged in the middle of one night. One more member of the Irgun, 19-year-old Meir Feinstein, was on death row in Jerusalem. He had driven the getaway car when the Irgun blew up the Jerusalem train station (as usual, the Irgun posted signs on the bomb warning people to keep away). At his trial, Feinstein told the judges who were about to sentence him to death:

Officers of the invading army! A regime based on

gallows—this is the regime you want to establish in this
country, whose destiny it is to serve as a lighthouse for
humanity. In your stupid wickedness you assume that
by this means you will succeed in breaking the spirit of
our people, the people to whom the whole country has
become a gallows. You are mistaken. You will learn that
what you have come up against is steel, steel tempered
by the fire of love and hatred: love for the homeland and
freedom, hatred for the oppressor and invader.

How blind you are, British tyrants. Have you not
learnt yet who you are fighting in this struggle, unex-
ampled in human history? Do you believe we are to be
frightened by death, we who for years heard the rattle of
the trucks that bore our brothers, our parents, the best
of our people, to a slaughter that, too, had no precedent
in history? We, who asked and ask ourselves every day,
how are we better than they, than millions of our brothers? In what lies our virtue? For we could have been
among them in the days of fear and in the moments that
came before death.

To these recurring questions our conscience makes
one reply: We were not spared in order to live in slavery
and oppression and to await some new Treblinka. We
were spared in order to ensure life and freedom and
honor for ourselves, for our people, for our children and
our children's children. We were spared in order that
there should be no repetition of what happened there and
of what is still likely to happen here, under your rule, the
rule of treachery, the rule of blood.

That is why we shall not be frightened. We have
learned—and at what price in vain sacrifices!—that there
is a life that is worse than death and a death greater than
life.[113] And if you fail to understand this phenomenon
of a nation that has nothing to lose but the chains of its
slavery, but the prospect of a new Maidanek, it is a sign
that you have been stricken by blindness in order to be
removed from the stage of history, from which Provi-
dence removes all those who rise against the Eternal
People to destroy it. Assyria and Babylon, Athens and
Rome, Spain and Germany preceded you, and you will
follow them.

> This is what I wanted to tell you, British officers, you
> and those who sent you. As for me, I am a prisoner and
> I demand to be treated as a prisoner of war.[114]

He was joined by 20-year-old Moshe Barazani of Lehi. Barazani had been sentenced to death for carrying a hand grenade. His trial lasted 90 minutes.

Barazani spoke only once during his trial, to tell the British:

> The Hebrew nation sees in you an enemy, a foreign
> regime in its homeland. We, the Fighters for the Freedom
> of Israel, are fighting you to free the homeland. In this
> war I have fallen your prisoner and you do not have the
> right to judge me; you will not frighten us with hangings,
> and you will not succeed in destroying us! My people,
> and all peoples oppressed by you, will fight your empire
> until its destruction.[115]

Barazani was sent to cell 18 in the Jerusalem prison while awaiting trial. Anshel Spielman asked him if he would be prepared to attack the British even from the gallows, should he be sentenced to death, and even if such an action would certainly result in his own death; to die as Samson did, taking the enemy with him. Barazani readily agreed.[116]

After Barazani's trial, Spielman asked cellmate Eliezer Ben-Ami to concoct a bomb from materials available in the prison. Ben-Ami suggested hiding explosives in a pair of phylacteries worn during morning prayers, but these proved too small. Ben-Ami next tried an orange. He cut off the top of the orange and ate the contents. He used wood shavings from the leg of a table to sew the top back on. Any protruding wood was pushed back in with a pencil. He presented Spielman with several oranges and asked him to try to identify the bomb by sight. When Spielman failed, Ben-Ami thought, "I wasn't crazy to think I could make a grenade out of an orange."[117]

Irgunists smuggled explosives into the prison in food packages, and Ben-Ami added shards from the prison's carpentry shop. Spielman guarded the cell door while Ben-Ami worked on the grenade in a corner. Meanwhile the prisoners began sending baskets of fruit to death row, to get the authorities accustomed to the traffic in citrus fruit. Since Feinstein's arm had been amputated after being shot when he left the train station, he asked to share a cell with Barazani, who would be able to help him get dressed. The two of them kept a hefty stock of fruit in the cell, and one day two grenades were added to it.[118]

One night, with no prior warning, the British authorities called Rabbi Jacob Goldman to recite final prayers with the two fighters. On entering the cell he was surprised to find the two young men, who had only hours ago been told they would die the next morning, in a cheery mood. They told jokes and sang. The two boys did at one point ask about the Jewish view of suicide, which they of course knew was forbidden. The rabbi assumed they were referring to their refusal to appeal their sentences, since they had not recognized the right of a British court in Eretz Israel to judge them. Rabbi Goldman therefore made reference to Rabbi Akiva and the many other martyrs for Israel who bequeathed their people a tradition of heroism.

The rabbi asked Barazani and Feinstein to recite the "Adon Olam" prayer with him, and they surprised him by refusing to recite it—but they immediately added they would agree to sing it. The guard posted outside later said he had never heard or seen anything like this last night on death row. Feinstein and Barazani liked this guard, and had already decided to abort their plan were he to be present at the hanging, so as not to hurt any British official who had been friendly. Now Feinstein handed him his Bible as a parting gift.

Rabbi Goldman could not bear the thought of the two being hanged alone with the enemy, so he promised to return in the morning. They failed to dissuade him and had to alter their plan.

If they could not die as Samson had, they could at least show that as Jews they held their fate in their own hands. They would not let the British hang Jews in Jerusalem. They would die as the Jews had died at Masada.

After the rabbi left, Barazani and Feinstein hugged. They placed a grenade between their hearts. With a cigarette, Barazani lit the fuse.

Two weeks later, the Irgun blew a hole in the wall of the Acco prison and dozens of Irgunists and Sternists escaped. Including criminal inmates, over 250 prisoners escaped, but almost all those not involved in the underground, who had not prepared safe houses, were quickly recaptured. The breakout was one of the heaviest blows to British prestige since the war for Hebrew liberation had begun. The British responded by sentencing three Irgunists caught during the operation to be hanged. The Irgun took two British sergeants hostage and warned the British not to hang their men, who were POWs; if the Irgunists were executed, the Irgun said, it would respond in kind. The British hanged the Irgunists anyway and the Irgun hanged the sergeants. After that, no more underground fighters were hanged in Eretz Israel.

In November, an Arab tipped the British off to the address of a house in Raanana where Lehi youth were training. The British police entered without being fired on and shot two young men and three young women to death. Five others were arrested. Lehi announced it would avenge their blood and in the course of the next week six British policemen and soldiers, and four civilian oil officials, were killed, and thirty-five more police and soldiers were wounded.[119]

After the breakout from the Acco prison, the British moved Jewish prisoners from Acco to Jerusalem. In the Jerusalem prison, cells were exchanged: The Hagana prisoners were being released legally because the Hagana had cooperated with the British, so the Hagana got the smaller Irgun room, cell 19; the Irgunists moved to a larger room, cell 31; Lehi got the larger Hagana room, cell 23. There were so many Lehi prisoners the authorities had to add bunk beds.[120]

In Acco, the Irgun had executed the escape, and so by agreement, twice as many Irgunists as Sternists were on the escape list. Now Lehi was able to repay the favor in Jerusalem. They were digging their way out of the Jerusalem prison and invited the Irgun to take one-third of the spots on the list of those destined to crawl out. The Irgun agreed. The Hagana prisoners were also asked if they wanted to escape, but they declined.

Joshua Zetler was in charge of Lehi operations in Jerusalem. He had earlier been transferred from the Jerusalem prison to Acco and was one of the escapees from there. Once free he rejoined Lehi's forces and was given charge of its combat unit. He moved to Jerusalem and took charge of operations in the city after the United Nations voted in November 1947 to partition the country between Jews and Arabs. One of his first moves was to send a message to the prisoners in the Jerusalem jail: he would get them out.[121] Matityahu Shmuelevitz, who was one of the Jewish prisoners transferred back from Acco to Jerusalem, took charge of digging a tunnel out of cell 23.

They dug in the corner, under Moshe Svorai's bed. Eliezer Ben-Ami, their engineer, was waiting in another cell for his expected release. When the diggers in cell 23 ran into technical difficulties their engineer was missing. So they concocted a story about his being their math and physics teacher and won prison permission for Ben-Ami to sleep in their cell two nights a week, when he would tutor them. Tutor he did, in the construction of support walls for the tunnel and in getting fresh air into its depths.[122]

A Jewish employee of the Public Works Department brought a map of the sewage tunnels near the prison and cement for the tunnel. Big stones

that were dug up were covered in blankets and carried into the prison courtyard. Eventually ten large stones were gathered there and no one ever asked
where they came from. Two stones were too big to carry to the yard; a prisoner brought a wooden plank from the carpentry shop, which they laid
across the two stones to create a table. This worked for while, until the day
a search was conducted, when the British were not pleased at the presence
of the table. Shmuelevitz said, "If you want us to remove it, we will remove
it." So they were able, under watchful British eyes, to remove the stones
they had been unable to remove until then.[123]

Still, there was too much sand and stone coming out of the tunnel.
Shmuelevitz suggested to the authorities that a pit be dug in the cell to collect the dirty water when they mopped, to obviate the need to carry buckets of water out of the cell and across the prison every morning. The warden loved the idea, and again, no one seemed to notice the huge amounts
of sand transported by wheelbarrows every day, far more than could have
come from the new pit. When even this ruse was not enough, the prisoners built a double wall in the prison's shoe shop, behind which the refuse
from the tunnel was dumped.

A Canadian prison expert was called in to search for tunnels. He announced that digging was underway and he would find the source.
Shmuelevitz looked worried and replied that he feared the Arab prisoners
were digging their way toward the Jewish cell to attack. Shmuelevitz was
given permission to post a Lehi man at the entrance to the cell as an early
warning station; one night this guard even staged a phony alert and anx-
iously called the prison officers, to convince them of the Sternists' worries.

Several searches of the cell were conducted, yet the tunnel was not discovered. The prison posted one of its guards on the roof, from where he
could look through a hole and watch the goings-on in the cell. The prisoners managed to keep out of his sight and the digging continued. They
had begun digging in December 1947. In February 1948, eight Sternists,
including Shmuelevitz and Svorai, and four Irgunists crawled from the
prison into the sewage pipes in the yard and emerged dressed as Public
Works employees. Inside, prison guards who got too near the tunnel were
taken into custody by the remaining prisoners and sequestered in another
cell; they were told, "We are running the prison now. We will release you
when we have finished our business." Outside, prison guards, smelling the
sewage-soaked escapees from afar, waved them on as they walked out of the
prison yard. By the time crawler number 13 was on his way out, the guards
outside knew something was wrong and put a halt to the escape. Inside the

cell they found Shmuelevitz' beard, which he had shaved so as not to be recognized outside the prison. "The f....g Jew left his beard here!" exclaimed the sergeant who found it.[124]

The escapees joined their friends outside whose fight lasted another three months, at which point the British evacuated their personnel from Eretz Israel. Those last few months the residents of Eretz Israel, the Jewish undergrounds included, were perplexed by British signals. While preparing to abandon the country, the British were also bringing in fresh troops from Egypt to replace some of those being sent home. Some British officials made no secret of their expectation, which many Jews read as a hope, that as soon as the British left the Arabs would make short shrift of the Jews and, in the ensuing chaos, England would be asked to return, restore order, and remain in control of Palestine. Jewish public opinion was inflamed by the perception the British were assisting the Arabs. The commanding general of the Arab Legion was Sir John Glubb, known as Glubb Pasha (who in May would lead the Arab Legion to take the Old City of Jerusalem, expel its Jews, and occupy the West Bank). Overall, 233 British soldiers and officers were serving with the Arab forces, motivated mostly by promises of pay.[125] At 6:30 A.M. on February 22, two days after the breakout from the Jerusalem prison, a British captain and corporal escorted Arabs in three British trucks full of explosives through Jerusalem's roadblocks and checkpoints and onto Ben-Yehuda Street, blowing up several blocks and killing some sixty people. A week later, still unsure whether the British intended to remain in Eretz Israel, determined to oust them, and now also eager for revenge, Lehi mined the rails on a bridge outside Rehovot and blew up a train carrying British troops from Egypt to Eretz Israel, killing 28 soldiers.

Recalling his Lehi activities more than sixty years after he had headed the Sternists' military operations division, Yaacov Banai told an audience in Tel Aviv that he had put together a list of operations conducted during the last phase of Lehi's war, from September 1946 until the British fled in May 1948. Needless to say, since Lehi was an underground and records were not kept, the list did not purport to be complete, but it was as comprehensive as he was able to make it. He recorded, he said, some thirty attacks on representatives of the government; thirty on government offices and buildings; thirty on transport lines and trains; eleven on cables; sixteen robberies and confiscations; all told, some two hundred attacks by Lehi on the British forces and government in that last period.[126] Not a single one of these attacks, or any of the operations conducted by the Sternists from the day the organization was formed by Abraham Stern in September 1940 until Jewish independence was won in 1948, targeted bus passengers, passers-by, women, or children. In their entire bloody, "terrorist," supposedly no-holds-barred war against the British, not a single British woman or child had been killed by Stern's group (some women were working in the country and many family members accompanied males stationed there). Lehi may have, once, deliberately murdered civilians, in retaliation for the British attack in Raanana in November 1947. But the circumstances of the murder are unclear, for the perpetrator had been given the license number of the victims' car and warned to exercize particular caution as they were dangerous.[127] Undoubtedly, civilians—British, Arab, and Jewish—were killed as they are in any war, but Lehi's policy was to target only the representatives of the regime occupying the Jewish homeland.

There were two more parts Lehi would play before exiting from the stage of Jewish history: fighting on the Arab front and assassinating Count Folke Bernadotte of the United Nations.

An Arab Front

As Stern had written in the "Principles of Rebirth" eight years earlier, war meant "never-ending war against anyone standing in the way of realizing our destiny." Any foreign regime in the country, no matter whose, had to be opposed, and any non-Jewish people or government laying claim to the country was an enemy. When the United Nations voted in November 1947 to divide Eretz Israel, the Jewish establishment welcomed the move and accepted the terms; the neighboring Arab countries and local Arabs opened attacks on Jewish towns and on individual Jews. This forced the Jewish fighting units to divert forces from the war for independence from England in order to defend Jewish areas from Arab attacks. Over the coming months the Arabs upped the scale of violence into a full-fledged war, which was made official when Arab armies invaded and attacked the one-night old Jewish state as soon as it had been born.

The Hagana bore the brunt of the Jewish community's defense burden, but the Irgun and Lehi wanted to do what they, smaller in numbers and poorer in equipment, could. Banai admitted, "To tell the truth, we weren't very ready for this front. Having focused all our deeds and concentration on the British enemy and its imperialist regime, feelings and thoughts had popped up about the desirability and possibility of cooperating with the Arabs against the 'common' British enemy...."[128] Banai said the Lehi fighters were divided on this issue, with some hoping for such cooperation and others determined to fight the Arabs as they had fought the British, but the situation on the ground forced everybody's hand, since if they did not defend and counterattack, the Arabs were going to make good on their oft-repeated threat to slaughter the country's Jews.

In December 1947, Lehi began allotting some of its forces to the war with the Arabs. A newspaper that incited against the Jews was blown up in Jerusalem. Vehicles belonging to the Arab Legion were attacked in Jerusalem and Haifa. Attacks were carried out in Jerusalem and in Arab centers. The railway into Jaffa was sabotaged. In January 1948, Lehi participated in the battle for Jerusalem being waged by all three fighting units; Lehi attacked and freed part of the Katamon neighborhood and defended and took part of Malcha. Lehi's biggest operation that month was the destruction of the "Saraya" building, the headquarters of the Arab Higher Committee in Jaffa.

Lehi's intelligence unit had made contact with three British detectives whose job was to listen to telephone calls to and from Jaffa. From these detectives, the intelligence operatives learned that Arab commanders from around the country were set to meet in the Saraya. They proposed to the Lehi Central Committee that Lehi bomb the building at that time, and Lehi went into action.[129]

A Sternist nicknamed Rigoletto cased the Saraya and the streets around it. Three days later, he drove toward the target in a car filled on one side with explosives and on the other side with fruits concealing the explosives. Two metal poles blocked the road to the building's rear where he had intended to park. He had no choice but to drive up the main street to the front of the building. When he drove up, the local taxi drivers demanded he stop blocking traffic. He tried to turn around, maneuvering around the car behind him, and soon found himself blocked in front by a truck. He drove onto the sidewalk in front of a café and was attacked by its clients. He sped off, now being chased by several Arab cars, which, luckily for him, were shot at by the area's Arabs, who thought they were Jewish cars.

Lehi fighters made another try and were prevented by Arab security from reaching the building. They set out on a third attempt determined to succeed, regardless of circumstances. This time it was pouring and the street clear; they parked and pretended to seek shelter from the storm. As they walked away, dressed as Arabs, the car blew up, destroying or damaging the headquarters of the Arab forces and the Arab Higher Committee, two neighboring banks, a warehouse and several homes and stores.[130] Dozens were killed, over a hundred injured. According to British reports, some children were being sheltered in the building at the time and were among the victims.[131]

The most famous or infamous action of Lehi and the Irgun on the Arab front, carried out with the approval of the Hagana, was an attack on the Arabs of Deir Yassin, a village that was technically at peace with the Jewish population but that had allowed Iraqi forces to encamp within. Because the village overlooked the road to Jerusalem, the Hagana wanted it taken.

About eighty Irgun and forty Lehi soldiers sent a car with a loudspeaker to warn the villagers they were about to be attacked. While this meant losing the element of surprise, it was hoped the move would encourage many of the residents to flee and get out of the fighters' way. The car overturned on its way up to the village, giving the villagers warning that something was up but, since no message was delivered, not exactly what. The village was therefore on alert. The attacking Jews were fired on from every house and ended up shooting and throwing grenades into many of these houses. Eventually the Jewish forces captured the village and hundreds of villagers, some of them combatants and others innocent. These prisoners were taken across Jerusalem toward the Old City and the Arab-controlled areas to be released.

Approximately one hundred Arabs were killed in Deir Yassin. The Arabs and the Jewish establishment called this an unprovoked massacre and added fictitious stories of Jewish fighters raping villagers and parading survivors through the streets to shame them. Because of the establishment's slander and the Arab exaggerations, Israel has forever had to defend itself from the charge of the crime, and the names of the Irgun and Lehi were darkened. But Irgun and Lehi veterans believe one unintended outcome of the defamation was beneficial, as they see it, to the Jewish state: local Arabs were so terrified of what would befall them after hearing about what occurred in Deir Yassin that many fled rather than fight, making the Israeli army's job easier and saving many soldiers' lives.[132]

Bernadotte

The final scene in Lehi's eventful history was also on the Jerusalem front. In mid-1948 Count Folke Bernadotte of the United Nations began brokering cease-fires between the warring parties in Eretz Israel. He came up with a plan to resolve the conflict, part of which included removing Jerusalem, the Negev, the Haifa port, and the country's airport from the Jewish state. Bernadotte sought to prevent the immigration of adult Jewish males to Israel; to this end he intended to station his own representatives in foreign ports to supervise departures for the Jewish state. On June

29, Ben-Gurion wrote in his diary that Bernadotte seemed to be acting as an agent for Ernest Bevin, Britain's much-hated foreign secretary.[133] The Lehi Central Committee approved Bernadotte's assassination.

Two seven- or eight-year old boys, Uri Scharf and Yoram Katz, were the only witnesses to the deed. They were playing on today's Palmach Street in Jerusalem. A jeep with four sunglassed and mustachioed "soldiers" was idling opposite the corner of today's Gedud Haivri Street. The boys asked the men in the jeep what kind of guns they had. One said he had a Norwegian Bren, one said a Czech Sten. The kids thought the men were joking. A few minutes later the "soldiers" told the two boys to go away, traffic was coming. The boys suggested they stay by the side of the jeep, but the men insisted they leave. As the boys were heading toward the corner of today's Chopin Street, they heard shots. Looking back, Scharf saw the jeep blocking three white cars. People were running from the jeep to the different cars. They ran back to the jeep, in which they sped past the boys. Scharf noticed one of them changing a cartridge. The white cars also passed them, and in one Scharf saw one of the passengers treating another. The boys returned to where they had been playing and collected some bullet shells.

The police checked the surrounding houses for possible witnesses. Scharf and Katz enthusiastically volunteered. They were questioned and the shells taken from them. Scharf told his parents the story when they returned home. His father took him to the bathroom and asked him if he could identify the shooters. He said he could. His father warned him, "They are bad people and if they find out they might...break our windows." The father wanted to frighten his son, but not too much.[134]

General Aage Lundstrom, who was sitting on Bernadotte's left, reported that the shooter pushed a Tommy gun through the window on his side of the car and fired repeatedly at Bernadotte. The French colonel on Bernadotte's right was also killed (either deliberately or because the driver, who suffered powder burns, tried pushing the gun away from Bernadotte). Lundstrom was uninjured, as was an American officer sitting next to the driver.[135]

Ben-Gurion, now prime minister of Israel, was opposed to Bernadotte's plan as was most of Israel. As prime minister, though, he had to play on the international political field, condemn the killing, and take action to show he was in charge. Ben-Gurion, however, had a deeper motive for acting against Lehi. He was determined that within Israel, there would be only one army, the state's, and one policy, the government's. Though Jerusalem was not yet technically part of the state, and thus the different undergrounds were still operating there, he was slowly dismantling them all: He had attacked an Irgun arms ship *Altalena* and essentially ended the Irgun's separate existence; he would soon dismantle the independent-spirited elite unit of his own Hagana, the Palmach; and he used the Bernadotte assassination as an excuse to arrest hundreds of former members of Lehi. Most were imprisoned. Most of these escaped from their overcrowded prison in Jaffa. Several Lehi veterans were released legally in order to staff the new Lehi political party, called the Fighters party, which was headed by Yalin-Mor. Others escaped and worked underground for the party. Still others, such as Eldad, remained all the while underground and waited for other Sternists to find their way to them. Yalin-Mor and Matityahu Shmuelevitz were put on trial by the army for violating an anti-terror law enacted after Bernadotte's assassination and given retroactive force by the cabinet. The Fighters party won one seat in the elections of January 1949, for Yalin-Mor, who was in jail at the time. Two weeks later a court ruled that it had heard no evidence of Lehi's involvement in the assassination and could not convict Yalin-Mor and Shmuelevitz of the deed, but it did convict them of membership in an illegal "terrorist" organization: Lehi. Yalin-Mor was sentenced to eight years in jail and Shmuelevitz, to five. Almost simultaneously the government issued a country-wide amnesty for all criminals in honor of statehood, and they were released.[136]

The man who pulled the trigger on Bernadotte was Joshua Cohen. Thus, the teenager who had given Lehi life after Stern's death had also fired its last shot.

5

People with Principles

Joshua Cohen may have been an extraordinary individual and fighter, but almost by definition, so were all nine hundred or so members of Lehi. Each had the temerity to think himself capable and worthy of declaring war on England. Each had the political awareness and self knowledge to fight for Hebrew independence when most of the people around him were going about their regular business.

The Sternist Yaacov Heruti refers to himself as just one of "several hundred Lehi members, and several tens of thousands of youth, members of all the fighting organizations, who were the silver platter on which the state was presented to the Jewish nation," and adds that

> Each of the fighters has the life story of a fighter, who knew he might give his life in the struggle—and many of them gave their lives, in the war and in ascending the gallows. All my brothers in Lehi, all my classmates in school (15 of 100 fell in the war to establish the state), and everyone who had a part in the Jewish people's war for its homeland are worthy of respect. Those who fell and those who lived dedicated their lives to the Jewish people and its homeland, Eretz Israel.[1]

In the chapters above many of these fighters appeared in their role as fighters. They were encountered in battle or in jail. The following pages will explore whence these and others came to the battle and why, and what became of them afterward. Lehi's three leaders will appear, followed by ten anonymous soldiers representing the run-of-the-mill Sternists rather than the few who attained fame by dint of deed or martyrdom. These profiles do not pretend to be exhaustive, either in content—entire books could be (and, in some cases, have been) written about more than one of those profiled below—or in numbers, since any selection from over nine hundred people, even if intended to be a cross-section, must be somewhat random.

Yitzhak Shamir: Chief of Operations

Israel Eldad, co-leader of Lehi with Yitzhak Shamir and Nathan Yalin-Mor, was undoubtedly a revolutionary theorist and agitator. Menachem Begin, Commander in Chief of the Irgun, was certainly a rebel, having declared the "revolt" against the British and led it for four years. But arguably, Shamir—though less theoretical than Eldad and commanding fewer forces than Begin, who would later precede him to Israel's premiership—was the most revolutionary personality to come to power in modern Israel or to attempt to do so. He chose as his nom de guerre during the revolution he led "Michael," after the Irish Republican Army leader Michael Collins, whose courage in fighting the British he admired.[2] Forty years later, regarding his service in the Israeli government, Shamir said, "Politics is war by other means," and he meant it.[3]

Yitzhak Shamir was born in 1915 in Poland to a traditional Jewish family and provided with a Hebrew day school education. His father was a leather worker and head of the local Jewish community. His original family name was Ysernitzki; Shamir was the name on a forged identity card he carried underground, and it stuck. He liked it because Shamir has two meanings in Hebrew: it is a "thorn, which stabs and stings; the question is who" and it is a "hard precious stone capable of breaking steel."[4]

Shamir joined Polish Betar after the 1929 Arab pogroms in Palestine. When the time came for college he enrolled at the University of Warsaw and took up law, but writes, "What became my raison d'être, what moved me and was to rivet my attention, undiminished, for the rest of my life, was the return of the Jews to the Land of Israel—a drive so intense, an idea so powerful, that all other options before me in Warsaw could in no way compete."[5]

Shamir dropped out and made aliya in 1935. His father, mother, and sisters were murdered by the Germans and Poles during the Holocaust.

In Eretz Israel Shamir found employment as a construction worker and later as an accountant. He enrolled in the Hebrew University of Jerusalem, but when the country's Arabs again attacked its Jews in the late 1930s, he again left school, this time to enlist in the Irgun. In 1938 he was active in a unit responsible for executing reprisal attacks against Arabs and was also involved in intelligence work. When Stern and the Irgun split, Shamir sided with Stern. Stern, he writes, "raised a banner only unfurled in Israel before by men like the hero whose name he took for his nom de guerre: Elcazar Ben-Yair, the first century leader of the Zealots who, for three years, held out on Masada...."[6]

Shamir served as deputy to the commander of Tel Aviv and in December 1941, on his way to visit his commanding officer, he was arrested. He was interrogated by Sergeant Thomas Wilkin and impressed enough with Wilkin's knowledge of the supposedly covert underground to know that Wilkin was a dangerous man. Shamir sat in the Jaffa prison and then in Acco; he was sentenced to three months in jail for possession of a rubber stamp used to forge documents, but since he was simultaneously under unlimited administrative detention, the three months did not particularly bother him. He was transferred to the Mizra Detention Camp, where he and Irgunist Menachem Lewin were assigned to collect the camp's garbage and cart it off to a nearby beach.[7] When Stern wrote to the prisoners urging escape, Shamir took it personally and in September 1942, he broke out with Eliahu Giladi.

As he was crawling out of Mizra, he was thinking of Stern's hopes to assassinate the British Minister of State in Cairo and of how he and his comrades had earlier viewed these hopes as sheer fantasy. Now, Shamir was determined: "I thought as I got ready for my escape that we needed to set as a goal for our organization that we be able to assassinate the British ruler in the Middle East."[8] It would take him two years.

According to *Lehi: People*, a sort of official album published by the Lehi veterans, Shamir

> found the organization in a difficult position and immediately set to rehabilitating it: he renewed the connections that had been lost; absorbed people, new immigrants, who had come from abroad; set up a branch in Egypt, whose members sent arms and ammunition;

made the administration efficient; heightened the secrecy; and recruited underground supporters who were
prepared to assist in providing hiding places, store-
houses, and housing. He also organized fundraising activities; ordered the formation of courses in theory and
in weaponry; and set up new branches throughout the
country and later abroad. Eventually he established the
Lehi Central Committee with Dr. Israel Eldad and
Nathan Yalin-Mor, on which he coordinated the organizational activity and was in charge of the combat division.[9]

Eldad, in his memoirs, recalls that Shamir had a tendency to immerse
himself in any subject or mission he took upon himself and to
micromanage it. This trait was displayed at the time; he insisted on personally interviewing almost all the recruits. Eldad says this was perfect for
Lehi at that stage, as Shamir raised it fighter by fighter from the ruins, but
the trait slowed the underground down when the number of potential fighters grew.[10] Another example of Shamir's style came during Lehi's attempt
to eliminate the High Commissioner in Jerusalem. Shamir dispatched
Joshua Cohen to do the job, then followed to check out the details.[11]

In the summer of 1946, Shamir was caught during a four-day massive
curfew and dragnet spread by the British over Tel Aviv. A British policeman
saw beyond his rabbinical beard and suit and recognized his bushy eyebrows. (As with Wilkin who had interrogated Shamir after his first arrest,
this policeman with the sharp eyes and memory for faces was deemed dangerous by the underground, and his days were numbered.) Shamir was
locked up in the Jerusalem prison, in solitary confinement, where, he says,
"I rested. I slept day and night. I was tired...."[12]

Shamir was soon put on a plane for Eritrea. At the end of August, following a six-hour flight, he found himself behind the barbed wire of a detention camp, longing for the "always warm and bright" Eretz Israel, so
unlike "here, where it's gloom, rain, and mud, and even when the sun
breaks through the clouds for a minute, the heat is stifling—not like our
homeland."[13] He longed for freedom, too, "that wonderful thing that will
allow us to build our lives, walk, stand and sit, love and hate as we and not
others wish."[14] And he longed no less for his wife—his former underground
contact, Shulamit—and his son, born in 1945 and named Yair; his longing
for them was as physical as it was spiritual, and it may not be coinciden-

Polish immigrants in a Jerusalem high school. Second row, center: Abraham Stern.

Abraham Stern in 1936

Abraham Stern and Roni (veiled)
under the wedding canopy

Abraham and Roni Stern on their
wedding day

David Raziel at 18

Abraham T'homi, first Commander
in Chief of the Irgun

*Joseph Trumpeldor in an officer's uniform
with the Zion Mule Corps, Gallipoli, 1915*

Contemporary depiction of the death of Joseph Trumpeldor, 1920

Poet Uri Zvi Greenberg, 1932

The editors of Hazit Haam, May 2, 1932. Left to right: Abba Ahimeir, Joshua Lichter, Joshua Yevin.

*Autograph manuscript of "To the Gangs of Crazies" by Abraham Stern
(see page 80)*

Destruction of CID headquarters in Jerusalem, December 27, 1945

An explosive ambush in Jerusalem, November 9, 1946

British soldiers amidst the ruins of Haifa's CID station, January 12, 1947

British soldiers surveying remains of police telephone exchange in Sarona, April 25, 1947

Vladimir Jabotinsky addressing the Third Betar Conference, Warsaw, 1938, at which Israel Eldad defended Menachem Begin's militant stance. On the dais, left to right: Yaacov Hoffman, Peretz Lasker, Menachem Begin, Joseph Glazman, Menachem Arber, David Warhaftig, Zalman Levenberg, Arieh Ben-Eliezer.

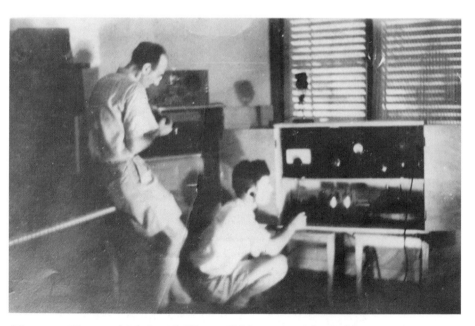

Matanya Ginosar (right) and Eliezer Sirkis prepare the Lehi transmitters for a broadcast, Tel Aviv, 1948. The photograph was taken in Ginosar's home at 115 Rothschild Blvd.

*Joshua Cohen (right) and Irgunist
Israel Ben-Amitai shortly before
their release from a detention camp
in Gilgil, Kenya, 1948*

*Joshua Cohen (right) with former prime
minister David Ben Gurion, Sde Boker, 1962*

A new member of Lehi in training, at the beach

Lehi soldiers attempting to reach the Old City of Jerusalem in 1948

Nathan Yalin-Mor (center) and Matityahu Shmuelevitz (left) on trial after the assassination of Count Bernadotte, January 1949

Nathan Yalin-Mor (rear) as a member of Israel's first Knesset, 1949. Front rows, left to right: Uri Zvi Greenberg, Yaacov Meridor, Menachem Begin.

The Lehi convention, March 1949. Left to right: Nathan Yalin-Mor, Yitzhak Shamir, Israel Eldad.

On Israel's Memorial Day in May 2011, a ceremony organized by the Lehi Heritage Society at the "Lehi Monument" in Mishmar Ayalon attracted hundreds of teenagers. Abraham Stern's son Yair eulogized his father's fallen comrades.

tal that just as he referred to the warmth of the homeland he often referred to the warmth of his little son's body. Indeed, at one point he explained that

> I don't recognize or see the boundaries between the personal and impersonal; you might say, everything is personal, one whole, one tome with different chapters: Love of homeland and love of a precious beloved wife; missing one's brothers, the strong sons of the homeland, and missing one's sweet, cute son, flesh of my flesh. The boundaries are blurred, everything is beloved and precious, so attractive and so missed.[15]

At night he lay awake staring into the dark, imagining Shulamit lying awake staring into the dark, and their son calling out in the knowledge that his mother and father are awake.[16]

Five months after his arrival, he wrote his wife a relatively brief note to "say only this: I love you very much, I love my son, love my homeland and my whole, whole family. And such a love obligates one."[17] Two days later, on January 14, 1947, he escaped with four Irgunists. He and one of the Irgunists crossed the border to Ethiopia, and from there to Djibouti in Somalia, where they were arrested. The British demanded their extradition, but the French were friendlier and, notwithstanding many delays, provided passage on a ship to France. On May 1, 1948, over a year after his escape, Shamir was finally a genuinely free man. Two weeks later Israel was established, but the British, who still had soldiers posted there, and the Israeli government, which was led by opponents of the Irgun and Lehi, were not putting out a welcome mat for the exiled fighters.[18] Lehi fighter David Shomron sent Shamir a forged passport, with which he flew to Israel.[19]

Looking back at his and his fellow underground fighters' years of prison and sacrifices, Shamir deprecated them, asking, "Can we speak of a readiness to sacrifice? What kind of a sacrifice is life or everything in it compared to saving a single Jewish child?" And as for the "goal of goals: freedom for all the mothers and fathers, brothers and sisters, boys and girls who comprise the people, our people, guaranteeing them freedom and beauty and human dignity, is anything more noble than this, more worthy of love and sacrifice?"[20]

Enclosed behind barbed wire, exiled from his home and family, he had written that there a person understands

> he didn't make sacrifices in the past. On the contrary,

he won his happiness. Everything he gave, every effort
he made, everything he suffered on behalf of his brothers—were all drops of happiness, which watered his life's
path and gave him moments of satisfaction and pleasure.
The suffering and worries of life's struggles are better
than the lack of worries and lack of even lack in a "nir-
vana" detached from life.[21]

Now, after the formation of Israel, Lehi was breaking up. Shamir joined
with Eldad and Yalin-Mor to transform it into the Fighters party. Shamir
became the party's secretary general. Tempers ran high at party meetings
as Eldad pulled to the right and Yalin-Mor to the left. Shamir tried to keep
things together. "You are my only brothers, my family," he told the former
revolutionaries.[22] But the split in the party's ranks was stronger than
Shamir's wishes or love; Shamir sided with the majority leaning toward
the left, but even it broke up not long after.

As did all the former fighters, Shamir had to earn a living, in his case
to support himself and his family. In addition to his wife, who had been a
prisoner of the British in the Bethlehem Women's Prison, and his son, a
daughter had been born in 1949, named Gilada. Shamir claimed she was
named for the mountain region east of the Jordan River, in today's kingdom of Jordan, which once belonged to the Hebrew tribes of Reuben, Gad,
and Menasheh, but one must wonder what unconscious currents led him
to give her the name of the friend with whom he escaped from Mizra, whom
he then had to kill, Elihau Giladi.

Shamir tried to get a job as a clerk at the Interior Ministry but Prime
Minister Ben-Gurion thought the government would be better off without
a former Stern commander clerking for it.[23] Instead, Shamir tried running
a chain of movie theaters in Ramat Gan and Givatayim. When that did not
work out as well as he had hoped, he formed a construction company with
Lehi vets Yalin-Mor, Shomron, and Shlomo Ben-Shlomo. The first road they
built led to Sodom, then came a road to Ashkelon, and a sidewalk in
Beersheba. But all things considered, business was not for Shamir. In 1948
he had told his Lehi faithful, as they considered what to do after emerging
from the underground, "Personally, I am miserable when everything is in
order and quiet. Seriously, it's hard for me, when I can go home quietly, go
to sleep, and get up in the morning without fear and tension. I feel alive
inside only when obstacles are arising that must be overcome and eliminated."[24] Now he told former Lehi bomb expert Yaacov Eliav, "I feel like I'm
not being useful."[25]

Eliav had already been recruited by Israel's secret intelligence service, the Mossad. He suggested Shamir apply; Shamir doubted the government would allow him to join but was willing to try. Mossad chief Isser Harel cleared it with Ben-Gurion and interviewed Shamir. Harel had two questions for Shamir: "Do you want to join?" and, "Can I rely on your loyalty?" Shamir's affirmative guarantees were enough for Harel. Shamir had one request, that he not be forced to do anything that was against his conscience. Harel replied that Shamir could call him if he were ever asked to. They worked together for the next decade and Shamir never made such a call.[26]

Harel then drafted several other Lehi vets, including David Shomron, who was sent to Paris and who supervised Mossad operations in Morocco. Secrecy was such that Shomron met Shamir in Paris, where he, too, was stationed, without knowing they shared the same employer. One of Shamir's first missions was to try to prevent a Soviet-sponsored arms deal between Czechoslovakia and Egypt, a mission at which he did not succeed. He then established and ran a special operations unit that placed agents or "moles" in hostile countries. He was also on the Mossad's General Staff and created its Planning Division. Shamir left the Mossad about six months after Harel resigned in 1963. Harel's assessment of his work was that "Shamir did his job excellently. He displayed exceptional operational skill and thinking. Had he remained in the Mossad, he could have been its deputy director or even its director."[27] Agent Mike Harrari, who served under Shamir in Europe, says, "I learned from [Shamir's] underground methods in handling fighters. These were original and unique methods, which I used in my operations and taught my agents and fighters." Harrari says Shamir's methods are still official doctrine today.[28]

Back in Israel, Shamir once again tried his hand at business. He managed a rubber factory in Kfar Saba. Once again, he was restless. He joined Menachem Begin's Herut party in order to help work to win freedom for Soviet Jewry. When Dov Shperling, a Latvian Jew convicted of studying Jewish history and disseminating information about Israel and sent to a gulag for two years, made it to Israel in 1968, he met with Shamir. Shperling recalls describing for Shamir Soviet Jews dancing at a synagogue on the eve of the Simchat Torah holiday. "Shamir's eyes welled with tears and I saw what true love of Israel is," says Shperling. Shamir opened the doors of journalists and politicians to Shperling, who was trying to get Israel to adopt a more activist stance in the effort to free Soviet Jews.[29]

In 1973 Shamir was elected to the Knesset. In 1977 he was elected

Speaker of the Knesset. He began by reading everything he could get his hands on describing parliamentary procedure around the world, another example of his immersing himself completely in any given subject or task. As Speaker, he abstained during the votes on the Camp David Accords and peace treaty with Egypt, the terms of which he opposed.[30]

In 1980 Shamir was appointed foreign minister. Able to speak to the pope in Polish and to Europeans in French, he promised Israelis that if confirmed as foreign minister he would do two things: improve his English and buy a tuxedo. He did both. Following Begin's resignation from the premiership in 1983, Shamir was chosen by Herut to replace him. The next year, he ran on his own right and split the vote with the Labor party, headed by Shimon Peres. The two reached an agreement to "rotate" in the premiership. Peres went first, with Shamir serving as foreign minister until he took over in October 1986. Shamir won the next elections in 1988 and again formed a national unity government with Peres. When Peres tried in 1990 to topple his own coalition in order to unseat Shamir, he was outmaneuvered, and Shamir remained at the helm for another two years, without Labor.

The last two years of his government were marked by several important events: the first Gulf War, during which Shamir acquiesced to U.S. demands that Israel not respond to missile attacks by Saddam Hussein, seemingly contradicting his commitment to reprisal attacks in the 1930s; the mass aliya of tens of thousands of Ethiopian immigrants; and the Madrid Peace Conference, held under the auspices of both Russia and the United States, with the participation of Arab countries. One need only look at the grim look on Shamir's face in photographs of the event to know how he felt about attending.

Shamir lost the 1992 elections to Labor's Yitzhak Rabin. A member of Shamir's party, Roni Milo, chided him for not being more innovative in dealing with the Arabs; had he pulled Israeli troops and residents out of Gaza, Milo argued, he might have won the election. Shamir answered, "I didn't give up a millimeter, and I'm not sorry about it."[31] Yet this conversation provides a hint as to why Shamir lost; he trusted people like Milo and allowed them to serve in his cabinet, though they did not share his values. Instead of uniting and inspiring the public, the government bickered.

Ephraim Even, an Israeli writer and analyst, once asked Shamir who he considered the greatest person he had ever met. Shamir replied, "Menachem Begin was the greatest person I met." Shamir explained, "Begin was the man because of whom the British left Eretz Israel. Had he not come in the early 1940s, there wouldn't have been a real war with the British and they wouldn't have been chased out of Israel." Even—a veteran Irgunist—nevertheless took offense on behalf of Shamir's own troops and asked, "But there was Lehi?!" "Lehi alone wouldn't have succeeded; and neither would the Irgun without Begin!" responded Shamir.[32]

In the 1999 elections, Shamir supported Menachem Begin's son, Benny, who had left Shamir's own Likud and Herut parties to run on a more nationalist platform. Shamir reduced his public appearances in the coming years, though playing a typically proud Jewish father to his children, often noting, "My son is doing great in business," or, "He calls me every day."[33] His attempts to convince his son to go into politics have so far not borne fruit. Since 2004, Shamir has not been in good health and is confined to a nursing home.

Toward the end of his autobiography, Shamir writes, "If history remembers me at all, in any way, I hope it will be as a man who loved the Land of Israel and watched over it in every way he could, all his life."[34]

Israel Eldad: Paving the Road to Redemption

When Israel Eldad was told that Israeli author Ada Yevin was writing his biography, he sighed to a friend that he saw it as a pointless endeavor, as there was nothing of interest to write about. "Biographies should be written about leaders, like Yair, who deserves one. But I never saw myself as a leader. I don't have organizational skills. I saw myself and wanted to be by the side of leaders."[35] Another time he said, "My ideas are my biography and my ideas have already been published."[36]

Others may find a life that includes setting one's own youthful oratory against Jabotinsky's, escaping from the invading Nazis together with Menachem Begin, fleeing from British policemen via a window and falling several stories, and escaping from jail exciting enough for a biography. Eldad acknowledged people wanted to read about his escape, "I know people are interested in stories, but history interests me only from the point of view of what it obligates us to today."[37] Eldad's real biography is, as he said, the story of his thoughts. His thoughts on almost any topic are diamonds to be held, turned over, and considered in different lights to discover their full worth. Some examples:

From an article published when Eldad was in his twenties, writing about an author he liked:

> The two-thousand-year Exile ended in castration and reversed the relationship between our spiritual forces. Normally, in an individual or a society the will is dominant because life is motion, and all motion springs from and derives force from the will. The intellect restrains and sets the direction. But the Exile wreaked psychological havoc with this healthy relationship in our blood, in both the individual and the community. The will was relegated to a forgotten corner and our life centered on the spirit, the intellect. Our lives focused and stood still; for without the will there is no movement.[38]

A warning from an essay written in 1961:

> If I become accustomed to thinking in categories of "miracles" then I will continue thinking in those terms in respect of the future as well and I shall rely on miracles.[39]

From an article written in the 1980s:

> The devil, in the person of Hitler, proved that the swastika—an outgrowth in some instances and countries of the cross—and the Nazi hatred of Jews, which used and misused the Christian hatred of Jews, were turned and were necessarily turned eventually against Christianity itself, insofar as that Christianity is Christian in its ideas and morals.[40]

An interpretation of a biblical incident: King Solomon prayed upon the dedication of the Temple in Jerusalem and said to God, "You would dwell in fog, I have built You a Home...." Eldad said God could just as easily have continued living in fog. God does not need a Temple; it is people who need something concrete to focus on, such as a Temple, or an ark inside it, to know that this is God's home.[41]

Asked once whether he was going on vacation, Eldad retorted, "A factory worker can take a vacation. What can I be on vacation from—my head?"[42]

Eldad's Lehi co-administrator Yitzhak Shamir pinpointed the importance of Eldad's mind to the Jewish people; Shamir said, "After Yair was murdered, Eldad took upon himself the task of being the Spirit."[43] Ironically, noted Shamir in a published eulogy, "we argued paradoxically: he, the man of the spirit and the book, put the emphasis on military operations. I, the 'practical one,' preferred propaganda. When the argument ended we agreed and began putting out a monthly bulletin called *Hehazit*....And a new spirit swept the rank and file. 'This is the child we prayed for,' said the old-timer fighters."[44] Shamir says he quickly learned that he "had underestimated Eldad's strength. He turned out not only to know how to write and to relate to the youth, but to be an ideologue with broad vision, a teacher, and a sharp debater who knew how to answer those who cursed the underground."[45]

Eldad (his original family name was Scheib; Eldad was one of his assumed names in Lehi, which he took from a ninth-century Jewish traveler named Eldad Hadani, who went searching for a free Jewish state where the ten lost tribes of Israel supposedly lived[46]) was born in 1910 in the Galicia region of Poland. At the age of four he was singing Bialik's "El Hatsippor," a poem about a bird from Eretz Israel bringing news of the redemption to a suffering Jew in the Diaspora, and the direction of Eldad's life was set.

His father taught him chess and Hebrew while they hid in an attic during World War I. He studied in a Polish elementary school before being sent to a Jewish high school, at which time his father, a man who loved education, culture, and Zionism, and his mother, who had the fiery spirit of her Hasidic family, also hired a tutor to immerse him in Judaic and Hebrew studies. At 16, Eldad chose to leave home to study in a Jewish high school where the lessons were taught completely in Hebrew. By the time he graduated he was attracted to philosophy, especially that of Friedrich Nietzsche, and also to the Zionism of Vladimir Jabotinsky. Eventually he would translate most of Nietzsche into Hebrew, a feat for which he would be awarded Tel Aviv's Tchernichovsky Prize. Eldad's translations are available in all Israeli bookstores and earned him royalties for decades. "I never thought I would be living off Nietzsche," he laughed.[47]

At 18, Eldad enrolled in both the University of Vienna and the Rabbinical Seminary of Vienna. He eagerly studied everything from Indian philosophy to the Talmud, from logic to midrash. He was awarded a Ph.D. for a thesis entitled "The Voluntarism of Eduard von Hartmann, with Its

Basis in Schopenhauer," but he did not apply for ordination.

He had at least two fateful encounters during those years: he met Batya Waschitz in 1932 and they were married in 1937, and in 1930 he read a poem by Uri Zvi Greenberg, "I'll Tell It to a Child," which was to him "an earthquake."[48] The poem was Greenberg's account of a would-be redeemer who stood on the edge of the site of Israel's past and future temples in Jerusalem, but who was chased away by those of his people who preferred to remain without grandeur. Eldad met the poet two or three years later and would ultimately be buried at his feet in Jerusalem.

Excited by Greenberg's version of Zionism, Eldad joined Jabotinsky's Betar movement and while teaching professionally in Volkovysk led that city's Betar chapter. In 1938 he attended the Third Betar Conference in Warsaw, where he supported Menachem Begin's call for a more militant Zionist stance than Jabotinsky was advocating. When Jabotinsky compared Begin to a useless squeaky door and Eldad responded by noting that a squeaky door is capable of waking people who are asleep and saving them, Jabotinsky applauded Eldad's rhetoric (literally; Jabotinsky joyfully exclaimed, "He got me!") but left the room before Eldad finished speaking.[49] At that conference, Eldad's Betar friend Nathan Yalin-Mor introduced him to Abraham Stern, who had sat in the balcony during Eldad's speech and had been impressed by his views.

These views soon lost Eldad his teaching job. A play was performed portraying the Maccabees as rebels who waved only paper scrolls and opposed the use of violence. Eldad wrote an article critical of the policy of restraint in general and especially of foisting nonviolent views on the Maccabees, of all people. He was fired. He took the opportunity to move to Warsaw, where he was put in charge of Betar's cultural activities.

He and Batya escaped from Warsaw one step ahead of the Germans and hid in a town outside Vilna with Menachem and Aliza Begin. In September 1940, the Soviet secret police arrested Begin while Begin and Eldad were playing chess. Begin conceded the game, but they agreed they would continue playing some other time. Traveling on forged documents, the Eldads reached Eretz Israel via Russia and Turkey in April 1941; Begin was still in a Soviet prison at the time and would by June be in a Soviet labor camp. When Begin and Eldad met again in Eretz Israel, Begin suggested they resume the game. Eldad's account of these events in his memoirs is highly metaphoric. Of Begin's original concession, he writes, "For the record....We were only on the seventh or eighth move. The battle was still before us." When they reunited, Begin then of the Irgun and Eldad of Lehi, Begin said,

"Nu....We will continue?" and Eldad answered, "We will continue, Menachem." But Eldad retells this story a few chapters later, noting there, "But we did not continue together."[50]

Eldad worked with Stern on his underground newspaper, then called *Bamachteret*, and later, Eldad, Shamir, and Yalin-Mor formed the triumvirate that ran Lehi. Eldad wrote for or edited Lehi's various publications, from wall posters to the newspapers *Hehazit* and *Maas* (The Deed). He was arrested fleeing the police when he fell from a fourth-story window and was imprisoned in the Jerusalem prison in a body cast.

He continued his underground work in his cell and in the prison's infirmary. Lehi prisoners took turns at his bed taking dictation and smuggling out of the jail his articles for the underground papers. When he was able to walk, he paced the cell, back and forth, for about 15 minutes, then recited an entire article to be written down by one of the prisoners. Those who recorded his words called him the "man of drawers," because he seemed to have all the world's information at his fingertips, categorized and neatly filed, and he knew from exactly which drawer to pull whatever information he needed on any subject.[51]

In September 1944, when Eldad's health permitted, he was transferred to the Latrun Detention Camp. The Sternists arranged his escape during one of his visits to his Jerusalem doctor in June 1946, and from then on he was free. Instead of writing in prison he wrote the underground papers in hiding, and now he lectured new recruits instead of prisoners. One Lehi member, Yoram Sion, recalls being sent with 17 fellow Sternists, all of whom had done a weapons course together, to a course in Lehi's ideas given by "the Doctor," the members' nickname for Eldad. They arrived two by two at the house of a Lehi supporter who had been asked to absent himself for the day. Eldad entered and without any introduction began speaking, which he did nonstop for almost three hours. "He hypnotized us," remembers Sion. "Our legs turned to stones, but it was enchanting; we were no longer of this world."[52]

During this period Eldad and Yalin-Mor formulated their foreign policy, "the neutralization of the Middle East," which called for a region free of superpower influence and imperialism. Within this region, Eldad wanted the Jewish state to pursue its own interests, beholden neither to the United States nor the Soviet Union, and certainly with no attachment to England. Yalin-Mor agreed but at some point began leaning toward the Soviet bloc, and this would be the major cause of the break up of what was left of Lehi after the establishment of the State of Israel.

Eldad was party to Lehi's decision to assassinate Bernadotte in September 1948. A year later, above ground without Lehi, Eldad recalled this decision:

> A year ago at this time I was not able to sit at a table in my home with my family, and seemingly I should be happy now, yet it is difficult to be happy with a whole heart. A year ago I was hunted by the hunters, and yet I was neither uneasy nor frightened, for I was not poor of deed, for goyim learned that Israel is not up for grabs. Now I am uneasy and frightened, for I am poor of deed and goyim are again opening their mouths to swallow us, to swallow the holy city of Jerusalem, and us with it. And I cannot rest here in my home if there is no rest for my beloved Jerusalem....Therefore my rest is not pleasant, and I do not want it at all.[53]

In Israel, Eldad wanted to preserve the ideological purity of Lehi and proposed Lehi become a political-educational movement, but he was in the minority. He founded a journal he called *Sulam* (Ladder), after the ladder in Jacob's dream that united heaven and earth, and that, according to Eldad, implied a firm Land of Israel underneath the ladder whose people reached for Heaven. The journal's full name was *The Ladder to the Kingdom of Israel*; it advocated the policies first propounded by Stern and later developed by Lehi. Eldad gathered Stern's poems and *Sulam* published the collection. Eldad gave Stern's eight-year-old son, Yair, a copy of the book, which he inscribed, "When the king, the messiah, comes, give him this book and tell him your father loved him and gave his life for him, and he should pay his respects to your father."[54]

Meanwhile, while editing *Sulam*, Eldad resumed his teaching career, until Prime Minister Ben-Gurion ordered him fired. Though Eldad was teaching Bible, Ben-Gurion was afraid he would spread Lehi's ideas to adolescents. Eldad went to court and won, but his career had been irreparably damaged by the prime minister's publicly expressed antipathy. It would be years before he would resume teaching, this time in various Israeli universities.

Instead he wrote several books, including one commentary on the Bible and a history of the world in newspaper form called *Chronicles*, which was translated into English and over fifty years later is still in print, as are most of his Hebrew books. For these writings, he was awarded Israel's Bialik Prize for Jewish Thought in 1988. His memoirs of the Lehi years were published in Hebrew right after the War of Independence and have gone through some five Hebrew editions, yet were translated into English only in 2008. His journal *Sulam* came out for 14 years. He was a regular columnist for the Israeli dailies *Yediot Aharonot* and *Haaretz*.

Eldad was one of the founders of the Greater Israel Movement calling for retention of the territories absorbed into Israel during the Six Day War, and in the late 1970s, in response to the signing of the Camp David Accords by Menachem Begin, he became one of the founders of the Tehiya (Rebirth) party (the name meant to allude to Stern's "Principles of Rebirth"). When General Rehavam Ze'evi founded the more extreme Moledet (Homeland) party, he offered Eldad the top spot on the list of the party's candidates for the Knesset. Eldad's only request was to know who else would be on the list. But Ze'evi refused to say, telling Eldad he would choose on his own and the names would appear in the newspaper a few days later. Eldad turned down Ze'evi's offer.[55]

In the early 1980s Eldad proposed that all the Zionist parties in Israel unite in support of a platform resembling the Allon Plan, originally formulated by Laborite Yigal Allon, calling for the retention by Israel of the Jordan Valley and other strategic areas. Eldad thought that this plan, which he considered the minimum amount of territory necessary for Israel but which Labor would consider the maximum, might be able to unite the divided Jewish community and allow Israel to speak with one voice. Nothing came of Eldad's proposal.

Eldad was approached by Yeshiva University about speaking or teaching a course in the late 1980s, and he proposed "an intensive seminar on the poetry of Uri Zvi Greenberg," explaining, "This matter weighs heavy upon me, as an obligation I must fulfill to others and to draw your students into a world almost unknown to them." Eldad asked to be granted 25-30 double periods in order to "impart the minimum amount of necessary material."[56] Yeshiva University must have had second thoughts, as the administration never followed up. In Israel, Eldad delivered several versions of this course in various schools and academies, and his lectures became the basis for a book about Greenberg's poetry edited by Eldad's son, Arieh.

Eldad bought a burial plot on the Mount of Olives adjacent to Greenberg's. He confided this was not the only option he had considered: "I couldn't decide whether to be on the Mount of Olives near Barazani and Feinstein or near Uri Zvi Greenberg. Then I realized, no one thinks of the graves of Barazani and Feinstein, they think of Begin who is buried next to them. They would say: 'You followed Begin.' And I never followed Begin.

So the choice was Uri Zvi Greenberg." Eldad added, "It is at the top of the Mount of Olives...there is a nice view."[57] Eldad died in January 1996 and was buried in that plot, where he rests today, overlooking the Temple Mount.

Nathan Yalin-Mor: A Revolutionary of the Left

"It is permitted to walk on grass and trample flowers. It is a historical necessity, if you want to start the great revolution.... Any talk about government's proper role and civil obedience is worthless," wrote Nathan Yalin-Mor.[58] He was not referring to Lehi and the Zionist revolution. He was writing 30 years after that revolution, which had created the State of Israel, and was referring to a social, economic, and political revolution that had not yet started. His belief in it and the policies he advocated for Israel distanced him from many of his former Lehi friends and almost all but the fringe of the Israeli political world. Yalin-Mor advocated an Israel allied with the Soviet Union, and called—beginning in the 1950s—for Israel to assist in the creation of a Palestinian state.

Yalin-Mor was born in 1913 in Grodno, in today's Belarus. His original family name was Friedman-Yalin, and he took Mor from his wife Frieda's maiden name when he got married, so they would both be contributing part of their new family name.[59] His father disappeared when he was one, drafted first into the Czar's army and then into revolutionary militias. Yalin-Mor grew up in his grandfather's home, in a town that was conquered some fourteen times by the time Yalin-Mor was seven. One writer says Yalin-Mor took away an undying gratitude toward the Soviets, whose army was the only one from which the local Jews did not have to hide in fear, and which even incorporated the Jews into active service.[60] But in Yalin-Mor's memoirs of his pre-underground years, he recounts "naturally" supporting the Fins when the Soviets invaded Finland in 1940, for "how can one not admire a small nation fighting for its life, rejecting the dictates of those bigger than it and ready to make many sacrifices, regardless of effectiveness, to defend the homeland and its independence?"[61] Perhaps a more accurate assessment of the impression the events of his childhood made on Yalin-Mor would be that Yalin-Mor took away from these events what he already had inside, a deep empathy for people fighting for freedom.

Even as a child Yalin-Mor had a diplomat's talent for turning a phrase. When classmates taunted him in elementary school, "Jews, go to Palestine!" he answered, "Of course I'll go there. What did you think, that I'd stay here near you?" and when, at the age of 13, inspired by Adam Mickiewicz and other Polish poets and by Poland's romantic struggle for freedom, he joined Betar and was scolded by his Jewish friends that Betar intended to use arms to liberate its homeland, he replied, "And why can't Eretz Israel be conquered with arms? Won't it work?"[62]

Yalin-Mor joined Betar's national leadership when he moved to Warsaw in 1933. In addition to his Zionist activities, Yalin-Mor studied engineering in Warsaw. He met Stern in 1937 and later said that this meeting made him a new person. Stern struck a chord in Yalin-Mor when he reported that the Irgun in Eretz Israel was turning into a force of Jewish national liberation that would free the country from the British occupiers. Stern told him that the Irgun was only the kernel, and that the real army would be raised among Jews abroad, who would be trained and would land on the shores by the tens of thousands when the Irgun made its move. Yalin-Mor says he pledged on the spot to dedicate the rest of his life to the Hebrew war of liberation in Eretz Israel.[63]

He began by crisscrossing Poland to establish cells dedicated to Stern's vision. He assisted in the organization of "illegal immigration" to Eretz Israel. He established (with Samuel Merlin, whose initiative it was) and edited the Irgun's newspaper in Warsaw, *Di Tat*, living in its editorial offices and often writing the entire paper, "from the headline to the last line."[64] With war coming, he closed the paper on August 25, 1939, and from August 28, served as one of the editors of another newspaper, *The Moment*. On September 5, five days after the Germans invaded Poland, in between air raids, he and Frieda convinced a jeweler to bring a selection of rings from his locked store; they chose one and were married that afternoon (Menachem and Aliza Begin were their best man and woman); that night Yalin-Mor put out the final edition of *The Moment*, and the next day they and the Begins fled Warsaw.[65]

Begin had just returned from the Romanian border, where mobs of Polish Jewish refugees had been turned back by the Romanians under pressure from the British, and Begin was now seeking another way out of Poland.[66] Begin and Yalin-Mor stuffed two packs as heavily as they could and another light one for their wives, to be carried by each woman in turn, and the four set off for whatever train they could catch. They were hoping for Lvov, which would at least take them south in the general direction of Eretz Israel, but they settled for Vilna to the north. The trains were already jammed and the doors locked. A friend pulled them through a window and they sat on the floor. The train spent most of the night and next few days standing still, halting and emptying during bombing raids, and crawling along to avoid running over shelled tracks. The two couples abandoned the train, a good target for German bombers, and walked most of the route. As they left the train and were strafed by the bombers, they realized that the Germans were aiming more for the refugees than the train. They took to traveling through fields at night. They finally caught a train for Lvov, then in Soviet-occupied territory. There they met up with Israel Eldad and his wife and other members of Betar and the Irgun.[67]

Several of them, including Yalin-Mor, made their way south to check out the border and were arrested. Yalin-Mor made up a story about going there to renew his studies that was surely not taken seriously, yet his interrogator and he both spoke Esperanto, a language whose supporters once hoped it would become a single international language, and in a comradely gesture he put Yalin-Mor on a train, under guard, with a warning never to return.[68] The Yalin-Mors and Begins, reunited, set off for Vilna. The train station was under guard and effectively under siege by mobs of potential passengers. A scout informed Yalin-Mor of a back fence near the tracks. He pulled Frieda out of the crowd and they found a hole in the fence; when they stepped through they found themselves in the town's sewage pool. Frieda was unable to walk without vomiting, so Nathan carried her, reducing his own breathing to a minimum to avoid his own collapse. On dry land he used an old newspaper to clean his shoes and found seats on the Vilna train. As the train rolled out, he says he drew the following lesson:

> Sometimes, the path to a goal is paved with mud, slime, and excrement. If you want to get there, there is no choice but to take it. Fastidiousness will keep your shoes clean but will also keep you from any hope of reaching an expanse, of reaching the life you want. Ultimately you may sink to your neck in refuse and repulsiveness and not be able to extricate yourself your entire life. Only after you reach your destination, can you wipe the slime off your feet and breath deeply.[69]

Later, Yalin-Mor added that if you hesitate and halt in the mud, then you, all you stand for, and all you want to contribute to others will be trampled by those who have no compunctions about marching on.[70]

Nathan and Frieda continued their long journey to Eretz Israel, where they arrived in August 1941.

On arrival, they both joined Stern's organization. Following a trip to Lebanon by Lehi member Naftali Lubinchik, who was tasked with making contact with the Germans, Stern sent Yalin-Mor to Syria for the same purpose; Yalin-Mor was supposed to cross into Turkey and find his way to a German embassy, there or in the Balkans.[71] While marking time in Syria that winter he was arrested by the British and returned to Palestine, where he was held in detention.

When a copy of Eldad's Lehi paper *Hehazit* reached him in 1943, he was beside himself with enthusiasm. He wrote Eldad a long letter of support, which included suggestions for improvements. Among other things, Yalin-Mor wanted Lehi's paper to focus on geopolitical issues. He foresaw the breakup of the Allied bloc of the war and wanted the Hebrew liberation movement to be alert to the conflicts of interest that would follow. He urged an attempt to unite peoples oppressed by the British such as the Indians, Boers, and French Canadians, and a "synchronization" of their struggles.[72] He hoped Eldad would include in *Hehazit* examples of other peoples' fights for freedom: the Irish, Poles, Balkans, Americans, and also Lenin's revolutionary activity after 1905 and the successful Russian Revolution of 1917. He also urged the inclusion of a literary section referencing such books as John Steinbeck's *Grapes of Wrath* and citations from Nietzsche's *Thus Spake Zarathustra* (the sections "On War" and "On Life and Death"). He advocated acknowledging the death of Zionism and casting Lehi as a native "Israeli liberation movement," which foreshadowed the ideas he would expound after the establishment of the state.[73] When Yalin-Mor edited the Lehi papers after Eldad's arrest, he was able to emphasize the geopolitical and other issues he raised in this early letter.

Yalin-Mor's seminal literary contribution to Lehi's development and to its folklore, his "Liquidate the Prisons" article, came during these early days, when the British were arresting or summarily executing Lehi members. The armed-at-all-times policy led to the deaths of many British policemen and not a few Lehi members, others of whom, when caught with guns, were sentenced to long prison terms. Nonetheless, it stirred the Lehi ranks as had nothing before, boosting their morale and organizational pride and helping create the image of daring, fearless Lehi fighters.

Yalin-Mor dug his way out of the Latrun camp with 19 other fighters in November 1943. He became Lehi's unofficial foreign minister, and participated in negotiations with the leaders of the other underground organizations. When the Hagana began threatening and hunting members of the Irgun and Lehi, and Begin, in order to avert civil war, ordered his Irgunists not to fight back, Yalin-Mor met with the Hagana chief Eliahu Golomb. He put a gun on the table and told Golomb that Lehi did not have kibbutzim on which to hold Hagana members were Lehi to kidnap them and did not believe in turning people over to the British, so it would do neither; instead it would execute those giving the orders to kidnap and torture Lehi members.[74] Afterward, the Hagana hunted only Irgunists.

After Shamir's arrest in 1946, Yalin-Mor shouldered most of the organizational burden of Lehi as well as editing, writing, and negotiating on its behalf. He propounded Lehi's policy of a neutralized Middle East but believed the Soviets would win what became the Cold War and thought Lehi should align itself with them and with the struggle of the proletariat.

Yalin-Mor was arrested after the assassination of Bernadotte in 1948 and while in jail was elected to Israel's first Knesset, representing the Lehi-based Fighters party. He served in the Knesset till the end of its session, in October 1951.

Afterward he tried various business ventures, and for 14 years he managed a cotton and deciduous fruit tree farm. But in the mid-1950s he joined other social activists, several of them also Lehi veterans, in establishing a movement they called Semitic Action. He helped pen its *Hebrew Manifesto*, which called for the establishment of a Palestinian state alongside Israel, with which Israel would enter into a federation. Because at the time—the 1950s—the areas known as Judea and Samaria and Gaza were occupied not by Israel but by Jordan and Egypt, respectively, Yalin-Mor and his associates called for Israel to fund and arm the Palestinians in order to help them create a national liberation movement.[75]

According to Uri Avnery, the impetus for Semitic Action was a phone call Yalin-Mor placed to him during the 1956 Sinai Campaign, a war which Israel fought alongside England and France against Egypt. "Yalin-Mor viewed this war as a disaster, as did I," says Avnery, referring to Israel's alliance with colonial powers. The members of Semitic Action decided that before they sought public support, they needed to turn their political and social views into a practical program. A dozen members participated in often heated discussions that led to the *Hebrew Manifesto*. When Avnery had first met Yalin-Mor in 1951, Yalin-Mor had not been supportive of the establishment of an Arab state in part of the Jewish homeland. However, over the years, and then in the course of the intense debates that gave rise to the manifesto, the members came to agree with each other about all the issues on the movement's agenda. Yalin-Mor's initial contribution to the movement was its foreign policy position, which he brought with him from Lehi: neutrality for the State of Israel and for the Middle East in the conflict between the Western and Eastern blocs. Avnery, Yalin-Mor, and the other activists went further and proposed that Israel orient itself toward the Third World. As the best Hebrew speaker in the group, Yalin-Mor was also responsible for the manifesto's final form and wording.[76]

Yalin Mor ran for the Knesset in 1969, not garnering enough votes to be elected.

Shamir recalls walking around the Mizra Detention Camp with Yalin-Mor when both were locked inside. Later he wrote,

> Yalin-Mor ("Gera," to use his code name) was an intel-lectual both by nature and by choice, an engineer by training and a proud Jew by faith....I was to...come to respect, admire, and depend upon his severe, practical, and exceedingly logical mind....
>
> [He] became increasingly extreme in his attitudes to-wards the Soviet Union and towards the Arabs. He once told me that a truly progressive man can only be judged by the way he feels about the Arabs, and he became pre-occupied by the East-West clash....He was a man who had changed and yet remained the same: involved, sharp, dedicated but at home nowhere....[77]

In 1969 Yalin-Mor cited a radio broadcast in which he debated foreign policy with former Irgunist Shmuel Tamir and noted that their "debate proves beyond a doubt that [our] earlier 'separatism' is neither common ground for nor a signpost to the views and beliefs of people alive today who are trying to solve the problems of Israel's future."[78]

Thirty-two years after the establishment of the State of Israel, in February 1980, its Ministry of Defense finally decided to award merit badges to the pre-state underground fighters. Yalin-Mor was too ill to make the ceremony. Lehi members Spielman, Shmuelevitz, Gepner, and Shomron took Yalin-Mor's badge to him at his home. Three days later he died.

One of Nathan and Frieda Yalin-Mor's two children is named Elisha, the code name of Yerachmiel Aaronsohn, one of the first Lehi fighters to be shot to death by the British in Tel Aviv, where he was trapped in a stairwell. Elisha Yalin-Mor was one of the founders of Peace Now in the late 1970s. Nathan smiled widely with pride one day when he reported to Elisha that "until now I've heard you called Nathan's son. Today I heard myself called your father."[79] Elisha views his father as a political analyst with great foresight. He remembers his father being pilloried by many in Lehi for not toeing the Lehi political line; when these veterans occasionally needed assistance, his father was there to provide it. Elisha says he learned from his father "never to sink to the level of others; raise them to your level."[80]

Joshua Cohen: No Surrender

When Joshua Cohen and Nehama, his future wife who had kept him alive while he kept Lehi alive in the "Orchard Days and Nights" of 1942, were on the run, he understood that his major contribution to Lehi was not this or that military operation, but being living proof that appearing on a British wanted poster did not mean the end of one's underground career, that there was an alternative to being arrested or surrendering.[81]

Cohen had been instructed in underground tactics and strategy in a course given by Eliahu Giladi. In one session, the instructor had been asked by the three students if he believed they could win the war in their lifetime. Giladi told them that the question was not would victory come in their lifetime, but whether they would contribute their part to victory. "If you fight, you will win," he said, "maybe in your lives and maybe not. But if you don't fight, you certainly won't win."[82]

Cohen admired and learned from Giladi's commitment to the underground and its war. Cohen was arrested in 1944. His interrogators asked if he understood that if he changed his ways he could lead a happy family life. Cohen answered that he desired that family life, but more than that he wanted to be sure that his son, should he one day go on a holiday walk or tour in the country, "would not find his path blocked because part of his precious homeland, soaked with the blood of its Hebrew children, is forbidden to him" based on the whims of a foreign ruler. "Whoever plans on being a Hebrew father," Cohen continued, "must be ready to answer the questions his son would pose in such an embarrassing situation. I would have to tell him what I did for my spiritual freedom and what he should do if this freedom has not yet been attained." The police also asked Cohen how he could cause his parents so much worry and suffering. He replied that his father was a priest, and "the Holy Temple, symbol of Hebrew strength and the site on which we serve the Lord of the Hosts of Israel, is his heart's desire," and given his parents' reliance on the Bible and the Hebrew prayer book, they surely sympathized with his chosen path.[83]

Cohen was exiled to Africa that December. His parents complained that his letters were full of generalities and questions about events in Eretz Israel, with nothing about how he was doing. He answered:

> 29 Nisan 5705
> In Exile in the Sudan
> Dear Parents, shalom,
>
> A few days ago I sent you a letter that unintentionally grants your special request for me to write about my "private" life. But today when I received your letter with the special request, I decided to write a second letter in which I'll say a few words about this request of yours.
>
> When I read your letter I remembered the prayer service of the last day of Passover when we reached the "Yizkor" memorial prayer. We happy ones whose parents are still alive left the synagogue hall and those from whom cruel fate had taken their dear ones were left alone. But, can I say that as I was leaving the hall, even though my parents are alive, I wasn't touched by the fate of my friends whose situation was different and tragic? In any case, I think that based on the education you gave me, and on what I learned from Jewish and other sources, *I shouldn't have left*. So now you can understand my situation. When millions of our brothers are buried under the European ice because they were not allowed to immigrate to Eretz Israel, I can't emphasize my private life in my letters. I can't write to you about things that aren't of primary importance to me.
>
> Now that I have explained the reason to you, I am ready to cut it short if it causes you distress, and to include more details about life. In any event, at least for now, in general, I am healthy, studying, and there is enough food. I am looking forward to getting the books.
>
> Regards to those who ask about me.[84]

He escaped once, with 53 others in Eritrean exile, and was captured. Despite the establishment of the State of Israel in May 1948, the British continued to incarcerate the detainees in Kenya. Cohen was one of the last deportees to be allowed to return to what had become the State of Israel—in July 1948, two months after statehood had been declared.

Following the assassination of Count Bernadotte, which he executed, Cohen enlisted in the Israeli army and became an officer. In 1952 he moved to and helped found Kibbutz Sde Boker in the Negev. Ben-Gurion visited a year later and Cohen told him to stay; the youth would follow and the desert would bloom, Cohen argued. Ben-Gurion asked what he would do there and Cohen suggested teaching, administrative work, shepherding—anything. Ben-Gurion moved in and Cohen became his de facto "bodyguard" and aide. Cohen also did agricultural and archaeological work in and around Sde Boker, and led groups on trips for a local field school. In the 1980s, he led a hunger fast at the Western Wall in Jerusalem to protest the Israeli government's destruction of Jewish cities in the Sinai Desert and the ceding of the desert to Egypt.

Cohen's wife Nehama died in 1985. Joshua died a year later. Their son was named for Joshua's brother Menachem, who was also a member of Lehi deported to Africa, and who upon his return was killed in Israel's War of Independence.

Cohen's son and daughter decided there would be no eulogies at Cohen's funeral, in deference to Cohen's earthiness. The mourners included Israeli right wingers and left wingers, members of the Likud and Hashomer Hatzair, farmers and students, Bedouin and kibbutzniks. One exception was made to the no-eulogy rule: a ghetto fighter and partisan who had fought against the Germans spoke. Cohen's son Menachem explained, "Dad felt that compared to the heroism of the Jews in that hell, the heroism of the underground fighters against the foreign regime in Eretz Israel was nothing."[85] In addition, says Menachem, his father wondered at the coincidence that as he and his comrades were facing the hangman in Eretz Israel, his brothers in Europe were rising against the hangman of the Jewish people.

Upon Cohen's death, his son discovered that Cohen kept next to his bed a note Cohen's father had written when Cohen was underground, asking, in the event of the father's death, that his children pay his debts and loans and take special care to be good Jews.

Also near Cohen's bed was a *siddur* (a prayer book) he brought back from a trip to Poland in the 1960s. It had belonged to an elderly Jewish woman killed in the Holocaust.

Also precious to Cohen were two pictures that he had hung on his wall: one, of the Roman emperor Hadrian, who had crushed Bar-Kochba's rebellion in the year 135, and the other of British High Commissioner Alan Cunningham, photographed saluting the lowered British flag as he left the country in 1948. Cohen used to say to the former: "Look where you are today and where we Jews are"; and of the latter he would say, "Here is the last British High Commissioner, in a salute to Eretz Israel."[86]

On one of Cohen's field-school trips he hiked up the mountain of Masada with a group of high school students. They sat on top in an ancient water cistern and talked. By torchlight they discussed Masada's meaning. Cohen read them a poem by Hannah Senesh, a Hungarian immigrant to Eretz Israel who had parachuted back into occupied Europe to fight the Germans and save Jews. She was arrested, tortured, and executed by a German firing squad in November 1944. Cohen read her most famous poem:

> My God, My God,
> May these never cease:
> The sand and the sea,
> The rustling of the water,
> The lightning in the sky,
> The prayer of man.

Cohen stressed the wish, "May these never cease," and adduced that Senesh wanted to live; "she loved life so much, yet the minute they told her in prison that she was going to die and the only way to save herself was to beg for mercy, she answered with contempt: 'From you, the murderers of my people, never!' In other words, she said: 'As much as I love life, only I will determine its contents; I alone am master of my fate. A slave to you Germans? Never.'" Cohen concluded, "That's what Masada means to me. That's the way I see its fighters."[87]

Moshe and Tova Svorai: Felling One Flag, Raising Another

As the Stern group's radio announcer, Geula Cohen, was being driven to the Bethlehem Women's Prison, having been caught red-handed during one of her underground broadcasts, she was not thinking "of my arrest and fate, but I was excited that I would meet Tova Svorai there."[88]

 Tova Hochglick was born in 1915 in Warsaw. Her parents moved to Eretz Israel when she was eight, but when their two children fell ill they returned to Poland for a few years. In 1934 they came for good. Her uncle wrote Tova's father inviting the family to join him in London, but the father replied that when a Jew leaves one country in the Diaspora it should not be for another but rather for Eretz Israel. Tova's father accepted all the hardships of immigration with equanimity if not love. When once Tova's mother complained about a lack of sleep because of young people singing in the streets at night, her father replied, "They are golden children, they are far from their parents, and they have nothing to eat, but they are in Eretz Israel so they sing!"

Tova was already a member of Betar. On one mission for Betar she had been ordered to watch over another Betari traveling by train; even on her sea voyage to Eretz Israel, she had been assigned to keep a protective eye on a stowaway Betari, the only one aboard the ship to know who he was. She did her job well and no one on the boat discovered the illegality of his presence, but after the voyage he was caught waiting to disembark and was sent back to Europe, where during the Holocaust he died as a partisan.

The night before she left Poland a friend had told her stories about Eretz Israel, including one of how members of the League of Birionim had torn down the Nazi flag from above the German consulate. Tova promised her friend she would one day meet the young man who had done it. At a Betar party in Haifa she met Moshe Svorai, who had carried the shears to the roof and cut the flag from its pole. During the year 1938 he happened to be out of jail but his freedom of movement was curtailed. He suggested that since he was required to stay at home anyway, they might as well be married, so they were.[89]

Svorai was born in 1914 in the Ukraine and came with his family to Eretz Israel when he was 11. He enrolled in a religious teachers seminary in Jerusalem and was asked to leave when his level of religious observance fell below the institution's standards. He was welcomed by Labor officials who ran a secular teachers seminary and who assumed he was one of them. They, in turn, later tried to expel him because of his activities in the League of Birionim, but he managed to stay and graduate with a teacher's certification. As noted, he spent much of the 1930s in jail as a member of the League of Birionim, established "national cells" in Poland that prepared the way for Stern's Irgun cells, stayed with Stern when the Irgun split and was Stern's intelligence chief. Tova deposited unasked-for underground literature in Haifa's mailboxes and smuggled underground mail into and out of Mizra, on one occasion bringing the prisoners a gun in a package of honey.[90] When Stern had no place else to go, Svorai brought him home to his and Tova's apartment.

Tova says Moshe and Stern spent most of the time talking and writing. Together they talked about the fate of Polish Jewry; while the news was inexact, the killing had already begun, and they were worried. They prepared material for the underground paper and for radio broadcasts and tried to keep track of the fate of their hunted comrades. At night they left for underground rendezvous. They did not have much to eat, mostly bread and cheese, and they used to joke about the need to pass their single broken knife from one person to another (though Stern was happy to learn they had separate sets of dishes for meat and dairy foods, as required by Jewish dietary laws).[91] The Svorai's daughter Herut (the name means Liberty) joined them occasionally, at least until the apartment became so cold during the winter that it was unsafe for the child to remain. Until she left, Stern would take breaks from his writing to play hide and seek with her, or to act like a bear or any other animal she wished. He carried her around the room on his shoulders and laughed heartily as he played with her.[92]

Moshe left the apartment on January 27, 1942, and did not see Tova for years. He was shot when Morton raided Lehi's apartment at 30 Dizengoff Street and was hospitalized with the three other victims of that shooting. Two died; Svorai and Yaacov Eliav were sentenced to life in jail. It would be six years before Moshe would escape.

On February 12, Stern was shot to death in the Svorai's apartment and Tova was driven away by Wilkin. She spent the afternoon in a police station, never calming down; she told the policewoman who escorted her, "They murdered him. They think that means they've killed them all. They'll be bitterly disappointed. Hundreds will come to replace the one who died." When Morton entered the station and was pointed out to Tova, she jumped from her chair, yelling, "There's the murderer—Morton!" Nonetheless, he received congratulations and back slaps from all the police in the room. At night Tova was interrogated. All she said, or more precisely, yelled, was, "Murderers, despicable murderers, I'm not saying anything. You'll feel our blows. You may have killed a leader but others will rise and continue on his path."[93]

Tova was carted off to the Bethlehem prison. "When I arrived in the Bethlehem prison I felt very lonely," she later wrote. "Yair was murdered, Moshe was wounded and in the Jerusalem prison. And I was alone, without my daughter; totally, totally alone."[94] In prison she sometimes imagined Herut running from one end of the apartment to the other, but at other times she imagined her asking, "Mother, where have you gone? Where have you gone?"[95] Tova says the women in the Bethlehem prison (in the course of the underground war some 150 women fighters were incarcerated in Bethlehem) "persevered despite the prison walls around us. We laughed, joked, read, worked on arts and crafts, and occasionally cried in secret." The women were torn between their personal "longing, worry, and desire to be free" and the "hope that very soon the underground would grow stronger and we would fight and expel the British from our country and establish the Hebrew state."[96] Given Tova's frequent and serious bouts of illness, she calls her four and a half years in Bethlehem the "hardest years of my life."[97] Her mother pleaded for her release on medical grounds and was told by the police that Tova would leave the prison "only on a stretcher."[98]

Tova's mother and siblings were all involved in the national struggle, whether by choice or by virtue of their relation to her. The Lehi youth knew the address of Tova's mother: Yaacov Banai went to her place to eat whenever he was hungry, and when Nehama Srulovitz, Joshua Cohen's future wife, ran out of glue while hanging broadsides, she dropped by and Tova's mother cooked up another pot of glue.[99] Tova's brothers were arrested; one as early as 1938 but the others after Tova's arrest. She received family letters from the Acco prison, Latrun Detention Camp, and finally from African exile.[100]

Despite the British threat to let her die in prison, Tova was eventually released for medical reasons. She was told she might get out before the Passover holiday of 1946 but there were many delays and it was only two months later that the hall of the prison resounded with shouts of "Tova! Tova! Tova *fraj* [free]!" Her fellow inmates sang and danced around her and she thought, "I'm really going home!...But they're not. Julie, Nelly, when will they be free?"[101] Her cellmates packed her things and Rabbi Jacob Goldman, who had come to deliver a Bible class but who found himself intruding on a celebration for Tova's release, walked her out, with two policewomen in tow carrying her bags, and the women in the prison standing at the windows or sitting on the sills serenading them as they left. Rabbi Goldman stopped the car at Rachel's Tomb and made Tova a gift of a book of Psalms. At the tomb she prayed for the release of her husband and her brothers. She spent her first night of freedom in the Jerusalem apartment of former cellmates Bella Zetler and Ruth Amikam and visited Rabbi Arye Levin, the spiritual father of the inmates of the Jerusalem prison. One month later, in the middle of the night of July 22, 1946, there was a knock at Tova's door and she was taken away for a month in a detention camp.[102]

On February 20, 1948, eight-year-old Herut burst into the home where she lived with Tova and Tova's mother, waving a newspaper and exclaiming, "Mother! Grandma! Daddy escaped from jail! It's here in the paper!"[103] Moshe had dug his way out of the Jerusalem prison with 11 other fighters, through the sewer pipes adjacent to their cell.

In Tova's words,

> When we reunited that first time, he told me that the day Yair was murdered, Yashke [Yaacov Eliav] and he were in their hospital beds. Morton took Yashke to the morgue room and then took Moshe there. He showed Moshe Yair's corpse and said, "We killed him in your house."
>
> This was a terrible shock. Moshe had been sure Yair was in Jerusalem, because we knew there was an apartment readied for him.
>
> Then Moshe told me that earlier that same day, Yashke's mother had come during visiting hours, after ten in the morning. She was standing next to Moshe's bed talking over him to Yashke. Moshe asked her about me and she said she hadn't seen me, she didn't know where I lived. He gave her the address. When he saw Yair in the morgue, he thought, "I'm responsible for this."

Morton claimed to have found Stern because one of his detectives overheard Moshe giving the address in the hospital. Svorai apparently believed Morton's story to be true. Therefore, Tova says,

> He entered prison a broken man and shared his feelings with Joshua Zetler, with whom he had become close in Haifa, where they spent two years breaking the policy of restraint. Moshe shared all his pain with Zetler.
>
> But what were they thinking? Why didn't they say, first we need to check the story out with Tova?

Actually, once, in prison, she and a cellmate heard a male voice from beyond the cell wall. Her friend jumped to the window and saw a man in a prison uniform. He was an inmate from Jerusalem doing work in the Bethlehem prison, and he was singing in Yiddish, "...a letter for Momma." When the guards were not around, Tova's friend extended her arm and was handed a letter that turned out to have been sent by Moshe. He and Tova often addressed each other as *Abbale* and *Mommele* (Daddy and Mommy). It was a long letter, which ended with a casual, "By the way, the guys would like to know what happened in the apartment." Tova wrote in miniscule script an account of the day Stern was murdered and surreptitiously sent it to Moshe. The letter never made it out of the Bethlehem prison. A friendly guard told her it had been intercepted and she, the guard, had been asked to translate it. The guard had managed to tear off the signature before the warden saw it but, she said, the warden was still intent on finding out which prisoner was writing an illegal letter to her father ("Daddy"). Tova soon forgot the whole matter, and Moshe never followed up on the letter, asked her again about the day Stern was killed, or spelled out his fear. "I didn't know what they were thinking because they didn't tell me. If he had told me he would have spared us so much pain," says Tova.

> How could he not have told me something that weighed so heavily on him? He had often told me things that bothered him. For example, he said, "If you hadn't married me, you wouldn't have gone to jail, you wouldn't have been kept from your daughter." He meant it. He said I would have had a better life without him. But he didn't tell me this assumption of his that hurt him so much.

Tova remembers that when she and Moshe had been going out for a few months and they knew the relationship was serious, Moshe told her that to him, being a couple meant telling each other everything. Tova felt the same way and they agreed not to keep secrets, even if they were unpleasant. Now his secret led to hers. "I couldn't get it out of my head. Moshe had disappointed me," she thought, but she was unwilling to ruin Moshe's return and cause him more hurt by telling this to him. She reasoned, "Now he had escaped, and thank God he was okay, and hadn't been caught, and I was ill at the time and couldn't give him the grand welcome he deserved after all these years."

Tova was in for another surprise. She recalls,

> Though he had told Zetler, it never occurred to me
> that others were also talking about this. Later I asked
> Julie, "Tell me, did the women in Bethlehem know?" She
> said they did. She explained that she had not shared the
> story with me because it was based on a mere rumor.
> She, Moshe, everyone wanted what was best for me, so
> I never heard a word! Had I only heard! All the witnesses
> were alive then, I could have proved the story was untrue.

Tova kept silent then and afterward.

> For a long time I thought, how can I complain to
> Moshe? First of all, I'm ill. Second, he's unemployed.
> They were hard times. Can I be angry with Moshe, when
> we don't know where we are going to get food, or where
> he can find work, and I am sick?[104]

The story became a cause célèbre in the State of Israel fifty years after
the events. An interview in the archives of the Lehi Museum recounted as
fact the story that Morton told. Moshe sued for libel and the matter came
to court, splitting the surviving Lehi members into two camps: those who
accepted Morton's story and those who accepted the Svorais' version. The
Israeli court considering the evidence ruled that Svorai gave his address to
Eliav's mother after ten o'clock, while the British police had reached his
apartment on a routine search well before that hour. But Tova remains sad.
"So much suffering could have been avoided, and some of our friends might
have stayed our friends if the other story hadn't been circulating unchal-
lenged for so long," says Tova.[105]

Eliezer Ben-Ami, one of Moshe's cellmates in the Lehi cell in Jerusalem, adds that one of the other inmates read a diary Moshe was writing in
the cell and learned what Moshe thought. He shared this information with
Zetler, who did what he could to calm Svorai. But Ben-Ami, too, faults
Moshe "for buying into the British report. And so did the other prisoners.
We didn't know Wilkin was at the apartment earlier and that he had already identified Stern, leaving so he would have an alibi that he wasn't the
one who shot him. Svorai bought the story the British disseminated. They
were often doing things like that, so we would suspect each other or wonder if there were a traitor in our ranks. Maybe sometimes it was true, but

usually this kind of thing was fabricated, it was disinformation."[106]

After the establishment of the state, Moshe wanted to resume his pre-war teaching job, but the political powers that be forbade hiring a former Lehi member. He worked at various jobs but for a few years was often unemployed, telling Tova that if he were to begin selling shrouds, people would stop dying. A relative in the United States provided them with a car and Moshe began driving it for pay, until he upgraded in 1951 to a job with Egged, Israel's public bus company. At the same time, he began studying law after work. In 1958 he became a lawyer, retiring in 1985.

In 1981 he and Tova traveled through northern Samaria and were impressed with the views but depressed by the paucity of residents. They chose an area with a few nearby Arab villages, brought together some young couples, and formed a new settlement. At the age of 65, the couple spearheaded the founding of Shaked, which is today a community of 200 families.

In the late 1980s and through the 1990s Moshe often traveled by bus to Jerusalem to participate in demonstrations and protest marches—the trip necessitated three bus rides over several hours in each direction. At these rallies one could still hear his voice, as deep as it had been when he read Stern's first words over the underground radio.

For millennia Jews have wished each other a long life with the Hebrew phrase *Ad me'ah ve'esrim*—May you live to be 120 (this was the age at which the biblical Moses died). When friends say this to Tova, she demurs; not that she is opposed to living until 120, but she has formulated a wish and hope of her own, which focuses on the quality and health of one's life: *Ad hasof tov*—May it be good until the end.

Moshe Segal: Sounding the Trumpet of Redemption

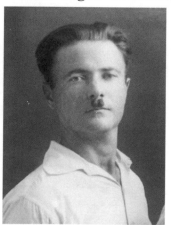

After the Russian Revolution, Moshe Segal had the option of joining the Communist Youth League and supposedly ensuring himself a future. Instead he joined the pioneering Hehalutz movement and started agricultural training so he would be able to till Eretz Israel.

Having survived the post-revolution famine and having taught Torah when it was banned by the Soviets, Segal made it to Eretz Israel in the mid-1920s. Ever the maverick, Segal and a few friends were expelled from the Hagana in 1927 for insubordination. At a standard roll call, they had been asked the purpose of the Hagana; a cadet was expected to recite: "To defend lives and property." Segal answered: "To become a Jewish army for a Jewish state."[107]

To further this goal, Segal signed up as the seventh member of Betar in the country. He enrolled in the Betar Officers Training School, the first Jewish military school in nearly two thousand years, and on the fast day of Tisha B'Av in 1929 he led its members and thousands of others who followed on a march to Jerusalem's Western Wall. On this march they sang Hebrew songs, carried the Hebrew flag, and proclaimed the Wall to be Jewish property and the British only temporary residents in the country. When establishment Zionist leaders tried to dissuade him from launching the parade, he replied that the youth would decide for itself what must be done. On the return march, Segal was lifted onto the demonstrators' shoulders at Zion Square, as the British governor of Jerusalem watched from a balcony. Segal exclaimed, "We will chase you from this land and establish a free Hebrew state!"[108] The Arabs opened a series of pogroms around the country at the end of the month. Some Jewish commentators blamed the Betar rally for inciting the rioting, though similar pogroms had taken place in 1920 and in 1921, and the current dispute over the Western Wall had been initiated a year earlier by Arab agitators and British officials.[109]

During the 1929 pogroms, Segal and the body of the Officers School defended various Tel Aviv neighborhoods. Segal convinced one recalcitrant woman to leave her neighborhood for her own safety by pointing a gun at her head. Afterward, he served as a watchman in the Jordan Valley and Galilee, then became a middleman matching farmers short of labor with unemployed members of Betar. He tried to enlist in a border guard unit stationed across the Jordan River because, "I've always wanted to see those regions on the way to Amman that my people conquered on their way from Egyptian slavery to the Promised Land."[110]

On the Day of Atonement in 1930 Segal broke the British ban on sounding the shofar at the close of the holy day. Standing before the Wall, he asked himself, "Can we skip the shofar blast, symbolizing the redemption of Israel? True, in itself it's only a tradition...but here, at this holiest of all spots, at this holiest of all moments...?"[111]

He borrowed a prayer shawl from another worshipper and hid a shofar under it, and fifty years later he was able to say, "I still recall the pleasant feeling that filled my heart in those moments. The prayer shawl above my head created a cubit-by-cubit tent, my personal space, sort of the territory of a Jewish state, where a Jew stood and made a sovereign decision, which he executed without regard to the opinions of gentiles."[112] He felt he could "do as I please, despite the foreign ruler outside, which prevents my brothers from freely worshipping God....I am free to do God's will."[113]

Segal blew the shofar and was arrested. At midnight his police guard went home, so he did, too. Every year afterward someone blew the shofar at the Wall and either evaded the police or went to jail for between three and six months. Many of these actions were organized by Segal. They became the underground's longest running operation: for 17 years shofars were smuggled by young men and women, people were trained to sound them, and others were trained to protect the shofar blowers. Jews throughout the country ran to their radios at the end of the fast, and abroad they waited for the newspapers, to learn if the youth had succeeded in defying the British Empire once again. For these people, the Wall became a symbol of heroism rather than wailing.

A few days after he sounded the shofar, Segal participated with other members of the League of Birionim in a rally against the British deputy minister for the colonies, who was visiting Tel Aviv. At Ahimeir's instigation, they decided to continue marching and singing *Hatikva* even if they were ordered to disperse, and thus they consciously chose to go to jail as Zionists, the first people in the country to do so since Jabotinsky had founded the Hagana in 1920 and had been arrested for defending Jerusalem. After their release, they continued their activities with the Birionim and soon, with the Irgun.

In 1937 Segal sat on the High Command of the Irgun then headed by David Raziel. He helped Raziel plan a series of reprisal attacks against Arabs during the 1936-39 years. In the summer of 1938, Segal joined a Jerusalem club called the League of Hasmoneans, which he soon turned into a national semi-underground. He had its membership card list seven principles, which he obviously professed then and until the end of his life:

> A Hasmonean is faithful to the God of Israel and is ready to give his life to sanctify God's name, Torah, people, and land; hopes for the coming of the messiah and longs to establish the Kingdom of Israel; loves every individual Jew with all his heart; intends all his actions to be for the sake of Heaven and is of exemplary character and behavior; continues in the tradition of the Hasmoneans and Zealots and is prepared to enlist in the war of liberation; scoffs at cowardice and surrender to an enemy

and reinstates Israeli heroism and pride; and obeys the
orders of his officers.[114]

Segal viewed the Hasmonean war that culminated in the holiday of
Hanukah in the year 165 B.C.E. as being a war of both national liberation
and religious commitment. He denied that these were two separate goals
or categories. To him, every action that advanced Jewish liberation was a
religious obligation. Nonetheless, in later years he took issue with those
religious Jews who believed that after 1948, God was beginning to bring
divine redemption and this was the reason they should support Zionism;
Segal agreed that the era was the beginning of redemption, but his commitment to Eretz Israel and a Jewish state was based on the nation's need
for these, rather than any reading of a divine plan for history.

Segal was arrested in 1939 and sat in jail with the Irgun High Command. On that year's Day of Atonement he watched Abraham Stern pray
in the left corner of their cell, "prayer book in hand, not moving an inch."
At service's end Stern and Segal sat at a table in the middle of the cell and
studied the passages of the ancient Mishna that describe the day's service
in the Holy Temple.

Out of jail, Segal resumed his Hasmonean and underground labors. He
stayed with the Irgun during the split. Arrested again and detained without trial in Latrun, he led Talmud lessons there. When he got out he answered Shamir's call and joined Lehi, bringing a good number of his young
Hasmoneans with him. Segal was appointed Lehi's representative in Jerusalem, with Joshua Cohen his deputy. Segal and Shamir, the latter's beard
dyed red as a disguise, continued to meet, often in a synagogue in
Jerusalem's Rehavia neighborhood, with open volumes of the Talmud scat-
tered before them to camouflage their discussions.

In 1948 Segal was a member of the semi-official Jerusalem Committee that managed the besieged city; he was in charge of food distribution.
In the 1950s he moved to Kfar Habad, where he established a woman's
seminary and managed the school. In 1967 he became the first Jew to move
back to Old Jerusalem following the Six Day War. He cleaned out the old
Habad synagogue and turned it into a functioning house of prayer. To
friends, the media, and the public, Segal became known as Rabbi Segal. He
had earlier run the religious Hasmonean movement, more recently managed a seminary and rebuilt a synagogue, now traveled around the country teaching Torah, and also taught the writings of Rabbi Abraham Isaac
Kook to small gatherings in his Jerusalem home; although he never referred

to himself as a rabbi, no one in the country, from its Chief Rabbis to secular kibbutz farmers, referred to him in any other way.

In the 1970s and 1980s, Segal joined the settlement movement and offered spiritual guidance to its members. In his late seventies, in 1981, he moved to Yamit in the Sinai Desert and locked himself in an underground bunker hoping to help prevent the turning of the territory over to Egypt. As the Israeli army's tear gas seeped in, the soldiers determined to dislodge the rebels and dismantle the city, the young activists with whom Segal was holding out suggested to him they might unlock the door and surrender. He answered that if their purpose was to avoid a violent clash with the Jewish soldiers trying to eject them, he would assent; if their motive was to spare him (the oldest of the lot) the gas and the fight, he would prefer to stay. Eventually, they opened the doors. After Yamit's destruction and the Sinai's transfer to Egypt, Segal, back in Jerusalem, supported Jews who engaged in reprisal attacks on Arabs in response to new terrorist incidents and wrote prayers to be recited on their behalf. He lobbied rabbinical authorities to endorse their deeds, attended their trials, and visited them in jail.[115]

He continued to sound the shofar at the Western Wall until the year of his death, 1985. At that time his shofar blasts were to protest that the Israeli government was not allowing Jews to worship above the Wall, on the Temple Mount itself. In 1980 he taught a young man to blow the shofar and, following Segal's own blast outside the gate to the mount, Segal handed the shofar to the man who, with a friend, smuggled it onto the mount and blew it there for the first time in centuries.[116] Regulars at the annual service at which Segal blew the shofar were friends of his from the Hasmonean league as well as Irgun and Lehi veterans. Eldad came every year and he was there in 1980 to congratulate the young shofar blowers on their return from the mount.

Segal and Eldad respected each other and cooperated on various projects over the years. But Segal took Eldad to task when in Eldad's later years he attempted to unite public opinion around the Allon Plan. Segal accused Eldad of stepping off the ladder leading to the Kingdom of Israel. Segal put little store in public opinion, believing that if a correct policy were adopted, people would follow; thus during the unpopular war with Lebanon in the 1980s, when most Israelis wanted to bring the troops home, Segal brought together a group of young people who offered to move to Lebanon to settle the land, which Segal and they considered part of the biblical Land of Israel.

Despite his uncompromising views, Segal did not raise his voice in argument, nor try to impose his views on others. When someone disagreed with him, he held his peace. He was often invited to lecture to audiences who were far from his views, and he was respected by his political opponents for his character and contributions to the country.

Segal headed several organizations working to restore the holiness of the ancient Temple site. The final year of his life, Segal helped found the Temple Institute, dedicated to reconstructing ritual vessels for use in the Temple service.

Segal died, fatefully enough, on the anniversary of his appearance on the stage of history, the sacred day of Yom Kippur. He literally bit his lips in the hospital, refusing to display the pain he was in. Only once did he reveal some of what he was thinking when he confessed the frustration he felt at his imminent death: "There's still so much to do...."[117]

Segal was once asked to sum up his political outlook. He said he aspired to a "maximum of unity among Jews. But one must never concede a matter of principle." Then he added that "with an enemy one must never concede anything, even if it's not a matter of principle."[118]

Moshe Moldovsky: A Vegetarian Sternist

Until his death in 2010 at the age of 101, Moshe Moldovsky was one of the last living founders of the Irgun, if not the last, and one of the last people alive who had played a major role in breaking the establishment Zionist policy of restraint in the face of Arab attacks in the 1930s. At first he had acted on his own, and for his breach of discipline he was "exiled" by the Irgun to the Galilee. This proved a boon for the Irgun in the Galilee, which gained an experienced and apparently fearless commander. He led attacks himself, trained others in use of arms, and organized operations throughout the Upper Galilee and as far south as Tiberias.

Molodvsky joined Eretz Israel's Betar movement before it was called Betar. He served in that organization's *Plugat Giyus* (service platoon) in Kfar Saba from 1931-33 and guarded Jewish-owned land that became, as a result of the guard duty, part of today's city of Netanya. He helped establish the Irgun in the Sharon, Shomron, and Galilee regions, and took over the Jerusalem branch in 1939, following the arrest of its commanding officer, Benjamin Zeroni. He decided on the execution of the British sergeant who had tortured Zeroni. He was eventually exiled to Africa in 1944, and was allowed to return home only after the Jewish state was established in 1948.

Moshe's widow Esther is a descendant of Don Isaac Abarbanel. She was allowed by her parents to sail alone for Eretz Israel as a teenager when she stopped eating. Her doctor assumed she had a case of unrequited puppy love and asked her if she were in love. She answered, "Yes, I am in love with Eretz Israel."[119] The doctor told her parents that if they wanted to save her they had to let her go. Given the Holocaust in the offing, his diagnosis proved correct. Esther met Moshe years later when he returned from his forced exile. They lived together for some sixty years. They were vegetarians and attributed their health and longevity to a natural diet. They grew their own produce organically, and according to one of the eulogists at Moshe's funeral, a species of avocado has been named after him. They usually took visitors out back to their sweet-scented garden to show off their vegetables and fruit. Moshe also liked to point out that he had planted two of the garden's trees for a different purpose: he was waiting for construction to start on the Third Temple in Jerusalem and would then donate their wood.[120]

Meanwhile the Moldovsky's donated their time and energies to the poor of Netanya. Moshe was late for one interview with a journalist, who instead heard Esther's account of the Abarbanel family history, an account that began before the Expulsion from Spain in 1492 and concluded in 1937 with her dancing on deck with her shipmates when they spotted a "microscopic dot in the distance that we knew was Haifa."[121] The then 98-year-old Moshe finally showed up, dragging a heavy sack, which, the journalist discovered when he offered assistance, contained dozens of books. When Moshe was temporarily out of earshot, Esther explained that he looks for discarded books on the street, which he collects for those who cannot afford them. The couple also collected used clothing for distribution, which Esther mended when necessary.

Moldovsky was fiercely committed to life in Eretz Israel. When he was a child in Russia, Russian children threw snowballs at him as he walked to school in winter, and in summer they threw rocks. He fought back until his mother warned him, "This is *their* land. Don't hit back. The Exile is a curse God has given the Jews. When the messiah comes we will be in Eretz Israel, our own land. Then—hit back."[122] Given Moldovsky's role in breaking the Jewish self-restraint of the 1930s, it would seem he imbibed the lesson. He even invented a mine that proved effectual, though he claimed to have known nothing about electrical connections or mines, and thus any inventing, he says, must have been the work of God.

Another supposedly divine incursion in his life took place the night before his deportation to Africa, when, he says, he was visited by his white-robed late grandmother who warned him about the surprise the British had in store for the morrow. He assumed the message was a reward for his having canceled a visa to the Unites States in 1929, when he preferred to remain in Eretz Israel to defend communities under attack by Arabs. The message so impressed him that after his return to his country in 1948 he vowed never to leave again. Only once did he break the vow, with "rabbinical" dispensation from Moshe Segal. In the early 1950s a relative of Esther's was scheduled to be married in South America and the Moldovskys were invited. Moldovsky consulted Segal about the vow; Segal allowed the trip provided Moldovsky would encourage those he met to move to Israel. Moldovsky was given the floor before the wedding ceremony, and he urged the guests to relocate.[123]

Julie Torenberg: Ready for the Knock at the Door

Julie Torenberg was an interviewer's dream and nightmare. She was a dream because she remembered details and wanted to tell all the anecdotes she had stored in her memory; she was emotionally committed to every point and story. She was a nightmare because, as she put it, she had an "associative mind"—her conversation was a flowing stream of consciousness, in which a word or sentence brought to mind other stories and years and subjects, and several stories later the original subject would reappear, usually without introduction or warning.[124]

Julie Torenberg (née Elazar) was born in Bulgaria in 1917. She was educated in a Jewish elementary school where Hebrew, Bible, and Jewish history were taught, then in a state high school, where Latin, philosophy, ancient Slavic prayers, and the lives of the Christian saints were taught; she was the only Jew in her high school class. In 1935 she and her parents, a twin brother and a younger brother joined her four sisters who were already in Eretz Israel—the four sisters had immigrated without British permission and were considered "illegals." In Eretz Israel, Julie's education was of a different sort; on a CV prepared in 1989 for a publication highlighting exceptional Israeli women, she noted she had no academic degree but listed her university studies as "four and a half years in a British prison for women."[125]

Her road to prison began innocently enough. She had been a member of the Maccabee youth movement in Bulgaria, where she engaged in gymnastics and danced, sometimes in public performances. Maccabee was not as militant as Betar but was strongly Zionist. On her arrival in Eretz Israel she felt she had actualized her ideals and could rest easy. Less than a year later, she was asking herself, "So I actualized them; what next? We have a political situation here, a complicated situation; strange yet understandable given the population of Arabs, Jews, and the English." This was April 1936, and the country's Arabs had just begun what would become three years of attacks on watchmen, civilians, and crops. Torenberg asked, "I am here and happy and my parents, since they are Zionists and good Jews, are happy because they are here. Now we are being attacked; how can I contribute to the war effort?"

Jewish towns and farms had been employing Arabs until April 1936, when Arab leaders declared a strike and the Arabs left their employers. Betar tried to help the suddenly short-handed farmers by sending its members to substitute for the Arabs in the fields and to double as guards against attacks, theft, and arson. Early in 1937, Torenberg left her parents' home and joined Betar. She was sent to the Betar chapter in the Galilean town of Rosh Pina. She went to work in tobacco fields, a rock quarry, and olive groves. "There were about eighty of us in planting season. We got up every day at three in the morning, drank some tea, had a piece of bread—when we were lucky it came with jam—and headed to the acres which had to be planted with tobacco. We worked till about three in the afternoon." Ditches were dug first. Torenberg recalled that Shlomo Ben-Yosef was one of their best ditch diggers. Other people followed those who dug the ditches, each person carrying two buckets of water with which he or she wet the ditches, from one end of the field to the other. At the far end they received more water from the farmers and doubled back. Following behind those with the water were the planters.

Tobacco was only one of Betar's concerns. Many Betar members in Poland had joined the "national cells" or the Irgun there, and the same was happening in Eretz Israel. Torenberg was one of them. She was the only woman in the unit commander's course she took and was soon instructing others in the use of light arms. ("We didn't have any heavy arms," she noted.) Her instructor was Moshe Moldovsky who had been "exiled" following his reprisal attacks against Arabs in Tel Aviv, and one of her students was Ben-Yosef, who would soon attack near Rosh Pina.

Torenberg thought along the same lines. One day Moldovsky called her down from a tree from which she was picking fruit. He gave her a grenade and told her to follow him. They climbed over walls and stone-terraced hills, through fields and woods and reached their target. He threw a grenade but told her to keep hers. Then they returned the way they had come. Back home she asked why he had stopped her from throwing her grenade. He explained one had been enough; for her this had been training—to be ready at a moment's notice to take action.

Not all the training in Rosh Pina was physical. Torenberg recalled that "Rosh Pina was birthplace to endless arguing. My commander ordered me to go to sleep early, so the arguing would stop and people could get some rest. Better they should work well with the tobacco than argue with me. But after that I pointed out to him that when I got into bed, they all gathered around and we argued there. He gave in. The hard work didn't affect us, we were young. After the hard work in the tobacco fields we trained with guns. Then after that we argued on and on. Each of us was determining his own position. Because of the political situation in the country, these were turbulent yet lively times for the Betar youth."

One day Torenberg feigned illness and did not go to the fields. She headed instead for the northern settlement of Metulla, where she picked up some arms. She miscalculated the travel time, and by the time she had snuck past Rosh Pina's customs station and the British police, her friends and commanding officer had been searching the area in the hope she had not been kidnapped and killed by the Arabs. They knew her well enough to know, when she turned up healthy and out of breath, that she had been up to something surreptitious. She and two accomplices were brought up on charges and expelled from the unit. She was "exiled" to the city of Tiberias, on the shores of the Sea of Galilee.

Not much time passed before Moldovsky found her again. He handed her a small suitcase with a mine inside and told her where to plant it, in a gravel pit. He assigned her a partner she had never met before and never saw again. They dug a deep pit and planted the mine. She recalled her thoughts as she carried the mine: "If anyone tells you there's no fear—No. There is. You think, 'The whole world hears every move I make.' You cough and think they are going to start searching. What might they be thinking? That this strange couple couldn't find a better place to sit and talk? The fear is that you will be discovered before you have time to finish the job. Or maybe the mine will go off early and you will be injured. Maybe something will go wrong and you'll get hurt or die. Maybe." Torenberg credited Moldovsky with preparing her for such times; she had already carried arms to actions and smuggled contraband for stashing, walked stealthily without being discovered, clambered over hills with explosives, and even experienced the let down of not using her ammunition despite all the preparation.

The mine she planted exploded the following morning. The police arrested two Betar members who had nothing to do with it. Coincidentally, Torenberg was renting a room from their mother. Moldovsky told her to get out of Tiberias quickly but instead she went to the police station claiming she was sent by the boys' mother. Torenberg reasoned that she was preparing an alibi since the police would not expect the guilty party to come to the police station complaining.

When the Irgun split and Stern formed his own underground, Torenberg went with him. Two or three years earlier, in the nighttime Rosh Pina disputations, she and her friends had argued that the Irgunists should not take orders from Betar. They saw themselves and the Irgun as an independent national liberation movement. Stern was now implementing what they had wanted to do then, so Torenberg left the Irgun with him.

Torenberg taught the use of arms, clandestine behavior, and political thought. She distributed underground literature and followed British police officials. When Shamir was arrested in late 1941, she was tasked with contacting him in jail and debriefing him. She pretended to be his fiancée and met with him a few times in the Jaffa jail.

Torenberg recalled her mindset when she was in the Irgun and Lehi: "We weren't afraid of being in prison. In Lehi it was clear to us, either you would be killed on a street, or be locked up in a jail, after you had either been put on trial or not stood trial. The only element of surprise was when the knock on the door would come or when you would be arrested, or when you would be caught on a street. Having set out on this kind of a war against the English, nothing that happened could be a surprise, only the timing: when they knock, or when a British policeman puts his hand on your shoulder."

Torenberg was arrested a month after Stern was killed, when someone tipped the British off to her home address. She was interrogated by Wilkin and sent without trial to the Bethlehem Women's Prison, where she spent four and a half years. Shortly after her release the Irgun blew up the British military headquarters located in the southern wing of the King David Hotel, and she was picked up again. She was released a month and a half after that. She resumed her pedagogic role in Lehi and traveled from city to city lecturing.

After the creation of the state she used forged identify papers to get past the roadblocks and join Lehi's units in Jerusalem. On Lehi's Jerusalem base she was put in charge of "cultural" activities: she lectured and also arranged for various specialists and dignitaries to lecture to the young fighters in between battles. In July, she was attached as a nurse to the fighters trying to break through to the Old City. The attempt failed.

That same month, one of her former compatriots in Rosh Pina, Nehemiah Torenberg, returned from four years of British-imposed exile in Africa and enlisted in the Israeli army. In November of that year they were married. After the war, Nehemiah worked in a textile factory; in 1968, he and Julie opened a stationary store, which they ran until 1980.

Julie Torenberg joined Eldad's coterie in the 1950s as it kept the Lehi flame alive and published the monthly *Sulam*. She joined and was active in the Gush Emunim settlement movement in the 1970s and was secretary of the Tehiya party's Tel Aviv branch.

The Torenberg's second son is named Yair. He settled on a seashore of the Sinai Desert. After Nehemiah's death in 1981, Julie moved to the Sinai to be with her son when the Israeli government removed all the Jewish residents. The night before they were evacuated, her son set their home on fire. They spent the night on the beach watching and weeping.

Soon afterward, Julie Torenberg joined the Tsomet party (now defunct), and she served on the board of the "Bet Yair" Lehi Museum located in the building in which Stern was killed.

When Lehi fighter Aryeh Kotser was on his deathbed in 1995, Torenberg visited. At his request, she stood by his bed and sang Stern's anthem, "Anonymous Soldiers," one last time with him.

Julie Torenberg died in 2003.

Nelly Lengsfelder: In and Out of Jail

Growing up in Vienna in the 1930s, Nelly Fisher attended a state school; given that the state schools taught Catholicism, the Jews were exempt from morning prayers and were expected to attend their own services on the Sabbath. Nelly's family was well assimilated and secular. For the first time in her life she found herself attending synagogue every Sabbath. The

synagogue was across the street from the local Betar clubhouse. The Betar youth were also at the services and soon became friendly with Nelly, and before long, Nelly had joined Betar. When the Germans invaded Austria in 1938, Nelly and her brother joined a Betar ship taking Jews from Europe to Eretz Israel, albeit according to the British, illegally.[126]

Her parents had made her promise not to join the Betar service platoons, for fear the work would be too difficult. Instead she worked as a maid in Tel Aviv, work that she herself found difficult. A Betar friend visited her and praised life in the service platoons, where despite the hard labor, "we have a ball." Nelly enlisted in a platoon and, once there, in the Irgun. When the Irgun split, representatives of both sides trekked to Nelly's group in Zichron Yaacov to win over its members. Nelly's boyfriend, Eliahu Giladi, was with Stern's freedom fighters and after many long discussions, he convinced her to join them.

She served under Moshe Svorai's authority, mostly in carrying messages and material from one person or place to another. She maintained contact between the underground and lawyer Max Zeligman, who represented many of Lehi's arrestees in court. Later she brought messages from Stern to the detainees in the Mizra Camp. Giladi was interned there. Nelly would plant the messages in a tube of toothpaste or a double-bottomed box and visit him. The box would be given to a supervisor at the gate for the prisoner, and when Nelly sat with Giladi she would tell him where to look. On these visits to Mizra she met and began a friendship with Tova Svorai, who was there visiting Moshe. Coincidentally, Moshe had once broadcast a Lehi radio show from Nelly's apartment; no one had informed Nelly of the event, she had simply come home and found her friends dismantling electrical equipment.

Having accompanied Stern on one of his nighttime walkabouts in south Tel Aviv in 1942, after which she had let him sleep in her apartment, Nelly saw Stern for the last time when she dropped mail for him at Tova Svorai's apartment and took his messages for Mizra.

After Stern's death Nelly continued bringing messages from other fighters to Mizra. On one such mission, she stayed in Haifa, planning to set out the next morning; the British raided the Lehi safe house before dawn and arrested Nelly and four other Lehi members, netting something like one-fifth of the city's Lehi chapter in one fell swoop.[127] Nelly was soon sharing Tova's cell in the Bethlehem prison. "My parents thought I was completely innocent," she recalled. "I was very quiet and obedient. They couldn't imagine my being a terrorist." She did not see her parents for several years. They were deported from Eretz Israel as illegal immigrants and sent to a British internment camp in Mauritius. When they returned after the end of the World War, Nelly was still behind bars, and so their reunion was held in jail. "My mother cried so much," Nelly said. "I was so embarrassed. I told her it isn't so bad to be in jail."

Nelly used her time in jail to good effect, taking Hebrew lessons from Tova that were so successful, other inmates asked to join in. She, Tova, Julie and the other underground fighters led more than one "rebellion" in prison to protest overcrowding or other conditions. During the first such revolt, they refused to return to their cells. The woman in charge of the prison enlisted the criminal inmates (mostly Arabs but also Jews, and mostly thieves and prostitutes) to push them in. Once they had been forced inside, they decided to barricade the door to their cell with a table and made as much noise as possible, calling to the women on the floor below them, which served as an asylum for the insane, to join the fracas and better their own lot, too. Policemen were called in as reinforcements. They broke into the barricaded cell and removed the prisoners, relocating them to other cells where they remained for six weeks, with Tova and one other inmate kept alone.

The women's conditions were in some ways worse than those of the male inmates in the Jerusalem prison. Nelly and her Lehi friends were detainees; since they had not been charged with anything and not been tried or convicted, they were without rights. Being without rights, for the next two years they had no visitors and no packages delivered. Eventually, as their number increased, they were granted visiting and other privileges and transferred to an adjoining building with better conditions. The prisoners called the building the "villa."

After about three years in jail, when letters were coming and going— both by British post and by underground couriers—Nelly remarked to her friends that when she got out, she would pay a visit to her boyfriend Eliahu and call him to account, for he had not written even once during her absence or sent her any other kind of message. It was only then that her friends, who had been incarcerated after her and who therefore knew what had happened "outside," informed her that Giladi was no longer alive. They may not have known the details then, but they knew he had been eliminated. In hindsight, Nelly did not hold this against the Lehi leaders. She knew Giladi was dangerous and understood them, but she did fault Shamir for not telling her about it.

Nelly was released from prison in July 1946. A month later, British military headquarters in the King David Hotel in Jerusalem were blown up by the Irgun and the British arrested everyone they suspected of working with the underground. Nelly was detained in Latrun for six months. Following her release she rejoined Lehi and took instructional courses in light weaponry and codes. With her new skills she maintained contact with the Lehi prisoners who had been exiled to Kenya. She wrote letters with regular ink and additional sentences in starch. The prisoners knew to brush the letters with iodine to make the starch visible. In addition to being in invisible ink, these sections were always written in code. The British searched Nelly's home and found stacks of letters, among which was a line in someone else's handwriting that served as the key to the code Nelly used. Nelly was arrested yet again.

Yet again she helped lead a revolt. As the date set for the British withdrawal from Eretz Israel drew near, the danger to the prisoners increased. She noted, "We were kept in Bethlehem, guarded by Arab women and men. We said we wanted to be in a Jewish area. When we got no answer, we revolted. We broke into the office, cut the phone lines, and so on, until the police came. Thomas, the warden, remembered me from my previous term and involved me in the negotiations. First I complained that the police were beating us with clubs, so they were ordered to put the clubs in their belts. Then we demanded that both we and the mentally ill patients below be moved out. They agreed. We informed the detainees by our usual means of communication—shouting from the windows—and returned to our rooms. It turned out the date set for our move was Boxing Day [December 26], so we were asked to agree to move on another date, which is what happened."

The women were relocated to the Atlit Detention Camp, as were the Jewish inmates of other prisons.

After the establishment of Israel, Nelly served in an armored unit of the army. When she went to live with her parents in Ramat Gan she met an old acquaintance she had known in Betar in Vienna, Gershon Lengsfelder, who had come to the country on the same boat as she. He had enlisted in the local police force in 1939 (in the coming years he occasionally assisted the Irgun). When Lengsfelder's wife passed away, Nelly paid a condolence call. In 1951, they married. Major Lengsfelder interfaced with Interpol and headed a security detail at Israel's airport before being given charge of the Israeli police unit concerned with tracking Nazi criminals. He died in the late 1970s. Nelly died in 2010.

Yael Ben-Dov: A 14 Year Old with Many Questions

Before there was a Sternist named "Yael," and before she married a Sternist named Ben-Dov, there was a 14 year old named Chaya Brandwyn. She was born in Jerusalem and came with rabbinical pedigree, an offspring of the families of Rabbi Isaiah Horowitz, a six-teenth-century kabbalist known as the "Holy Shelah," and Rabbi Israel Baal Shem Tov, the eighteenth-century founder of modern Hasidism.[128]

As she remembers it, she and her mother were walking in Jerusalem's religious neigh-borhood of Mea Shearim near Sabbath Square when they saw two boys pasting broadsides on the walls. The British po-lice descended on the square, the boys escaped capture, and the "whole crowd sighed with relief." Chaya asked her mother why everyone was happy—"aren't the people being chased by the police criminals?" Her mother responded with a sharp "Quiet!" The teenager went over to the remains of the broadside the British had ripped down, and read: "We won't go like sheep to the slaughter. Britain will pay for the blood that has been shed." At the bottom of the poster was the name "Lehi." She asked, "Who's Lehi?" and the crowd sharply "Shhh"ed her. Her mother admonished, "Don't ask questions." "But," says Yael today, "at fourteen and a half when you're told not to ask, you ask."[129]

Chaya assumed that the boys would eventually hang more broadsides and waited for them to return. That second time she recognized one of them; he was her counselor in the League of Hasmoneans youth move-ment. The next time the youth group met, she decided to attract the counselor's attention and delivered a long speech about a ship called *Patria*, which had carried eighteen hundred immigrants from Europe to Eretz Is-rael in November 1940. The British considered the refugees "illegals" and ordered them deported to Mauritius. The Hagana smuggled a bomb on board, designed to cripple the ship and forestall the deportations, but the ship was too weak to withstand the blast and sank, killing over 250 of the refugees. Chaya's impassioned speech frightened her friends, who called to her, "Quiet—it's too dangerous," but it impressed the counselor, who recommended her to his higher ups in Lehi and brought her in.[130]

Brandwyn was soon traveling with a team of youth pasting her own stack of Lehi broadsides on Jerusalem's walls. One day the Sternist fighter Dov the Blond approached her: "Do you want to kill the commander of the British forces in Eretz Israel?" Of course she did, she said, but how? He answered: "With a woman's wiles." Looking back, she comments, "Not much before that, I was in kindergarten; all of a sudden I was a woman with wiles? I was no Queen Esther, how was I supposed to kill him?" Dov instructed her to dress as a nanny and appear with a baby stroller near the home of General Evelyn Barker, the British commander. (Barker was known as an anti-Semite. His policies included forbidding social interaction between his soldiers and Jews and calling on his troops to "punish the Jews in the manner this race dislikes the most: by hitting them in the pocket, which will demonstrate our disgust for them."[131]) Brandwyn's job was to walk by Barker's home (today the residence of the Israeli prime minister, on Jerusalem's Balfour Street) every morning and report the time Barker emerged. Every day, she reported, he left at 8:30 for his headquarters at the King David Hotel, less than a ten-minute walk. At that point the baby in Brandwyn's carriage was switched for a doll made of explosives. Brandwyn was supposed to pass by Barker and press a button. Undoubtedly this would have worked, she knew, but she would blow up with Barker. Lehi never approved an operation unless its fighters had a means of escape. They offered her a few seconds' delay and a motorcycle but, she says, "I was scared to ride a motorcycle...." Her superiors laughed and realized even "Yael" was afraid of something. Instead they planted a mine at an airfield from which Barker was scheduled to fly to Tel Aviv; it was discovered before the flight. Barker ordered that all his routes be checked and soon another mine was discovered on the Jerusalem-Tel Aviv road where his car was expected to pass. Ultimately Barker left the country before Lehi was able to reach him.[132]

Yael served as Lehi's lookout during Eldad's escape. After the owner of a café alerted the police to her identity she was forced to flee the city and essentially abandon her ill mother. She was never caught and continued her Lehi activities until the establishment of the state. She ended up in charge of a squad of young recruits in Jerusalem. In Israel, Yael married Shabtai

Ben-Dov, a member of Lehi who had been exiled to Africa (and who had escaped from the internment camp there, though he was recaptured). Shabtai wrote for Eldad's journal *Sulam* in the 1950s and later authored several works, including one entitled *The Redemption of Israel as Reflected in the Crisis of the State*, and another, *Prophecy and Tradition in Redemption*. Following the 1967 Six Day War, Shabtai and Yael moved with six other Jewish families, including Lehi members Ezra Yachin and Shimon and Aliza Barmatz, to an Arab neighborhood in East Jerusalem. Shabtai died in 1978; Yael was a nursery school teacher and then a special education teacher until her retirement, after which she volunteered assisting troubled youth. In recent years she has been spending one day a week at the Museum of Underground Fighters in the former Jerusalem prison, where she leads tours and teaches tourists and students about the underground.

Benjamin Gepner: A Sternist in Greenwich Village

Overheard: 95-year-old Lehi veteran Benjamin Gepner in a crowded auditorium in Jerusalem in 2010, in conversation with an appreciative reader of his recently published autobiography:

— "You're Benjamin Gepner, no? I couldn't put your book down. It's great. The book is written with grace and humor and tells an important story."

— "That's because I didn't write it, Charles Dickens did. I just put my name on it."

— "I'm glad you put the time and effort into it."

— "It's a good thing I did. If I hadn't I would've been out chasing women."[133]

Gepner's one-liners give way to somber thought when an interviewer focuses on his past activity with the Sternists. Looking out over the Mediterranean from his seaside apartment south of Tel Aviv, Gepner says wistfully, "Every word you spoke then had meaning. You were always attentive, you needed to think about everything you said and did."[134]

Gepner has been paying attention to Lehi for a long time. After the underground's war, he brought a tape recorder to Israel from the United States, with which he taped his fellow fighters while their memories were still fresh. That accomplished, "some internal compulsion," he says, caused him to fly to England, at his own expense, three times, to interview the "other side." Decades later, these tapes were donated to the Lehi Museum, run by Israel's Ministry of Defense. In fact, Gepner had been something of a pack rat in the underground, saving any scrap of paper that came his way if it could be hidden without posing a mortal danger. He preserved Stern's last letter in the knot of a tie. All the scraps he saved—six carloads according to Gepner—were donated to the museum in 2010.[135]

Even in the underground Gepner was forced to *talk* about Lehi. Nathan Yalin-Mor told him he intended to send him to the Unites States to found a Lehi branch there. Gepner pleaded for "action" in Eretz Israel, but Yalin-Mor insisted he would be more useful writing material for journalists or spreading the word in New York. Meanwhile, Gepner wrote poems for the underground papers (his first, written as if by a man waiting to be hanged, he gave to Yalin-Mor without comment; Yalin-Mor put it straight into a drawer, also without comment, seemingly ignoring it. Two weeks later it was posted on the country's walls as part of a Lehi broadside).[136]

Until he left for New York, Gepner was assigned to write articles for a newsletter being distributed to foreign journalists. Finally he cornered Yalin-Mor and asked how he could go to the United States to talk of Lehi's activities without having engaged in any such activity. Two weeks later, without advance notice, a young woman, Leah Granek, knocked on his door and told him to follow her. As they got into a waiting car, three young men jumped in with him, Gepner wondering from where they had come. Gepner tried to make small talk with Granek and failed miserably. She curtly ordered the driver to set off, ignored Gepner during the ride, ordered the car to stop when they were in south Tel Aviv, stepped into a store, and returned with two mines and some other packages. She handed Gepner one and said, "Pepper." Again, Gepner attempted a humorous retort, to no avail. Without explanation, she told him to sprinkle the pepper on the ground after the operation.[137]

Several miles further on they stopped on a dark road and planted the mines. Granek asked Gepner whether to detonate them under the front or the rear of a British convoy. He advised the front, saying the higher ranks would be up front. Her response was, "I'll blow up the rear." Gepner asked for her reasons but by then there was no time; she ordered, "Heads down," and after five cars had passed the mines went off. She ordered Gepner to sprinkle the pepper (to throw track dogs off the scent) and they ran, stopping for some water about half an hour later in a house near Bnai Brak.

As they were about to leave, a man ordered them to stop; it was the owner of the house, who had opened his doors to the Lehi fighters and now insisted on laying his hands on their heads and blessing them before they left.[138]

Gepner soon left for the United States, able to tell of participating in such missions. He set up office in the Julius Café in New York's Greenwich Village, there interviewing potential volunteers. Later they took an office in a small hotel near Times Square. Gepner was assisted by a diverse crew: Nicholas Kisberg, a leader of the Teamsters; Shepherd Rifkin, a bohemian novelist; Mike Frankel, a poet and confident of author Henry Miller, and others.[139]

At Gepner's first press conference, Rabbi Baruch Korff, a colorful figure in his own right, protected Gepner's identity by having him speak from behind a half-closed door in a midtown hotel room. A former FBI agent was hired to identify current FBI agents posing as journalists. One such was ejected; a second, allowed to remain.[140] Gepner says that despite Korff's successful ploy and his own constant caution, "Lehi wasn't something hidden in my pocket, it was my life. No matter how discreet I was, at least a hundred people knew I was in Lehi." On a visit by Gepner to relatives in Kalamazoo, Michigan, the local rabbi even introduced him to his Sabbath congregation as a representative of Lehi, blowing any cover Gepner might have hoped to maintain.[141]

At the party to which Henry Wallace invited him, Gepner not only heard the former vice president adopt Lehi's goal of a neutralization of the Middle East, he also met his future wife. They did not talk at the time, but he recognized her a few years later when she visited Israel, and they hit it off then.[142]

Gepner had come a long way to be partying for Lehi in the United States. He was born in Poland in 1914, came to Eretz Israel in 1936, enlisted in the Irgun in 1937, and was arrested in November 1939 during an Irgun training course. That landed him in the Acco prison and Mizra Detention Camp for two years. Though he switched to Lehi in jail, on his release Gepner declined Shamir's request that he serve Lehi because, he says, "I didn't believe Lehi would beat the British while they fought a World War." Instead Gepner enlisted in the British army to fight the Germans.[143]

Gepner served in the A-Force, which helped Allied POWs escape from behind enemy lines, and was cited for bravery. On his first foray onto a battlefield he found a fiancée's letters next to the body of a dead Italian soldier and carried them throughout Italy looking for the woman, perhaps to console her. He finally found her, much to his surprise preparing to wed her soldier boyfriend. The letters he had carried so carefully had not belonged to the dead soldier.[144]

On a furlough in Eretz Israel he met with Hagana commander Eliahu Golomb, whom he tried to enlist in an effort to save Jews in Europe, and with whom he discussed the local undergrounds. Golomb shared his views of the Sternists with Gepner: "The Freedom Fighters for Israel are idealists. They combine the messianic fervor of Polish Jews with the hands-on wisdom of Eretz-Israeli Jews."[145]

Gepner met with Shamir again, who tried to convince him to desert and join the now advancing underground. Gepner refused to desert but could not turn Shamir down cold, so he volunteered to set up a Lehi cell in Cairo where he was going with the British. He organized a cell from among Palestinian soldiers and Egyptian Jews.[146]

The British caught up with Gepner after Moyne's assassination. He was arrested, exiled to Sudan and later Eritrea, and taken for interrogation to Maadi Prison near Cairo. Gepner was kept in solitary confinement for 90 days. Of that time, he writes:

> Who are in the cells next to mine?...Throughout the length and breadth of the British Empire the rebel movements of peoples awakening to new life are stirring. How I would like to shake the hands of my neighbors, to tell them there is hope, even if they are still weak and maybe there are not many like them in their lands. "In my country, too, there are not many like me," I would tell them. "People like to lead quiet and pleasant lives. They call people like me the 'Stern Gang.' In the language of officialdom, only those who oppress us and those who obey them are called decent people. And many of my own people might agree."
>
> If my eyes could fell these walls, I would see them all. Though I do not understand a word of their languages, I "speak" with them every day. They are my brothers. And maybe they, too, wonder who the man stuck in cell number eight is, what he is made of, what his hopes are, what wars he and his people are fighting that have brought him here, between these thick dark walls.[147]

It was after his release from Maadi and his return from his year of forced African exile—he claimed to have eye trouble and was allowed back to Eretz Israel—that he was "forced" by Yalin-Mor to write and edit for Lehi and then sent in 1947 to the United States.

Given that Gepner had studied agronomy but had, he says, his "professional career hijacked by Lehi," he found himself unemployed in 1949, the year after Israel's establishment. He chose to study filmmaking in the United States, failed to make a go of that when back in Israel, and instead founded a publishing company. "I spoke seven languages," he recalls, "so assumed I could read all the books being published elsewhere in the original and select what was worth publishing in Israel." Once he had saved a little money he decided to preserve the story of Lehi, so he began taping the former fighters and their former enemies.[148] Eventually, he turned the publishing company over to his son, who is still republishing the books his father put out years ago.

On the one hand, Gepner has done quite a lot to preserve the history of Lehi, some of the time almost as if he were on a one-man crusade to do so. On the other hand, Gepner, at least these days, is sometimes reluctant to immerse himself in Lehi matters. "At this point Lehi is a subject about which people get sentimental; once, it was a subject that people acted on."[149]

"Lehi," says Gepner, "was fire. You try to talk about it today and you can't even touch it."[150]

Rabbi Abraham Ravitz: He Heard the Shots and Joined

Abraham Ravitz was eight years old when he and his classmates in a Talmud Torah (private parochial school) in south Tel Aviv heard shots fired a few blocks away. It was February 12, 1942. Ravitz ran downstairs and asked the gathering crowds what had happened. In a speech to the Knesset the year before his death, Ravitz recalled:

They all answered, "The British police killed a Jewish robber and murderer." I went

back to the class and my friends asked what had happened. I mumbled what I had heard on the street. The
rabbi who was our teacher was weeping and said—I remember it until today—"Avroymel [a Yiddish nickname
for Abraham], it was not a murderer and not a robber they
killed. It was a self-sacrificing Jewish hero." This rabbi
was Rabbi Isaac Yedidya Frankl, who later became Chief
Rabbi of Tel Aviv, the father-in-law of [former Chief Rabbi
of Israel] Rabbi Lau.

The class was surprised and fell silent. How could
this be? We were in shock. Then I began to think. I
swung back and forth between the terms "murderer,"
"hero," "robber," "self-sacrifice," and I came to conclusions that engraved themselves on my heart and built
my young personality: not everything adults say is true,
and not everything the majority believes is always right.

Thanks to Yair I knew that ahead of us lay a war
against the British occupiers of our land, the few against
the many and the weak against the strong, in order to
establish a Jewish home for those persecuted in the European Exile. Lehi entered my heart as a seed that had
sprouted. I labored and found my path with the fighters
in Lehi's ranks. And I merited being able to fight most
of the war in Jerusalem.[151]

Ravitz was then and he remained a Haredi (ultra-Orthodox) Jew. He
knew that his rabbis looked with disdain on the underground movements
because they threatened to draw young people away from their Torah studies. But, Ravitz pointed out, a good number of ultra-Orthodox joined Lehi.
The Hagana, he said, was part of the establishment and the Irgun represented various ideologies that sounded foreign to the ultra-Orthodox,[152] in
addition to which the "map" for which the Irgun was fighting was that of
British Mandatory Palestine. Both sides of the Jordan River (today's State
of Israel as well as kingdom of Jordan) were on the map, but Ravitz preferred to distribute maps based on the biblical promise of a Jewish state
from the Nile to the Euphrates. In any case, he said, "Lehi was the only
underground that spoke pure truth. They talked about expelling the British from the country so Jews could immigrate freely, and this spoke to our
concerns. We and many other yeshiva boys were pained by the plight of the
Jews, and this is what drew Haredi Jews to Lehi."[153] Ravitz enlisted when

he was 13 and hung Lehi broadsides and newspapers on the shop windows and billboards of Jerusalem. Then he worked at getting new recruits. At the age of 14, he also enrolled in the Hebron Yeshiva (located in Jerusalem), where he was the youngest student and one of six who were also members of Lehi. During the War of Independence, Ravitz fought with Lehi's religious unit.[154]

In the 1950s Ravitz taught Torah to new immigrants. Sometimes, underground methods had to be adopted; the government had an unofficial "melting pot" policy of secularizing the new immigrants. Ravitz consulted with Rabbi Abraham Yeshayahu Karelitz, a sage known as the Chazon Ish, who handed him money and told him to buy skullcaps and *tsitsit* for the newcomers. Ravitz brought sacks of the head coverings and fringed garments to the compounds where Yemenite arrivals were kept behind barbed wire, and at night he and his associates dug under the fences and distributed the religious apparel. The next morning the tables had turned in the camp; the Yemenites had resumed their ancient practices and were wearing the skullcaps and garments. Ravitz informed the authorities that he and his friends were there to stay and demanded a room to teach Torah, which he was granted.[155]

Professionally, Ravitz earned his living as a building contractor, but he continued his volunteer activities teaching Torah. He was active in the Yad L'Achim organization dedicated to bringing wayward youth back to Judaism. He became an ordained rabbi who was principal of a high school in Jerusalem and a seminary in Pardes Hanna. In 1984, he campaigned for the Sephardic party Shas, and in 1988 he was elected to the Israeli Knesset as a representative of the ultra-Orthodox Agudat Israel camp. He served until his death 11 years later. He was a member of the Knesset's caucuses for Jerusalem, for the environment, and for treating rare genetic diseases. From 1999 to 2003, he served as Deputy Speaker of the Knesset. Beginning in 1990, he served at various times as Israel's deputy minister of housing and construction, deputy minister of education, and deputy minister of welfare and social services.[156]

Yaacov Heruti: Long after Lehi, the "Most Dangerous Man in Israel"

When the Zionist establishment opposed the undergrounds fighting to liberate Eretz Israel from foreign domination and forbade the dissemination of their literature, teenager Yaacov Heruti's curiosity was piqued. "Stolen waters are sweet," he recalls, citing an ancient talmudic dictum to

explain why he began reading underground newspapers. "We wanted to know what we were forbidden to read."[157]

Nonetheless, after high school Heruti enlisted in a British-approved constabulary that essentially represented the establishment Hagana. He planned eventually to study law in England. Then, during the summer of 1944, Heruti read in the general press the courtroom declarations of the Lehi fighters. When Lehi assassinated Lord Moyne in Cairo and tried to assassinate High Commissioner for Palestine MacMichael, Heruti respected them even more. Thus, when Ben-Gurion, then chairman of the Jewish Agency and leader of the Histadrut, took action in November 1944 against the fighters and ordered children suspected of sympathizing with the underground expelled from schools, adults fired from their jobs, and Irgun and Lehi members captured and turned over to the British, Heruti says, "I knew kidnapping Jews and turning them over to the enemy is tantamount to treason. It was clear to me I would not find my glory with the Hagana."[158]

Heruti was breaking with his roots. His father, Mordecai, did find glory in the Hagana. He belonged to the leftwing Hashomer Hatzair movement in Poland and adopted the family name Heruti, meaning "liberty," when Hashomer encouraged its members to exchange their Polish names for Hebrew ones. Under the impression that the Jews of Eretz Israel did not need more intellectuals, he changed his career plans, too, and became a blacksmith's apprentice. He moved his family to Eretz Israel in 1920, enlisted in the Hagana, subscribed to the Histadrut's newspaper, and served with the British during World War II. In the 1950s, while his son Yaacov was in jail in Israel, Mordecai was deputy chief justice of the army's military tribunal.

After the Moyne and MacMichael attacks, Yaacov Heruti sought contact with the underground. A friend passed his name to the Irgun, but someone from Lehi knocked at his door. Heruti told him he had hoped to join the Irgun, but he did ask his visitor what differentiated the two movements. The Irgunists "are vegetarians," he was told, they only blow up buildings and refrain from hurting soldiers; but "we are at war." Heruti agreed to join and was taken to an open field near the local zoo. A committee interviewed

him from behind a screen or a sheet. He was asked why he was not joining the Hagana or the Irgun, and replied that he opposed the Hagana's restraint and once he had decided to fight he did not want to fight "halfway"
as the Irgun did. A voice from behind the screen asked if he understood that
the underground is not something one enters and exits at will, but that he
was enlisting for life; was he ready to give that life? He was, and he was
in.[159]

His first work was in Lehi's "technical department," building bombs.
He was taken to a room and ushered to a bookcase that, when two loose
wires were touched, opened to reveal a laboratory behind it. He expected,
he says, to be trained by the country's leading chemists. Instead he was
ordered to "figure out" out how to create explosives and spent his time
"underground" sitting in a public library researching the subject. His first
mine was assembled on a rooftop in south Tel Aviv. When that worked he
was given a building in an orchard and was soon producing tons of explosives every month.

In October 1947, Heruti enrolled as a student in London and headed
a Lehi branch there. He was involved in unsuccessful plans to assassinate
Foreign Minister Ernest Bevin, General Barker, and former Palestine policeman Roy Farran, who had abducted Alexander Rubovitch, a Jerusalem teenager who had been carrying Lehi broadsides. Farran and his squad pulled
Rubovitch from near Jerusalem's Ussishkin Street, pushed him into their
police car (Farran's hat namctag and all—fell off and thus revealed his
complicity), and apparently tortured and murdered him outside the city.
Heruti decided that since Farran lived far from his Lehi unit, in a city with
no Lehi safe house, the attack would be by means of a letter bomb. This
was inserted into a fine edition of Shakespeare and the package was marked
"Personal." Farran's brother opened it and was killed. Heruti says, "This
was a frustrating failure. We were out for the murderer, not his brother."[160]

"During those months I became friendly with many British people,"
writes Heruti. "I felt no contradiction between these friendships and the
mission I was given, not even for a minute. Lehi's military strategy totally
ruled out attacks on innocent civilians. Our goal was to strike at the British authorities, those that took from the Jewish people its right to establish an independent state in its historic homeland. The people we wanted
to strike at were the decision makers and executors of the policy, certainly
not the 'man on the street.'"[161]

When the State of Israel was established in May 1948, Heruti joined
a boatload of refugees and returned. Yalin-Mor wanted him to take a re-

fresher course in explosives and return to England to continue the fight, because Yalin-Mor expected England to do an about face and return to the country it was supposedly fleeing. Heruti was less than enthusiastic and was relieved when Shamir suggested he join the front lines in Jerusalem instead, where Arabs and Jews were fighting for every square foot.[162] In Jerusalem, Heruti led a Lehi unit in an attempt to penetrate the Old City.

Heruti was picked up by the Israeli authorities during the mass arrests of Lehi members that followed the assassination of Count Bernadotte. He had a saw in his backpack, though, which inexplicably remained with him in jail. At night he cut through the bars of his Jerusalem cell and together with several others, laid a blanket over the glass shards atop the compound wall and jumped to freedom. With the Israeli army's approval, he enlisted, hoping to put his past behind him, but instead the military authorities rearrested him. When visiting-day privileges were revoked in the Jaffa prison, he and his cellmates broke through a wall and were again free. In November 1948 Heruti again enlisted in the army. He brought his professional military career to a close only later, after a commanding officer singled him out for mistreatment as a Lehi vet.

Trying to eek out a living holding down three jobs—translating for a newspaper, copying documents for a law office, and working for a notary—Heruti also began to study law. But in late 1951, Rudolf Slansky, the General Secretary of the Communist party in Czechoslovakia, was arrested on Stalin's orders as part of a purge. Slansky and thirteen others were put on trial in November 1952; all but three of the fourteen defendants were Jewish. Slansky was executed in December. That same month, Stalin declared that Jews were agents of American imperialism and ordered the arrests of Jewish doctors he accused of trying to poison Soviet leaders. Heruti writes,

> We saw a great flight from the principles we held. We had fought to liberate Eretz Israel, the homeland of the Jewish people, and what did we get? A state that relied on the mercy of other nations and was afraid to offer a sovereign response to its bitter enemies. Arab terrorism runs amok, the Fedayin walk freely in our country, they shoot, kill, and escape, and we remain silent; in Czechoslovakia, Jews are executed and Israeli citizens are also arrested on false charges, our Jewish brothers in the Soviet Union are doomed to destruction, and no one says anything or even whistles...."For this we fought?" we asked...as did many at that time.[163]

Heruti and Lehi vet Shimon Becher discovered that many of their former comrades in arms were upset that the government bowed to the wishes of foreigners and related to the homeland as "real estate" that was for sale to its neighbors. This circle of Lehi veterans looked to the ancient Kingdom of David for inspiration and saw the modern return to Zion as a reincarnation of that kingdom. Thus the new group they formed became known as the "Kingdom of Israel Underground."[164]

The idea was to break the government's restraint. First they shot at Jordanian soldiers who were manning a post in Jerusalem's Old City, from which one of the soldiers had earlier shot and killed a Jewish woman hanging laundry. In February 1953, during the preparations for the doctors' trials in the Soviet Union, Heruti readied explosives in a building next to the Soviet Embassy in Tel Aviv. Another Lehi veteran brought guns, which he distributed to the members of the team. They cut the fence surrounding the embassy and planted a bomb in the yard, far enough away from the building to send a signal but not to destroy it or cause loss of life. Heruti hurried home and made sure to engage a neighbor in conversation in order to have an alibi. But someone who was arrested for a different crime in Jerusalem revealed he had also hidden guns and documents for Heruti's group. He named names, and Heruti and 14 others were arrested that June.[165]

The 14 refused to recognize the military court before which they were brought, demanding a civilian trial; they sang at their trial, stirring memories of bygone Lehi days but not ameliorating their sentences. The government had no evidence linking the group to the Tel Aviv bombing, but Heruti received ten years for belonging to a terrorist organization. In prison they focused their efforts on arts and crafts, and one of the group, an important archaeologist, was sent ancient specimens by the state Antiquities Authority for him to sketch and catalogue. Heruti also studied radio technology, built a radio from scratch for the prisoners, and resumed his legal studies. He asked permission to take all the university exams from which he had been absent, and while in prison took and passed some thirty of them, failing only one, which he had to make up. His wife divorced him on the grounds that he had been sentenced to ten years in jail; he agreed to the divorce. Two weeks later he was pardoned.[166]

The prisoners had hoped to be catalysts for change and by the time they were released they felt they had accomplished their mission. Ben-Gurion had established the army's new "Unit 101," whose mission was to take the offensive against Arab terror and to respond to attacks on Israelis.[167]

Now free, Heruti served as a legal intern and once again held several jobs in order to earn a living. In his position as a typist he was handed a manuscript by a woman who soon afterward became his second wife; they remained married for 45 years, until her death in 2000. Heruti also volunteered for Eldad's *Sulam* journal and club, where he and others he says "had not abandoned the dream of the rise of Israel in its land" worked to educate the public.[168] Many of the attendees at Eldad's lectures were actually agents of Israel's internal security forces, though not very good agents. Some tried to justify their investigations to their superior officers and fabricated stories of new undergrounds on the horizon. In March 1957 one went in the opposite direction and apparently left his government job and, with no connection to Eldad, took up arms: he killed Rudolph Kastner, a Hungarian Jew accused of collaborating with the Germans and facilitating the murder of Hungarian Jewry in return for the rescue of just over sixteen hundred Jews. Heruti, who had just begun his law practice and had nothing to do with the killing, found himself in jail, in solitary confinement, and on hunger fasts for the rest of the year. One newspaper's headline asked why he—dubbed "the most dangerous man in the country"—was being held so long and hinted the government was trying to break him. In January 1958 the judge in the trial ruled the government had failed to prove the existence of an underground and Heruti was cleared of all charges related to terrorism, but to justify the time he had been held, he was found guilty of insulting a judge in 1956 and sentenced to 18 months. With time off for good behavior he was out of jail a few weeks later.[169]

Heruti formed several lasting relationships during his stints in jail. He represented one of his cellmates, a conman, in court for the rest of the man's life, without compensation. He became friendly with the prosecutor, too, and with his judge, and even with Isser Harel, the chief of the security force and the Mossad, who had directed the case against him.

In the 1960s, Heruti was active in nationalist circles with Eldad to "encourage, renew, and revive the national consciousness among the nation of Israel and the Diaspora."[170] They published a journal called *Hehazit*, the same name as one of Lehi's journals. In 1968, this group sued for the right to worship on Jerusalem's Temple Mount but lost. In the 1970s Heruti began arranging purchases of land in Judea and Samaria. "I work with land," he says, "not real estate. Land is for growing food and building a home; real estate is easy money."[171] Heruti and his teenaged son set off together on two attempts to settle in the area of ancient Sebastia in Samaria, a Gush Emunim effort that eventually paid off when the then minister of defense,

Shimon Peres, approved the formation of a town that became today's Kedumim. When the settlement of Ofra was being built, Heruti was coincidentally moving into a new home. He invited members of the Bnei Akiva youth movement to the house he was vacating and had them take everything that could be moved—walls, ceilings, pipes, and even the street signs—which he sent to the builders in Ofra.[172]

Heruti declined the usual age-based discharge from the Israeli military reserves and instead extended his reserve service so he could serve as legal counsel at hearings on the legality of planned settlements. At the age of 71, Heruti wrote a doctoral thesis on the relation between land ownership and whatever governments were in charge of Eretz Israel throughout history, from the first human settlement at Jericho nine thousand years ago until today, concentrating on the determination of ownership and on taxation.

Heruti was politically active during the 1980s and 1990s. At the founding meeting of former army Chief of Staff Rafael Eitan's Tsomet party, Heruti was not only present, he brought and filled out the incorporation forms. Eitan committed his party to "renewing the basic Zionist values on which the State of Israel was established and built. Tsomet supports the entire Land of Israel (including the Golan Heights) and unfettered settlement in all parts of Eretz Israel."[173] The Tsomet party became influential in the 1990s, at one point winning eight Knesset seats, but several of its members bolted the party and today the party is not represented at all. Heruti also supported the Moledet party, led by another former general, Ze'evi, and once again Heruti was there at the founding, filing its legal papers. In this case he also suggested the name Moledet, which Ze'evi adopted.[174] Moledet's political platform is that a solution to the Arab-Israeli conflict should be based on population transfers: Jews from Arab countries should be absorbed in Israel, and Arabs from Israel should be absorbed in Arab countries (according to Ze'evi's theory, these transfers must be voluntary).

After neither Tsomet nor Moledet proved vital to Israeli politics and both collapsed amidst internal bickering, and after both Eitan and Ze'evi died unnatural deaths—the former killed by a high wave during a storm as he oversaw the construction of a new pier, and the latter murdered by terrorists in Jerusalem while serving as Israel's minister of tourism—Heruti lost his enthusiasm for politics. He had earlier been disheartened after the election loss of his former Lehi chief, Prime Minister Yitzhak Shamir, in 1992, to Yitzhak Rabin.

Heruti believes that, ironically, the establishment of a state eroded the tools of survival and progress the Jewish people had in hand until then. Israel, he says, needs to invest in revitalizing Jewish communities around the world, and these communities need to assume a role in Israel. The problem is that a conflict of interest seems to have arisen between the two.[175]

> An establishment, a small minority, completely disconnected from the people, was taking control of the homeland....Over the years it has become clear that this process not only hasn't abated but has accelerated. The vast majority of the Jewish people believes in our historic right to this land and wants a leadership that will return the Jewish people's property and inheritance to it, and especially—that will return its self-respect. The establishment, the Jews of little faith, busies itself with short-term political survival. It is not interested in honor but in honors.[176]

Heruti has devoted his recent years to supporting the University Center at Ariel, even helping arrange for it the donation of a particle accelerator. He still works at his Tel Aviv law office, where prominent on his walls are a portrait of Rabbi Arye Levin, the rabbi who visited the underground prisoners in jail, and an even larger portrait of Salvador Dali, which he bought from a street artist in Budapest. He breaks every afternoon to study a page of the Talmud with his staff.[177]

Heruti writes,

> My generation was educated on the simple and natural love of the homeland. The Book of Books, the Bible, was an inseparable part of our world and of the nation of Israel's right to Eretz Israel....We were prepared to fight and sacrifice our lives for the liberation of the homeland and the survival of the nation. We aimed toward the goal that the Jewish people saw before it for the thousands of years of Exile: to return to the homeland, liberate it, and keep it.[178]

The Family Breaks Up

The brief biographies of the relatively few Lehi fighters sketched above make clear that the group was not homogeneous. One became an ordained rabbi, one was called "rabbi," one had dropped his rabbinical studies to become a philosopher, at least one was an atheist; two were engineers, several were writers, one a clerk, two were housewives. While Julie Torenberg recalled being the center of attention, her friend Nelly Lengsfelder thought of herself as "quiet and obedient." Of Lehi's three leaders, Yalin-Mor was on the far left, Eldad on the far right, and Shamir began his political career allied to the leftist and ended it close to the rightist.

Abraham Stern's son Yair (he was born after his father had been shot and was named for him) recalls that his mother told him that had Stern lived, he would not have gone into Israeli politics but would probably have gone into academia, becoming rector of a university or perhaps the head of a Jewish studies department.[179] Yair the son's view is that his father was above politics, "it would have been too petty for him."[180] A few Lehi vets entered politics, some more successfully than others, and many of the former fighters volunteered for various political parties or causes and still do.

Lehi was an army of teens, adults, rabbis, atheists, writers, clerks, and housewives who chose to change the world, and so they became revolutionaries.

This diverse group was united as long as it fought single-mindedly for a state, but even so, the ideal state appeared somewhat differently to each fighter in his mind's eye. When the British were defeated the Lehi fighters took a breath; when the state for which they fought began to rise, the visions they had set before them reflected different dreams.

When Yalin-Mor and Shmuelevitz stood trial following the assassination of Bernadotte, Eldad disagreed with the defense they mounted. He said that Yalin-Mor, instead of calling witnesses in his defense, should have challenged the court: "Who are you and who are we? You are able to sit here in judgment thanks to us and you want me to prove that I am not a terrorist?"[181] But Yalin-Mor was already trying to show the establishment that Lehi was not quite so bad, pinning his hopes on winning acceptance and wooing the masses, while Eldad was planting himself as firmly as ever on his convictions and bucking the political tide.

The trial was not half as divisive as the dreams.

6

Lehi Looks at Israel
and
Israel Looks at Lehi

Stern's Principles after Stern

After Stern was killed his mantle was shared by three men totally committed to his vision, yet whose own visions were amazingly dissimilar. Yalin Mor and Eldad, whose different visions were propounded—during the underground war and after the creation of the State of Israel—with the most clarity and on the greatest number of newspaper and book pages, both tried to convince the Israeli public to follow them and failed to garner enough votes to win seats in the Knesset. The third man, Shamir, did not write any philosophical or political tracts, neither underground nor afterward in the Jewish state, yet a majority of Knesset members chose him as their Speaker and a plurality of Israeli voters twice elected this taciturn man of action to lead the country.

Stern, his three successors, and all nine hundred plus members of Lehi believed in liberating the Jewish homeland and establishing a Jewish state. Their plans for the war to establish the state and their deeds before and after this war have been described in the pages above. Their plans for the state have not—or have not yet—come to pass. They wanted a state; what did they want *for* the state?

Nathan Yalin-Mor

In "real time," as Lehi was emerging from the underground and debating its future format, Yalin-Mor summed up his views and those of his fellow fighters:

> Despite our differences of opinion, which have been expressed sharply during the debate, it has become clear beyond any doubt that all our members without exception see the war of liberation as a project that has not yet reached its conclusion, that is far from completion. The entire movement sees the continuation—in accordance with circumstances and current conditions—of the war of liberation as a mission with which we will be engaged until its realization. And it is also clear that the vast majority of the movement's members see a classless society as the solution to our people's social problems. Not a voice was heard at the convention demanding as a foundation a victory for social and economic inequality. No arguments were made in favor of the sanctity of personal property, or about capitalism or economic liberalism as the institutional basis for Hebrew society in the future. The differences of opinion were limited to one point: under the new political conditions, with the establishment of the State of Israel in part of the homeland, should the movement become a party operating in all fields of daily life or is it obligated to preserve its strength for a war for the entire homeland when this becomes feasible? Those who support this latter approach expressed their fear that when dealing with day-to-day matters we may forget the larger goal, we may stop thinking about it.[1]

Yalin-Mor wanted Lehi to commit itself to attaining a classless society based on socialist economic theory. He favored a planned, centralized economy and buttressed his argument by partially crediting the Soviet Union's military successes to such an economy. But for Yalin-Mor this was not just expediency or what turned out to be a misguided respect for the Soviet's economic health (the façade of economic health tumbled for the Soviet Union's own citizens 40 years later, taking the Soviet Union with it). Yalin-Mor wished for a particular type of planned economy. He condemned and wanted to eliminate the "parasitism" of local middlemen. Since he did not expect socialism to suddenly appear in Israel, he hoped to begin by setting limits to the profitability of private initiative and capital. Because he could not imagine massive foreign investments flowing to Israel in any event, he believed that such a policy would have no negative impact on investment. His goal, he said, was to blend a capitalist economy with planned, socialist control.[2]

Yalin-Mor's call for a continuation of Lehi's war of liberation did not mean social revolution alone; his further remarks leave no doubt he was still committed to the liberation of the historical Jewish homeland:

> Members of the movement, underground veterans, experienced soldiers, supporters and friends, all of them such as they are, are called upon to lend a hand in strengthening the movement and preparing it to fulfill the great roles that await it. And these are immeasurably greater than the roles we have filled in the past, just as the territories of the homeland held by foreigners are immeasurably wider than the small portion under Hebrew rule now, and just as the nation in the Diaspora is larger than the tiny number in the homeland.
>
> The outer form of our movement has changed in accordance with the demands of time, but its content remains unchanged. And its content is: Freedom for the homeland, freedom for the nation, and their standing on foundations that will guarantee the strength of the nation in its land.
>
> As we led the underground war in the past years, so are we able to lead the nation in the coming period—to the continuation of the war, to conquests, to achievements, to building a strong and just national society.[3]

Criticized during a week-long convention of Lehi fighters in late March 1949 by Eldad and others for diluting the movement's purpose with social issues, Yalin-Mor responded that the Golan Heights and the land across the Jordan (i.e., the land that had two years before the creation of Israel been incorporated into a new state, which had been named Jordan) was equally dear to all Sternists. None of the Sternists, he said, have betrayed the organization or its ideas.[4] Yet, he added, he rejected the idea that when the homeland would be liberated, the Sternists could rest. He told the gathered fighters, "I was under the impression that our role would not end with the liberation of the homeland, and I wrote and will say again and again, 'Is our role the concrete liberation from foreign domination and nothing more? I do not think this is our final purpose.'"[5]

He defined what he called "our destiny": "...not just to liberate the homeland; our destiny is to fill this homeland with content—economic and social, spiritual and cultural content. Our destiny is to ensure the nation's existence in this homeland...."[6] Ironically, Yalin-Mor defended himself from a charge he said he had heard leveled at him that his views were nearly Zionist. "Zionism was philanthropic, and I am far from standard Zionism. Our movement—and Eldad was the herald on this issue—moved the emphasis to the homeland,"[7] meaning to the liberation of the homeland rather than to providing a home for wandering Jews. The State of Israel could be a tool in this effort, "an Archimedean point from which we can change the world. With it we can expand borders and conquer the entire homeland. It is a tool. It provides an opportunity to have 200,000 Jews immigrate every year."[8]

Despite his apparently total commitment to liberating the entire Jewish homeland from whatever non-Jewish ruler or rulers governed it, and foreshadowing the *Hebrew Manifesto* he would co-author seven or eight years later, his preferred foreign policy was built on the view that corrupt governments in many Arab countries would allow their countries to become bases for foreign imperialism; Lehi—later he would say: Israel—should encourage revolutionary activity in such countries.[9]

Yalin-Mor submitted a proposed platform to the Lehi vets, which was accepted by a 49-13 vote, with 25 abstentions. The platform referred to Lehi's new incarnation, the newly formed Fighters party, as a "national liberation movement fighting for the complete freedom of the Hebrew nation in its complete homeland." The platform's first clause called for the liberation of the homeland and establishment of Jerusalem as its capital. This was followed by clauses calling for (in order) the return of all Hebrews to the homeland; sovereignty of the nation in the homeland; establishment of a socialist regime with state ownership of resources and means of production; and, then: identifying the interests of the working class with those of the war for national liberation; viewing the working class as the main factor in the war; favoring socialist state planning of the economy; maintaining the Histadrut labor union monopoly on labor and using it as a tool in the political and social wars; naming imperialism as the enemy of Hebrew liberty; and seeking the friendship of neighboring countries, this friendship to be based on national and social liberation and distancing the Middle East from imperialism and foreign power politics.[10]

Partly in tandem with nine of these points, but in seeming contradiction to the first and to the overall description of the party that preceded them, in later years Yalin-Mor supported the creation of a Palestinian state in Judea and Samaria. Just as Jews did not give up their desire for freedom for two thousand years, he asked, why should one expect the Palestinians to give theirs up in the course of a dozen or so?[11]

When he was then asked how the Jews could lay claim to cities currently considered Israeli such as Jaffa and Acco if the Jewish claim to Shchem, a city historically part of biblical Israel but now inhabited by Arabs and part of the disputed "occupied territories," were ceded by Israel, he countered by noting that the Jewish right to Shchem is no less than its right to Amman, today the capital of the kingdom of Jordan, and actually—to all of Jordan. One would need to choose between two arguments, he said:

One could argue that Amman might one day become part of the Jewish state. In that case, said Yalin-Mor, one would be lending credence to the standard Arab claim that Israel is expansionist; one could instead argue that for peace, he is willing to forego his right to Amman, implying that historical rights are not the litmus test of what territory should be under whose authority. One would then be expressing the idea that peace is a higher value than land or that it is more crucial to Israel's survival. But once one says this regarding Amman, he can say it of Judea and Samaria, too Yalin-Mor argued that Israel cannot buy peace with the territory of Jordan, which it does not hold, but only with the "occupied territories" it does hold.[12]

Yalin-Mor's longtime personal commitments are apparent in his argument. He continued to view the entire Land of Israel as falling within the state's borders, if only in principle; he supported national liberation; and he remained committed to the survival and growth of Israel. In the 1930s and 1940s, he believed that Jewish survival depended on liberating the homeland and achieving independence. In the 1950s, and through the 1960s and 1970s, he believed that peace and regional integration were necessary for survival.

> In my opinion, a person should always fight for what he sees as central to the life of our society. With all my heart I believed thirty years ago that attaining freedom, independence, and political sovereignty would be decisive for

our future....Now, too, I believe with all my heart that
at this time the great and holy goal is to inscribe the
State of Israel as an irrevocable fact....This we can do
only by means of peace with our neighbors, by means of
an historic rapprochement with them. To achieve this
goal I am willing to sacrifice a lot, as in the past.[13]

In the 1960s, Yalin-Mor found himself again accused of no longer being a Zionist, a claim he did not entirely dispute. In response, he noted that
the Jews do not have a pope to rule which school of Zionist thought is correct. He himself defined Zionism (which he rejected) as the desire to establish a state that would resolve the problems of those Jews who cannot
or do not wish to assimilate in other countries. Noting that he lived in Israel, met his civil obligations, and did not lead a life outside of Israel, he
asked, "Why should I call myself a Zionist?" Yalin-Mor declared calling
oneself a Zionist in Israel absurd and anachronistic. "I am a citizen of Israel," he continued. "I want my people to grow, and grow spiritually, so they
won't seek culture elsewhere." He therefore wanted to ease the way for Jews
abroad to join the citizenry of Israel. Instead of preparing for war, he felt,
better the citizens should busy themselves building the nation. He had no
objection to others calling themselves Zionists as long as they took the
trouble to define the term, and he asserted, "My views are not Zionist."[14]

Israel Eldad

In the course of the 1949 Lehi convention, most of which was a debate focused on the different world-views of Yalin-Mor and Eldad, Yalin-
Mor said of his former colleague and new opponent, "Eldad gave the movement most of its ardor and its energy, as well as much of its political
wisdom. Without Eldad we would be much poorer than we are. Eldad was
a spring constantly bubbling with ideas, he always shined brilliantly with
ideas." Yalin-Mor noted, smearing Eldad while seemingly clearing him, that
upon consideration Eldad occasionally abandoned some of these ideas, but
Yalin-Mor concluded by praising Eldad's "ability to overflow with
ideas...which has been a blessing to the movement."[15]

Nonetheless, he and Eldad disagreed. Yalin-Mor sought to transform
Lehi into a political party that would draw its support from the masses of
workers, while Eldad advocated its transformation into a revolutionary elite,
an intellectual salon focusing on the roots of the movement for Hebrew
liberation and spreading the word slowly, until such time as circumstances

again favored the retransformation of the ideas into deeds. In terms of their ideas, both seemingly favored the complete liberation of the homeland, but Yalin-Mor added a social revolution while Eldad sought to promote the biblical form of Hebrew redemption.

"The public wants from us what it can't find in another party, not this or that economic plan," Eldad told the audience of fighters.[16] He dismissed Yalin-Mor's attempt to widen the ranks of Lehi supporters by appealing to an amorphous working class. If the Jewish community in Israel is called upon to engage in some form of limited "struggle," Eldad gibed, the local socialist or communist parties, Mapai and Mapam, would lead it and

> the youth will stay with them. The workers and plain Jews are not seeking us. Those who seek us are sitting here, and maybe a few more. Each one of us is a personality, an idealist. That is the type that will come to us, those of high quality who are alert, or who have good instincts. That is how we grew before and how we will grow. Don't delude yourselves into believing that a miracle will occur and the masses will stream toward us. This is an illusion, they won't come. They want Mapai and Mapam. Our party has no chance as a party for the masses. We can be a large party that wants to take control of the government, or we can be, under current conditions, a framework for educational work. I want you to educate the worker that the war for the liberation of Israel is his war. If you speak to him this way, your work will be blessed. We need to keep seeking quality not quantity....[17]

Eldad shared Yalin-Mor's antipathy to imperialism, though his hatred and fear of imperialism had, perhaps, slightly different roots, limited to the needs of his own nation. He disdainfully said, "My view is the State of Israel is [no more] than the Zionist Organization with expanded authority. Certainly, there is an army, but a strange army that cannot move forward according to its strength, only according to the dictates of American imperialism." Continuing with his comparison of Israel to the pre-state Zionist leadership that needed England's approval for its activities and for Jewish immigration, Eldad mocked, "The state does not get immigration certificates from Britain but gets additional authorities from America. From every angle, this is an enlarged Zionist Organization."[18]

Eldad did not particularly reject the statism or socialism favored by Yalin-Mor, he rejected elevating them to the level of principles, and certainly to replacing other Sternist principles with them. He argued that if the fighters wanted to propound socialism, this was alright with him, "but please, within the framework of the vision" of Stern's principles, which should not be dropped.[19] He opposed capitalism in the same way he opposed socialism, as he opposed any "ism" imported to the Jewish revolution and placed in competition with Zionism. Later, Eldad was unenthused about the Israeli economic reforms of the 1990s, because "I am against all privatization, including economic privatization, according to which the individual becomes the measure, and happiness and wealth are the goals, while the larger picture is forgotten."[20]

Eldad's view best finds expression in an incident that took place in his cell in the Jerusalem prison. Moshe Svorai was arguing with Nissim "Nitchko" Reuveni over the future character of a Jewish state. Svorai was arguing for a state based on Israel's biblical heritage while Reuveni was arguing for a socialist state. Eldad interrupted, saying, "Children, children, what are you fighting about? You are fighting now? Splitting apart already? Let's create the state first, then argue."[21] He was a monist in Jabotinsky's tradition and, he would argue, in Stern's, and he sought to realize the goals of Revolutionary Zionism above and before any others.

He was undoubtedly closer to Svorai's view than to Reuveni's, but he and Yalin-Mor worked well together, as did all the members of Lehi, as long as they were focused on the first part of the plan: liberating the homeland and establishing Hebrew sovereignty in it. His counterproposal to Yalin-Mor's platform at the Lehi convention called on the state to realize the unrealized parts of the war of liberation and to establish *Malkhut Israel*, the sovereign kingdom of Israel. Lehi was to focus on training leaders; establishing agricultural and industrial towns; sending emissaries around the world to meet and encourage freedom fighters; creating an educational labor movement within the Histadrut labor union; publishing a literary-political journal; educating its members to be able to serve as leaders of a revolutionary movement-to-come; and it was to locate its headquarters in Jerusalem. Eldad's platform was rejected by a vote of 41-19, with 27 abstentions.[22] Eldad was convinced Lehi should expound its own views on the future of the Zionist revolution to a smaller audience and he proceeded to do so, with or without Lehi.

Most of the time, then and later, Eldad knew that "we are at the ground stage"[23] and the time had not yet come to realize his goals. "To speak of the necessity of Israel's borders being the Euphrates to the Nile to five people is okay. Maybe to ten. Twenty people would not understand," he said a year or so before his death.[24]

His use of the term *Malkhut Israel* for his goal was often misunderstood, since *malkhut* is Hebrew for "kingdom." The term "kingdom," he felt a need to explain, "is symbolic and is used to express the aspiration that Zionism be not only a Zionism seeking a safe haven for Jews and copying other national movements, but a Zionism that draws from the vision of Jewish rebirth."[25] Nonetheless, just as in 1949 he had not been opposed to socialism on principle (in later years he, and even more so the team he put together for his journal *Sulam*, would oppose socialism because it impeded the state's economy and the Jewish renaissance), he was not opposed to an actual kingdom. His final newspaper column, published a week before his death, was entitled "A King Is Needed." In it he wrote,

> A king is a force that creates his kingdom independently, even before any being has been created and this is the kind of king for whom we yearn. Where today are waves of such faithful longing created, yearning for true beauty? This Zionism, of yearning for redemption, for brotherly love, for love of Israel, for love of the Land of Israel—this Zionism is gradually disappearing. But the potential still survives. "David, the king of Israel, is still alive"—potentially, he still reigns over us and in our midst.[26]

Thus, both Yalin-Mor and Eldad rejected, as had Stern before them, what passed for Zionism. Stern avoided using the term, Yalin-Mor proudly renounced it, and Eldad advocated a different form of it. Zionism, he said, is a national liberation movement while the goal he saw before him is a uniquely Jewish one: redemption.[27]

Redemption, Eldad told a group of youthful followers in 1953, is itself a revolution, as was the redemption of the Jews from Egypt. The freedom fighters of the 1940s and their allies misled themselves by using words such as "liberation" and "revolution" instead of "redemption," which encompasses these and a complete revaluation of values as well. They talked of a state and when a state was created, they were faced with a crisis regarding its form and content. Had they spoken of redemption, the state would have been seen for what it is: one more modern tool to be used by the movement for redemption.[28]

Eldad called on modern Jews to reject the values of modernity and stop speaking in non-Jewish terms.

Ninety-nine percent of our thinkers say: Because our crisis is that of the entire world, we must solve the world's crisis, and then ours will be resolved. Socialism, democracy, the danger of world war—the resolution of our crisis will come with the resolution of the world crisis. This seems a logical solution. But the solution that should be proposed by our movement of national liberation is different: resolve both crises by separating completely from the foreign world and returning to our own.[29]

Eldad proposed returning both physically, from the Diaspora to Zion, and culturally, from the corruptive values of the eighteenth-century Enlightenment and from Descartes, who began modern philosophy with "I think therefore I am," to the beginning of Jewish thought, which is the knowledge, "In the beginning God created." God, not the individual, should be the starting point and what follows should be seen as national activity in history. The Jewish declaration that God created the world means history has a beginning, an order, and an intention.[30] God is called the God of Abraham, Isaac, and Jacob, who chose the Jews as His people. Eldad said the benefits of Jewish sovereignty cannot be won as long as the Jews do not know who they are and what they seek.[31]

Eldad sought to liberate the Jews from the Western and Eastern spiritual crises they picked up while wandering in Exile, especially after the old ghetto walls came down. He knew many Jews still had to be liberated from the actual Exiles and claimed, "The fight for [Jewish] rights in the Diaspora is an illusion and a distraction. It is planning for the present. If we want to view matters from a practical revolutionary point of view, we must always remember that the Torah says, 'Among the nations you will know no rest...,' meaning that in the Diaspora, things are going to be bad."[32] He postulated that the fate of Jewry in Exile was always either destruction or assimilation, but never good. He told Jews who lived in Exile, "My love and concern for Eretz Israel and for you obligate me to tell you simply and with gloves off: Your love is not enough for us. We call on you to come home, to Eretz Israel, to Jerusalem, to make aliya."[33]

The return to the land of Zion was to be accompanied by a return to the Heaven above it. A return to fulfillment of the Law, with a commitment to spiritual renewal, would be followed by the return of prophecy. Eldad was not satisfied with the revival of the Hebrew language wrought by Zionist activists like Eliezer Ben-Yehuda, the author of the first modern Hebrew dictionary, but wanted a return to the spirit which was fashioned by the language and land so long ago.[34]

All the various aspects of redemption are linked, according to Eldad. The spiritual revival will not come until Israel ceases to live off philanthropy, ceases to try to please other powers, and ceases to acquiesce to the continued existence of the Diaspora. The homeland will not be redeemed until all the Jews return both physically and culturally. Nor will all the Jews return until the homeland is liberated. The three together—the evacuation of the Exile, the liberation of the land, and the revival of Jewish values— were Eldad's vision of *Malkhut Israel*.[35]

Eldad thought that *Malkhut Israel* was being delayed both by self-imposed obstacles, such as Jewish and Israeli leaders' delusion that a Jewish state could not survive without foreign philanthropy, and real ones, such as wars and barriers to Jewish immigration from some countries. He believed that the Jewish people could choose to overcome these problems.

> The great Jewish revolution that will make a reality of the vision of *Malkhut Israel* will come about in spite of the real obstacles and difficulties, and not only the imaginary ones—when the vision pulses once more through the soul, when once again an awareness of the greatness and inevitability alike will awaken.
>
> And the State of Israel will be the mighty lever for removing those obstacles and preparing the road to *malkhut*, and to full and entire redemption.[36]

"I am considered a Zionist extremist," said Eldad, "but reality is always more extreme."[37]

Yitzhak Shamir

On the face of it, Shamir offered history no thought-out, well-presented ideology. But when asked once why he followed Yalin-Mor when Lehi split during and after the convention, he replied, "How do you know it wasn't Yalin-Mor who followed me?"[38] Shamir's remark was undoubtedly ironic, yet he did have a philosophy, which was, essentially, Sternist Zionism. As he put it, "The liberation of the Jewish people and its ingathering in Eretz Israel. In a state—Jewish, big, free, and independent."[39]

His stance during and after the convention, when he supported Yalin-Mor, through his tenure as Israel's prime minister four decades later, when he was close to Eldad, can only be understood in light of his personality.

If Yalin-Mor's tribute to Eldad at the convention included a jab at the man he was praising, his paean to Shamir is generous at his own expense. Yalin-Mor referred to his own underground article, "Liquidate the Prisons," which had been called a turning point in Lehi history that united the fighters under a banner, when he said,

> The article contributed something to the strengthening of our movement, but on this point I want to say that our movement was not strengthened by articles. It was strengthened mainly by one man who spoke in the debate yesterday, and who was a member of the Central Committee—Michael [Shamir]. If Eldad provided some of the ardor and energy and wisdom, Michael gave the movement the iron-will and masculinity with which it was blessed. I believe that without Michael our movement would have been much weaker in character. To a large extent, Michael strengthened it with his own will and his cruelty. I don't mean to say that Michael is without feeling; he is perhaps more sensitive than others, but he knows how to be cruel to others as he knows how to be cruel to himself, to achieve the goal.[40]

The ruthlessness inside Shamir allowed him to reject his comrades' fear of devolving from an underground into a political party and their fears they were not cut out to be party workers:

> It's not easy for us to devote ourselves to party matters. It requires a great spiritual effort. One doesn't change tracks easily....I once asked: even if we reach the conclusion that a party is what is needed now—are we the people who can do it? Today I say that after we have resolved our doubts [about becoming a party], this attitude is not revolutionary. It does not suit people who have a vision set before them. We have always taken upon ourselves that which was necessary and carried it out....If we will this and decide to do this—we can.[41]

Shamir told the gathering that "what matters is how much each step brings us closer to the goal."[42] The goal, as far as he was concerned, had nothing to do with other nations, oppressed or otherwise:

> Our member Judah Ben-David declared that the destiny of the Hebrew nation is no more and no less than to bring revolution to the neighboring countries. I do not believe at all in "destinies" of this sort, to be "a light unto the nations." The destiny of the nation is to grow, develop, and build its life and its sovereignty.[43]

Yet Shamir allied himself with Yalin-Mor. Perhaps he did so because, as he put it, "overthrowing the regimes in the neighboring countries is our most vital interest, a condition necessary to fulfilling our destiny, and an important means to it."[44] "The alternative to a progressive Egyptian people is not a rotten Egyptian people," he warned, "but British imperialism along the Suez and in Sinai, with its planes and navy."[45]

He called imperialism "the enemy" and urged that the group focus not on attacking it abroad but routing it from the area.[46] Shamir decreed that in order to be rid of the corrupt local regimes serving the interests of imperialism, "we must be an awesome power."[47] The Israeli army, he said, was "the main tool in the anti-imperialist war, and this war must be fought along the borders of the homeland...the front is in the homeland and the only force that can do it is the army of the Hebrew homeland."[48] He had long held this view, even before the establishment of the Jewish state or the debate within Lehi; from African exile he had written, "Freedom knows no borders. A freedom fighter hates *all* oppression," while making clear that "We can only fight for freedom, even the freedom of others, in our own homeland."[49]

Having said this and adopted Yalin-Mor's terminology, Shamir distanced himself from the latter's socialism while adopting it, too. He noted that one member had stated they were all socialists; Shamir demurred, saying, "such a thing cannot be decided quickly; the majority is not familiar with [socialist] thought and doesn't feel any special need to study it," while agreeing that they all supported economic planning in order to prevent exploitation. He expressed surprise that people were talking about the problems of a working class, which at the time in Israel really meant the members of the local communist and socialist parties, "while the entire Hebrew nation will one day be on its way here, and all of it, almost all of it, is a penniless proletariat. Tomorrow, almost the entire people will be one class, a working class."[50]

Shamir stressed that

during the entire underground period, during the entire
war against the foreign regime, we supported an absolute and complete focus on a clear war against the direct
enemy. We would not entertain and we rejected any problem or thing that might take our minds off this main
thing. We did not want to think about communal problems, we did not want to deal with issues concerning the
type of government in the state that would be established, we did not want to enter into the thicket of social problems, nor did we find time or opportunity to deal
with the Arab problem, which one might suppose we
would have encountered, because we had decided to focus everything on the war with the direct enemy.[51]

Shamir seems to have adopted the anti-imperialist views that were at
hand during the underground war but these, as his economic views, were
means, not ends. Shamir's consciousness was not Yalin-Mor's, and it did
not come from the same place. Shamir was, he recalled later,

influenced by the Bible and the Jewish history that I
learned as a child—from the moment I could understand
I knew I had to come to Eretz Israel. No one told me this,
except the Bible and history. When I grew up, I began to
read all that appeared in Eretz Israel—newspapers,
books. My poets were the poets of Eretz Israel, not the
poets of the land in which I was raised. My capital was
Jerusalem and not Warsaw.[52]

In the 1990s Shamir spoke to a meeting of Betar teenagers of having
fought for a Jewish democratic state. Eldad disparaged that cliché: "Nobody
in Betar knew back then what democracy was!" and added that Shamir was
"always the politician."[53] But Eldad may have been overly harsh in his judgment. Shamir's ideals, as Eldad's, were monist. All he genuinely cared
about was Zionism. When the people around him were talking about socialism, Shamir did, too; when they were talking about democracy, he
adapted. He was in that sense a good "politician" but he adopted this attitude only because none of it really mattered to him. Social issues needed
to be resolved insofar as they affected the possibility of realizing Zionist
goals. Even though, as far as Shamir was concerned, they probably should
not have had any effect.

Zionism is a revolutionary process. And in a revolution you must be ready not to think too much about
sentiments or human weaknesses....

When we fought for freedom, for the establishment
of a Jewish state, we didn't send a questionnaire to the
Jewish nation asking if it wanted a Jewish state or not.

It is permitted to liberate a people even against its
will, or against the will of the majority.[54]

Shamir's brand of Zionism means "more Jews in Eretz Israel. The
more Jews there will be, the closer we will get to the goal. This is our
struggle for survival. If we succeed in bringing millions of Jews to Israel,
we will be a Jewish nation. Other [Jews] will disappear." His program was
for Israel to "stand firm and have a good state—great, beautiful, organized,
and Jewish. We will spread our culture and beliefs in the world, spread Zionism, and influence Jews to build their futures in Israel." He expected
Israel to help Diaspora Jews to buck the current of assimilation by helping "youth to realize that not by bread alone does man live; that all the
things they think money can bring them are empty, they don't satisfy man
or give his life meaning." He called on American Jewish youth to "learn;
learn and understand Jewish history, the Bible, all the teachings....Learn
and understand and reach the only conclusion: to come on aliya to Israel.
Only this will save the Jewish nation."[55]

Remaining Loyal to Lehi

The handwriting of the chiefs of the Stern Group tells much about their
personalities. The letters of Yalin-Mor's words are pearls and the words are
strung together as symmetrically as a necklace. Yalin-Mor, as is known, was
the diplomatic voice of Lehi during the underground, hoping to make a
favorable impression on others. After the war, he pinned his hopes on winning over the masses and presented his ideas in ways he thought would
most appeal to them. Eldad's handwriting is lava, his pen could barely keep
pace with the flow of his ideas. During the war only two inmates of the
Jerusalem prison could decipher his writing in order to forward his articles
to the underground press. After the war, he advocated adopting an ideological purity in tracts that could be read by only a few. Shamir's words are
straight as soldiers on parade, with no left- or rightward slant. He pens
powerful downstrokes that give his writing a slightly angular feel, as if he
were cutting what needed to be cut, and some of his letters shoot forward

under a word, setting its direction. His signature is often followed by a period, as if he were saying, "this is what needs to be done, period." Perhaps most interesting of all is Stern's writing. He had two distinct scripts, one using block letters that communicated his ideas clearly but hid or eliminated his own personality, and another—also quite legible and beautiful—that was more personal.[56]

When asked if he had not strayed from the teachings of Stern and Lehi, Yalin-Mor replied, "The question is not what Yair said then, but what he would say if he were alive today."[57] Yalin-Mor thought Stern would favor peace and Israel's assimilating into the region in order to ensure Israel's survival.[58] He had known Stern and could offer insights into the question of what Stern would say today. But Eldad also knew Stern and he accused Yalin-Mor of being afraid someone would say he veered from Stern's path, so "What do you do? You look for socialism in Yair."[59] As far as Eldad was concerned it did not really matter if Stern was a socialist, for what mattered was what needed to be done at any given time, but he added that based on his own discussions with Stern, he could state that Stern was no socialist.

Tova Svorai, who knew Stern and was an early member of his crowd, and whose husband Moshe prepared Stern's articles and broadcasts with him, confirms that Stern was no socialist, because no one discussed socialism back then. She says it was only in the final year or so of Lehi that people began talking of socialism, perhaps influenced by an influx of young members who had not grown in the movement.[60]

Gepner explains, at least as far as his own case is concerned, that he was swept up by his opposition to British imperialism and therefore generalized to all imperialism, leading him to sympathize with various socialist anti-imperialist movements around the world. Once he had stopped fighting British imperialism, he lost his enthusiasm for socialism.[61] Similarly, fighters who joined Lehi after 1946 read the fiery articles Eldad and Yalin-Mor wrote against imperialism, instead of the fiery articles Eldad and Yalin-Mor had written in 1942-44 explaining the history and goals of Jewish independence. Even the older fighters were fed this same diet during Lehi's last two years. So from the leadership down, in 1948 all of Lehi wanted to be fighting imperialism. Perhaps this explains why in 1949 a majority of the Lehi veterans at Lehi's only convention voted to establish a socialist party to compete for the support of the country's workers, and why the party collapsed a year later and then ceased to exist.

When British imperialism was defeated, Eldad returned to emphasizing his and Stern's roots, which he had never abandoned. Yalin-Mor continued moving in the direction he had helped set; he pursued a war against imperialism, ever hopeful the other anti-imperialist forces in the world were as committed to freedom as he, a hope far from reality.

The great difficulty with Yalin-Mor's argument about what Stern would have said had he been alive is that given that Stern was dead, Stern's followers or others had only Stern's words to rely on when they attempted to determine what he would have said. If Stern is to be taken at his word, he was, as Eldad posits, committed to full redemption, and in 1949 even Yalin-Mor talked of liberating the entire land. (Apparently no one knew or remembered at the time that even before the formation of the underground, Stern had once, in 1934, boycotted the Ohel theater because he thought it was putting its energies into promoting socialism.) Also, while Yalin-Mor stressed the need to appeal to the masses, Stern was prepared for his followers to be labeled a "gang of crazies." Eldad followed suit and intentionally sought to found a small group—his journal had 1,500 subscribers[62]—which Yalin-Mor said would not last, or would have no effect. Instead, Yalin-Mor and the Fighters party disappeared with Lehi. Eldad's journal lasted 14 years. Indeed, Stern had believed that "A revolutionary combat organization should not and cannot set up institutions for itself" and "A movement that wants to redeem the nation...most definitely cannot sink into the mud of day-to-day reality...."[63]

Yet Yalin-Mor might well have had in mind Stern's editorial response to the letter from Eliahu Lankin, which Stern published in Lehi's paper; Stern rejected limiting Lehi's goals to the liberation of the homeland by force of arms, instead staking a claim to be a movement of material and spiritual redemption for all Israel until the end of time.[64]

Ironically, in the 1960s Yalin-Mor ended up editing *Etgar*, a leftwing journal that had fewer readers than Eldad's; also ironically, Yalin-Mor used the same printers who had published Lehi's underground papers.[65]

Yehuda Hakohen, director of the Zionist Freedom Alliance, an activist student organization, suggests that

> "Drifted" would be a more accurate term than "changed" to describe what happened to Yalin-Mor. His attitudes regarding Jordan and Egypt and his support for indigenous populations against Western-backed puppet leaders were a logical and natural outgrowth of Lehi's war to liberate the Jewish homeland from British occupation. Yalin-Mor's later position advocating the surrender of

portions of Israel, however, is extremely problematic as it conflicts with and appears to negate his earlier struggle to free the Land of Israel from foreign rule.

The story of Yalin-Mor needs to be understood as a warning. Eldad represented the undiluted eternal truth of the Zionist Revolution that burned in the Jewish people's national soul for thousands of years. Shamir transformed this vision into concrete actions against British imperialism. Yalin-Mor made a major diplomatic contribution by putting the Zionist struggle for Jewish liberation into the context of other struggles for liberation and justice. Focusing on that international context brought Lehi diplomatic success but it also led Yalin-Mor down a dangerous road. Without Eldad to balance him, he drifted further and further away from the initial truth that he had originally sought to present to the world. And the flip side is that without Yalin-Mor to balance *him*, Eldad drifted further and further away from being able to effectively "market" the uncompromising truth he carried with him until his death. The tragedy is that both men became largely irrelevant to the Israeli political discourse. Perhaps our task today is to reunite their spirits.[66]

Stern, as noted, was able to write clearly with two different scripts. Hakohen believes that Stern essentially united the different characteristics of those who followed him: Eldad's mind, Yalin-Mor's voice, and Shamir's hands.

Considering the decades that followed Lehi's war and disbanding, Shamir may have been the most representative member of Lehi, or at least the most effectual. He experimented with Yalin-Mor's approach, realized it would not do, and moved on. Not satisfied with Eldad's idealized smallness, but true to his ideals, and all the while politically flexible, he succeeded in politics as he had succeeded before in the Mossad, and as he had succeeded before that in the underground, all the time asking what role the revolution required of him and executing it. He won over Israeli voters, and while not promoting all of Stern's 18 Principles of Rebirth, he made progress on several. Before he began his somewhat meteoric ascent to the premiership, as he was about to join a government cabinet for the first time, he set his goals: bringing more Jews home to Israel, settling more in the land, and buttressing Israel's international position.[67] He accomplished all these during the next ten years: he initiated Operation Solomon, bringing fourteen thousand black Jews of Ethiopia to Israel in 1991, and helped open the doors of Israel to hundreds of thousands of Jewish refugees from Soviet persecution; he helped settle tens of thousands of Jewish residents in Judea and Samaria; and he opened diplomatic fronts that led dozens of countries from Albania and Angola to Uzbekistan and Zambia to establish or restore diplomatic relations with Israel.

Once the hunted leader of the Sternists, he was running the Knesset and about to become Israel's foreign minister when he said,

> Times change. When you start to fight and are part of a minority, you are not satisfied with that, to always be part of a minority. You tell yourself, "Okay, today I'm in the minority, tomorrow I'll be in the majority." Now we are the majority. This is natural, a natural process. I see nothing unusual about it. It is a revolution, but we deserved this revolution, sought it, and worked and fought for it. [68]

Shamir added, "All our life in this land is a revolution."[69]

The Legend

Seventy years after the "Fighters for Freedom" came together at the behest of Stern to die in the battle to liberate a homeland, they are the subject of museums, academic conferences, Ph.D. theses, high school essay contests, scholarly books, an "Israel Liberation Week," t-shirts, and youth movements. And some young Israeli mothers and fathers name their boys Yair. Even Prime Minister Benjamin Netanyahu and his wife Sara have a son Yair. His predecessor, Ehud Olmert, has a nephew with the name.

The original boy named Yair, Abraham's son, addressed a packed hall at the Menachem Begin Heritage Center in Jerusalem, on June 13, 2010, during an evening marking the seventieth anniversary of the establishment of Lehi. His remarks, in full, were:

> In the beginning was the split. And the land was without form and void, and darkness was upon the face of the deep. And then Yair came and lit the torch of liberty. He determined that England was the enemy and

must be fought to the end, until the attainment of Jewish mastery over Eretz Israel and until his eyes, which looked out at the valley of the shadow of death, would see the flares of victory.

You here and those who are no longer with us followed him and his vision because you believed the single goal was liberation of the nation. You were prepared to sacrifice everything as Yair did to attain the sacred goal, and 127 of you fell in the war against the foreign occupier, on the enemy's gallows, and in the ranks of the Israeli army.

Yair founded Lehi as a liberation movement, as a combat organization that would not accept political dictates, only the dictates of conscience. The underground held fast to this even after Yair was murdered.

His light has not dimmed. And the beauty of Lehi and Lehi's power was that under its wings gathered fighters who were Ashkenazi and Sephardi, religious and secular, leftists and rightists, ultra-Orthodox Jews from Mea Shearim and Arabs from Abu Ghosh. All of them fought to expel the foreign ruler and for Jewish sovereignty in Eretz Israel. And all of them enlisted in the Israeli army after the British flag was lowered. And when the land rested after the War of Independence, then ended the historic role of Lehi.

Lehi began in a tempest and now lives as a legend.[70]

For most of their lives, the majority of the fighters who served under or with Shamir, Eldad, and Yalin-Mor remained what Abraham Stern called anonymous soldiers. Stern had once jotted a note to himself that "The anonymous have their recompense in the knowledge that they have fulfilled their obligation toward their people and their people's destiny. Their wages have been paid, ahead of them lie—deeds."[71] Shamir had passed a normal man's retirement age before he won a cabinet post. When he became prime minister he was nearly 70.

But Shamir had to wait that long for recognition partly because for the first three decades of Israel's independence not only the names of Stern's fighters were forgotten but also their deeds, and this, perhaps, would have surprised or offended them more than the fact that their names were missing from the history books. This was no accident, however.

In 1952, Prime Minister Ben-Gurion ordered his government to award military merit badges to everyone he thought worthy, and he listed them all: "All those who did guard duty before Hashomer was founded, the members of Hashomer, the soldiers in the Jewish Legion of World War I, members of the Hagana from the time it was founded until the founding of the IDF [the Israeli army], those who served in the Jewish units of World War II, members of the settlements who were not soldiers in the Israel Defense Forces but who defended the settlements during the War of Independence, communities that excelled as units during the War of Independence (Jerusalem, Negba and the like), and all who gave their lives for the homeland though they are not listed above."[72] The Irgun and Lehi (as well as Nili) are conspicuously absent from this purportedly comprehensive list. Ben-Gurion earlier explained his refusal to accord military recognition to dead underground fighters by pointing out he could never equate them with the Hagana.[73] He denied Begin's claim to have had a role in establishing the state, declaring, "This land has a long history. Many foreign regimes were forced from it and yet a Jewish state was not established." He attributed the establishment of the state in 1948 not to the British leaving but to the pioneers who had arrived in the preceding decades and their agricultural work, and he called the Jews' return to physical labor in the fields and construction industry, "perhaps the decisive event that led to the establishment of a Jewish state."[74]

Leftwing politician and journalist Uri Avnery mocked the establishment's policy toward the Lehi vets as early as 1958, when he wrote that Ben-Gurion and his government think that the removal of the British flag from the country amounts to nothing, but it is thanks to the fighters who brought that flag down that they sit in their government offices.[75]

The British were clear about who drove them from the country. To mark May 14, 1948, the day they terminated their Mandate over Palestine and left the country, they issued the following statement:

> ...84,000 troops, who received no cooperation from the Jewish community, had proved insufficient to maintain law and order in the face of a campaign of terrorism waged by highly organized Jewish forces equipped with all the weapons of the modern infantryman. Since the war, 338 British subjects had been killed in Palestine, while the military forces there had cost the British taxpayer 100 million pounds. The renewal of Arab violence

on the announcement of the United Nations decision to
partition Palestine and the declared intentions of Jewish
extremists showed that the loss of further British lives
was inevitable. It was equally clear that, in view of His
Majesty's Government's decision not to enforce the partition of Palestine against the declared wishes of the
majority of its inhabitants, the continued presence there
of British troops and officials could no longer be justified.

In these circumstances His Majesty's Government
decided to bring to an end their Mandate and to prepare
for the earliest possible withdrawal of all British forces.[76]

The statement referred to getting no cooperation from the Jewish community. However, the Hagana and establishment Jewish Agency had cooperated, even turning members of the underground over to the British
police. The British referred to a campaign of terror, but the Hagana and
Agency had condemned this campaign and often sought to thwart it. From
October 1945 until August 1946 they cooperated with the Irgun and Lehi;
but before that their members served in the British army and after August
1946 they engaged in only a handful of "terrorist" actions, declaring that
they would limit their activities to illegal immigration. The British warned
in their statement of the intentions of Jewish extremists who rejected the
partition of the country, obviously referring to the Irgun and Lehi, who rejected partition, not to the Hagana and Labor leadership, who accepted it.

The dust bin of history got a shaking with Begin's election to the
premiership in 1977, and along with recognition of the accomplishments
of Begin's Irgun came recognition of those of Lehi. Arguably, Israelis today
may take more pleasure in remembering the Irgunists and the Lehi fighters than in remembering the Hagana, perhaps because revolutions are more
exciting than troop movements, prison breaks often excite the imagination
more than establishment protests, and the total commitment of revolutionaries to a cause seen in stark black-and-white terms stirs many people.

Jabotinsky, founder of Betar, backer of the "illegal immigration" of European Jews to Eretz Israel before the Holocaust, and Supreme Commander
of the Irgun, is the most commemorated person in Israel, with at least 57
streets, parks, and squares named for him. Herzl, somewhat of a revolutionary in his own right, comes in a close second, with 52. Famous personalities who led the state, but who represented the establishment, such
as Ben-Gurion and Israel's first president, Chaim Weizmann, have only 48

each. Ironically, Ben-Gurion and Weizmann's political nemesis, the Commander in Chief of the Irgun, Menachem Begin, specifically asked that nothing be named for him, yet the Israeli people has expressed its love for him, albeit not its respect for his wishes, by naming 43 places for him.[77] Stern has a town named for him, Kochav Yair in central Israel—home of many VIPs, including two former army Chiefs of Staff and several current or former members of Knesset. He has 16 streets named for him: 12 are named "Yair" and 4 are named "Abraham Stern."[78] Perhaps the lag in streets named for Stern is temporary, as for the first thirty years or so of Israel's statehood, Ben-Gurion and his political party ensured no streets would be named for him, and today many of those who wish to honor him are still too young to sit on city naming councils.

The Lehi Mystique

The annual memorial service at Ben-Gurion's grave is sparsely attended and Weizmann's is ignored. Yet hundreds of mostly young people are present at Stern's grave on the anniversary of his death every year, and sometimes more than one ceremony is necessitated, with younger, more religious teens fashioning their own service after those attending the official one have dispersed. Since 1985, the official ceremony has been a formal military one, with the army's cantor and soldiers paying tribute to Stern.

A memorial evening held in a Jerusalem auditorium on the anniversary of Eldad's death in 2005, comprised mostly of speeches, drew an overflow crowd of many hundreds who filled all the chairs, dais area, and open floor space in the building. In October 2010, a larger hall had to be rented to mark the centenary of his birth.

Almost four score years after Stern founded his Fighters for the Freedom of Israel movement, its spirit enthralls Israelis of various ages and political stripes, but mostly those too young to have personally encountered Lehi.

The Israeli daily *Haaretz* reported in July 2010 that recent years have seen an increased interest in the Irgun and Lehi among the younger generation of Israelis living in Judea and Samaria. *Haaretz* theorizes this generation is attracted by the personalities who sacrificed themselves for Israel. According to the newspaper, at the home of one grandson of an Irgunist, underground songs are sung at Friday evening Sabbath dinners (apparently in addition to the more traditional Sabbath hymns). "I see a connection between the underground members and our generation," the

grandson is quoted as explaining. "Both gave their lives for the Land of Israel and the Bible. Yair Stern's beliefs have a lot in common with our own."
Another teen living on a settlement said, "The underground movements
were a very small group of people who opposed everything accepted in that
period. They're like us in a way....We're trying to do something that will
make a difference and advance redemption."[79]

More studiously, Hebrew University, Haifa University, and Bar-Ilan
University held academic conferences in 2007 and 2008 to discuss Lehi,
and all the speakers spoke to jammed rooms. At the Hebrew University,
for example, Yair Stern (Abraham's son) spoke of his father's academic interests; political scientist Dr. Udi Lebel offered an account of the underground in Israel's collective memory; television anchorman Yaacov Ahimeir
told of discovering Stern's student file while on guard duty at Hebrew
University's Mount Scopus campus during the 1950s[80]; and Professor of
Classics Joseph Geiger discussed the Homeric roots of Stern's poetry—in
particular, suggesting an affinity between Stern and Achilles, the hero of
The Iliad, who is told by his mother that he can choose to meet his end by
fighting in Troy, in which case he will die with "undying glory," or he can
forego the glory and live a long life at home. Like Achilles, Stern chose to
pursue the enemy knowing it would hasten his own death. Geiger postulated that Stern's poem "Yes, I am a soldier and a poet" was based on this
story, as Achilles is the only one of Homer's heroes who also sings.[81] Yet,
in contrast to Homer's hero, Stern did not expect the "gifts and fair words"
proffered to Achilles as recompense for his sacrifice; he expected to die
anonymously and was even willing to be condemned by future generations,
as long as his deeds would help ensure Jewish survival.

The condemnation came and went; in February 2008, on the anniversary of Stern's death, his songs were read and performed at Tzavta, a trendy
club founded by the Hashomer Hatzair movement and known as the center of Tel Aviv's "progressive culture."[82]

More officiously, the Israeli parliament met in special session two
weeks earlier to honor the centenary of Stern's birth.[83] In 2010, the Knesset
went further and recognized the underground fighters in a special session
accompanied by day-long events. This was not the first time the Knesset
marked the accomplishments of the Irgun, Lehi, and Hagana, but March
9, 2010, was the first day the institution "saluted" (as the invitation to the
ceremony put it) the martyrs who were hanged by the British. Once again,
as with the memorial ceremonies held in Jerusalem or Tel Aviv and conferences in Haifa and Ramat Gan, an auditorium—this time the Knesset's

largest—was overfull. Among the speakers at the event were the former Chief Justice of the Israeli Supreme Court, Meir Shamgar, an Irgunist deported by the British and held in confinement in Africa; Knesset Speaker Reuben Rivlin; and the chairman of the Jewish Agency, Natan Sharansky, the former Soviet Jewish dissident. Sharansky told the crowd of his affinity for the martyrs by recalling his early life in Russia, when he was "alone, and wanted just to live." He would, he said, have signed any confession the Soviet authorities told him to sign. Then came the Six Day War of 1967. After that, he said, he felt "connected to a past, part of a great nation, with a history and with heroes, and connected to a future." All of a sudden he looked at his daily activities differently. He understood that "what you do will influence generations. Maybe you'll live only one more hour, or a day, or a week. You have to make that time meaningful."[84]

At five that evening, following the ceremony, the prime minister and the leader of the opposition both spoke in the full plenum in honor of the martyrs, followed by Member of Knesset Arieh Eldad, the son of the Sternist leader, who recited a poem by Uri Zvi Greenberg.

The next day some five hundred people gathered in the Cultural Center of Acco, in Israel's north, also in honor of the martyrs. This event included speeches by the mayor of Acco; Moshe Yaalon, Israel's minister for strategic planning and a former Chief of Staff; representatives of the army and Ministry of Defense; and entertainment by popular Israeli rock star Meir Banai. It opened with the Army Band playing a rollicking version of Stern's "Anonymous Soldiers." Stern had composed an anthem to inspire underground commandos, now his son and namesake was sitting in the first row, hearing a hip-hop version with hundreds of teens bobbing in the hall behind him.

Part and parcel of the acceptance of the underground by Israeli culture has been its literary reception. In the first years of statehood, the only books about Lehi were memoirs authored by its own members, such as Eldad and Shmuelevitz. These and many like them are still in print, six decades after publication, and similar memoirs are still appearing; as noted above, the then 95-year-old Benjamin Gepner finally wrote his in 2009, and Yaacov Heruti published his the year before. But recent Hebrew scholarship also includes Yaira Ginossar's *Not for Us the Saxophone Sings*, a study of Stern's poetry; the posthumous *A Tear and Glow, Blood and Gold*, by Israel Eldad, analyzing Greenberg's poems; Lebel's *The Road to the Pantheon: The Irgun, Lehi and the Limits of the Israeli Memory*; Ofer Regev's *The Prince of Jerusalem*, an account of Bernadotte's work and assassination; a massive two-volume Who's Who of Lehi fighters; and a new five-volume history of Lehi that dwarfs even the Who's Who.

The student activists of the Zionist Freedom Alliance wear t-shirts with Stern's face, reminiscent of the ubiquitous Ché Guevara t-shirts sported around the world. The Alliance calls itself the "student voice of Jewish liberation and the fulfillment of Israel's national aspirations." Its members say they are committed to Jewish national liberation as well as social justice and support the "right of all indigenous peoples to live freely in their own countries." The Alliance calls the Jews one such indigenous nation, which, it says, was "robbed of our right to land, liberty and peace by Roman imperialists nearly two thousand years ago." The Jewish people only recently liberated its land from British imperialists and now faces "attempts to wrest portions of our country from us" by other powers acting as imperialists. Regarding what has become known as the Arab-Israeli conflict, the Alliance writes in what it calls its Covenant of Freedom,

> The Middle East conflict is not between Jews and Arabs or democracy and terrorism but rather between the indigenous natives of our region and foreign powers that exploit, arm and fund Jews and Arabs while pushing us towards war and trying to impose superficial diplomatic initiatives from above. The political and economic elites of imperial powers have an interest in provoking regional conflicts and providing artificial solutions that ultimately further inflame the situation;
>
> "Peace" has become a cynical tool in recent decades for Western governments and multi-national organizations who seek to shrink and weaken the State of Israel. The United States, European Union, World Bank, United Nations and international media all have a hand in exacerbating the Middle East conflict while each push[es] their own imperialist agenda for the region....[85]

They warn,

> While the State of Israel should strive to maintain good relations with all other nations, we must be careful not to become too close to any one ally;
>
> A country cannot be politically independent while at the same time being financially dependent on a foreign

power. United States foreign aid has been a disaster for the State of Israel, delaying sound economic reforms and encouraging wastefulness. U.S. military aid is really just a form of corporate welfare as much of the money must be spent on products made by American corporations;

Only people with a superficial attachment to the State of Israel could defend a situation where our government depends on over $2 billion in American aid each year. A true supporter of the Jewish state would want the U.S. to extend the same honest friendship to Israel that Thomas Jefferson and the American founding fathers urged their people to offer all nations. True friendship does not include foreign aid—not to Israel nor to our potential enemies in the Middle East (which taken together receive significantly more money from the U.S. than Israel). Providing money and arms to both the Jewish state and our potential enemies in the region fosters the suspicion that the American government is not a true friend but rather a foreign power hypocritically hedging its bets in the Middle East.[86]

The Alliance is opposed to Israel's security wall, combats poverty and discrimination in Israel, supports the liberation movement of Kurdistan, and runs "Israel Liberation Week" on campuses across the United States.

Member of Knesset Arieh Eldad also runs a small pre-teen and teen youth movement, Ami Chai (the Hebrew name means "My Nation Lives"), which draws at least in part on the teachings of the senior Eldad and Lehi. The younger Eldad has elsewhere referenced Stern's principles and stressed the need to "educate the nation to love freedom and develop zealous loyalty to its eternal heritage. Implant the idea that the fate of the nation is in its own hands."[87] Eldad says "clear piercing light" from Stern's 18 principles of the rebirth emanates from the underground even today, "clarifying the darkness and the confusion of our lives, and marking our goals."[88] According to Eldad, "We who walk in Yair's path can never accept any foreign army, international auspices, Mandate, trusteeship, international forces, or foreign guarantees of any sort that purport to defend us and actually transform us into a nation of victims needing protection in our own homeland, or that are destined to be a buffer separating us from our enemies on a day when we would be able to defeat them decisively."[89]

Shabtai Ben-Dov's writings have recently been collected and republished. In *The Redemption of Israel as Reflected in the Crisis of the State*, he says the "Principles of Rebirth" leave no doubt that Stern expected Lehi to be quite busy after the establishment of a state. Ben-Dov recalls a high-ranking Lehi man telling him that Lehi had no pretensions to national leadership, existing solely to expel the British from the country, but this view does not jive with the principles, which cast Lehi as a "movement of political and spiritual redemption—almost in the full historical sense of this messianic concept." According to Ben-Dov,

> Looking at Lehi from this perspective, the acknowledged value of its prophetic role in having expelled the foreign regime remains, but this role becomes only one part of a movement that for the first time restored to a relevant political action platform the values of full redemption and building the Temple.[90]

As a result, writes Ben-Dov, Lehi should not only be considered one of the giants of the establishment of the state, but also the bearer of a spiritual message still needed within the state.[91]

Thousands of mourners gathering around the graves of those who died sixty and seventy years ago and mass gatherings at which hundreds join in singing "Anonymous Soldiers"—belie the death of Lehi. A not-inconsequential minority of Israelis believes that along with Ben-Gurion's socialist-Zionism and Jabotinsky's Revisionist Zionism, Abraham Stern's Revolutionary Zionism still has a role to play.

Uri Zvi Greenberg, the poet whose works of the early 1920s prophesied the Holocaust and whose works of the early 1930s prophesied Jewish underground fighters being led to British gallows, assessed in 1948, toward the end of the underground war, the war and the fighters, the "singing progeny of King David" whose voices were stilled when "they fell, swords in hand." The earth of their graves thanks God, Greenberg writes; it is, he says, the sort of earth from which man was first created and the sort from which Temple Mount and the Foundation Stone are made. The "select few" who fought and died are "resplendent" and express what is true in this world. All who remain after them live thanks to them, and

> Whoever looks upon their grave can no longer be a slave.[92]

Appendix A

Chronological List
of Lehi Operations

About the List

Compiling a list of underground operations is problematic because the men and women of Lehi were more concerned with attacking the British than with recording the dates of their attacks, and more concerned with evading arrest than with retaining proof of what they had done. Other tools often helpful in documentation are in this case equally lacking: there was no television news coverage of Lehi's war, radio broadcasts were not usually recorded, and newspapers reported only some of the operations, and even then, they did not usually know which underground organization was responsible. The British, too, often attributed actions of the Irgun to Lehi, and vice versa.

Abraham Stern was imbued with a sense of history and buried three caches of documents pertaining to the Irgun of the 1930s and to the early days of Lehi. Two of these caches survived the underground war and were dug up afterward. These documents are a mainstay of academic research into the underground in those years. After the war, some of the participants wrote memoirs or recorded their stories in print or on tape. Because of the dearth of surviving hard data from the underground war to assist the veterans in their recollections, these recollections are not always reliable in terms of dates and details. Eventually a concerted effort was made by historians to gather the historical data. The Jabotinsky Institute and the "Bet Yair" Lehi Museum were and still are at the forefront of this effort.

What follows is as comprehensive a list of Lehi operations as can be compiled today, given the limitations enumerated above. It is meant to serve two purposes: to be a chronological record of the selected operations recorded in this book, and as such to enable readers to put the events in context; and to provide the complete picture of Lehi's war, which was composed of hundreds of robberies, escapes, road mines, sabotage of the communication and transportation networks, and assassinations.

The list presents Lehi's war but does not purport to be a history of the entire struggle for Jewish liberation. Unless relevant to specific actions of Lehi, not included are British actions such as the imposition of nationwide curfews, random shootings of Palestinian Jews in their homes or on the streets, deportation of Jewish refugees from Europe back to Europe, the establishment in other countries of detention or prison camps for deported immigrants, and assaults on the underground; Irgun raids on British arsenals, destruction of government offices or military installations, and other Irgun operations; the blowing up of bridges, rail lines, and British anti-immigration patrol boats by the Hagana; and Israeli army battles in which Lehi members took part as soldiers after leaving the underground.

Format

This chronology was compiled from five lists published over the years by various Israeli and Lehi sources, buttressed with newspapers and other historical sources. The superscript following each event identifies the main source; when no superscript follows, the source is *The Chronicle of the War of Liberation*.

Until November 29, 1947, Lehi's war was fought against the British, and all soldiers and police listed below as injured or killed before that date were serving in the British army and police, and all military vehicles were British. On November 30, 1947, the Arabs attacked the Jews and Lehi began fighting on the Arab front as well as the British front. Following that date, the targets of attacks and casualties listed below are identified as British or Arab. Also, most British soldiers and police who were casualties of Lehi's operations were British nationals, but a minority were Jews or Arabs serving with the British. The religion or nationality of the casualties is not specified, in as much as, in the words of John Donne, "any man's death diminishes me."

Chronology of Lehi Operations

1940

June	Founding of Lehi, which was known then as the Irgun Tzvai Leumi b'Israel.[a]
September 16	Robbery of Anglo-Palestine Bank on Ben Yehuda Street in Tel Aviv; Joshua Zetler arrested and sentenced to 15 years in jail.
October 2	First official proclamation by Lehi.[b]
December 19	Bombing of immigration offices in Tel Aviv.

1941

May 26	Joshua Zetler and Yaacov Polani escape from Tel Aviv police station.[a]
July 15	Attempted robbery of The Arab Bank in Jerusalem; Eliyahu Amikam arrested and sentenced to five years in jail.
November 27	Moshe Svorai escapes from police escort in Haifa.

1942

January 9	Robbery of bank clerk in Tel Aviv, two passersby killed. Nissim Reuveni and Joshua Becker arrested; Becker sentenced to death, commuted to life imprisonment. Reuveni sentenced to 14 years in jail.
January 18	While under detention, Zelig Jack escapes from moving train.[a]
January 20	Mining of rooftop at 8 Yael Street in Tel Aviv, three policemen killed.
January 27	At 30 Dizengoff Street in Tel Aviv, British shoot and kill Abraham Amper and Zelig Jack and wound

	Moshe Svorai and Yaacov Eliav. Svorai and Eliav sentenced to life, later reduced to ten years each.
February 12	British police shoot and kill Abraham Stern in Tel Aviv.
April 22	Bomb attached to car of Deputy Inspector General of British police, Michael McConnell. His servant killed.[c]
April 22	Attempted assassination, by use of a road mine, of Police Inspector General Alan Saunders.[c]
April 24	Attempt on lives of police officers in Jerusalem.[a]
May 1	Attempted assassination of Geoffrey Morton on Haifa-Tel Aviv road.[a]
May 1	Israel Tevuah and Moshe Bar-Giora are captured in Givat Shaul in Jerusalem. They are sentenced to ten years in jail, reduced to seven.
August 16	Yitzhak Shamir and Eliahu Giladi escape from Mizra Detention Camp.[a]

1943

September 3	Trial and execution of a Jewish collaborator who turned fighters in to the Criminal Investigation Department (CID).[d]
September 15	Emmanuel Hanegbi escapes from Latrun Detention Camp.[a]
November 1	Twenty members of Lehi (including Natan Yalin-Mor, Matityahu Shmuelevitz, and Menachem Schiff) escape from Latrun Detention Camp by tunnel.
November 3	Latrun escapee Yitzhak Simantov killed by police; two policemen wounded.
December 23	Yaacov Eliav and Moshe Bar-Giora escape from Jerusalem Central Prison.

1944

February 3	Attempted assassination of High Commissioner Sir Harold MacMichael by use of a mine in Jerusalem.
February 14	Two policemen killed in shootout in Haifa.
February 24	Bombs attached to police cars in Haifa; three policemen wounded.
March 2	British policemen wounded in a shootout with Lehi members who are hanging wall posters in Tel Aviv.

March 19	Yerachmiel Aaronsohn shot to death by police in a building on Mazeh Street, Tel Aviv.
March 23	Two British police killed and one wounded in three attacks in Tel Aviv.
April 1	One British policeman killed, one wounded, in shootout with Lehi members in Haifa.
April 6	Two of the Lehi members involved in the Haifa shooting are discovered by the police in Yavniel and, after a shootout with British police, they kill themselves rather than surrender.
April 9	Bomb thrown at police station in north Tel Aviv. Three policemen injured.
April 10	Attempted assassination of Tel Aviv Deputy Superintendent of Police J. Fforde, in an ambush of his car.[c]
April 23	Attack on soldiers in Tel Aviv.[a]
April 26	Israel Eldad arrested.
May 10	Two Jewish police collaborators sentenced to death and killed.
May 29	Zvi Tavori, on trial for possession of a gun, declares that he does not recognize the authority of British courts. He is sentenced to seven years in jail.
June 13	David Hameiri-Begin refuses to recognize the authority of British courts, is sentenced to ten years.
June 20	Hisia Shapiro and Anshel Spielman refuse to recognize the authority of British courts and are sentenced to four and ten years, respectively.
June 28	Matityahu Shmuelevitz refuses to recognize the authority of British courts and is sentenced to death, later commuted to life imprisonment.
July 1	Attempted assassination of High Commissioner MacMichael in Jerusalem.[a]
July 10	Nehama Srulovitz refuses to recognize the authority of British courts and is sentenced to ten years in jail.
August 8	Attempted assassination of High Commissioner MacMichael on the road from Jerusalem.
August 18	Menachem Cohen escapes from Latrun.[a]
September 29	Assassination of T. J. Wilkin, in charge of the Jewish section of the CID, in Jerusalem.
October 18	Two hundred and fifty-one detainees, suspected by

the British of membership in or support of the Irgun and Lehi, are deported to exile in Asmara, Eritrea, in Africa.

November 6   Assassination of British Minister of State for the Middle East, Lord Moyne, in Cairo.

1945

January 27   Exiled detainees are transferred to a detention camp in Sudan.[e]

March 15   Three Lehi detainees escape from Sudan detention camp and are recaptured.[a]

March 23   Eliahu Bet-Zuri and Eliahu Hakim, assassins of Lord Moyne, are hanged in Cairo.

May 17   Arye Shalem escapes from a train taking him to Egypt.[a]

July 23   Joint unit of Irgun and Lehi blow up rail bridge near Yavneh, disabling the Cairo-Haifa line.

August 21   Lehi sentences to death and executes British agent for turning a fighter in to the police.

September 2   Attempted robbery of Discount Bank in Tel Aviv.[c]

September 28   Attempted robbery of a post office payroll in Tel Aviv, one policeman is killed.[c]

October 8   Robbery at the Gold Exchange on Lilienbloom Street in Tel Aviv.

October 12   Exiled detainees are transferred back to Eritrean detention camp.

November 1   Establishment of United Resistance Movement by Hagana, Irgun, and Lehi.

November 1   Attempt to sabotage oil refineries in Haifa. Moshe Bar-Giora is killed when a bomb explodes prematurely.

November 1   Joint Irgun and Lehi sabotage of Lod train station, destruction of tracks, locomotives, signal station, and warehouse. Two soldiers and four policemen and rail employees are killed.

December 2   Robbery of textiles worth 3,000 lira, in Tel Aviv.

December 22   Fifty-five more detainees are deported to Eritrea.

December 24   Attempted robbery of weapons from Tel Litvinsky military base.[a]

December 27   Joint Irgun and Lehi attack on CID headquarters in Jerusalem and in Jaffa. In Jerusalem, 7 soldiers and policemen are killed and 14 wounded, and part of the building destroyed, as is the building in Jaffa.

1946

January 17	Irgunist Eliahu Ezra and Lehi member Shaul Haglili are shot to death in random shootings by guards at the detention camp in Eritrea.
January 19	Joint unit of Irgun and Lehi attacks Jerusalem Central Prison in a failed attempt to free prisoners. Two policemen are killed and others wounded. Curfew is imposed on Jerusalem.
February 6	Lehi confiscates 4 mortars, 8 Bren guns, 24 submachine guns, and 70 rifles from a military base near Tel Aviv. In revenge, soldiers go on a shooting spree in Holon and kill three Jews.
February 15	Joint unit of Irgun and Lehi attempts to assassinate Superintendent of Haifa District police, Raymond Cafferata, who leaves the country shortly thereafter.[c]
February 18	Police arrest Lehi radio announcer Geula Cohen and another 19 members of Lehi during a broadcast. Cohen refuses to recognize the authority of the British courts and is sentenced to seven years in jail.
February 25	Lehi attacks Kfar Sirkin airport and destroys 8 Spitfire planes; at the same time, the Irgun attacks airports in Kastina, destroying 20 Halifax planes, and in Lod, destroying 4 Hansons and 7 other planes.
April 2	Lehi blows up Naaman rail bridge near Acco as the Irgun sabotages the rails near Yavneh and Ashdod. Rail service from Egypt to Lebanon and Syria is brought to a halt.
April 24	Confiscation of arms from a paratroop base in Tel Aviv.[a]
April 25	Attack on army parking lot on Hayarkon Street in Tel Aviv kills seven soldiers.
May 1	Attempt to blow up a British battleship in Alexandria.[a]
June 6	Israel Eldad escapes in Jerusalem.
June 11	Sabotage of rail line in Hadera.
June 17	Attack on and demolition of railway works in Haifa. Eleven Lehi members are killed during the retreat

and twenty-two are captured.

June 26	Robbery of diamonds in Pardes Katz.
July 1	Fifty-four detainees from the Irgun and Lehi escape by tunnel from the detention camp in Eritrea.
July 22	Irgun destroys government and military offices in King David Hotel in Jerusalem, 91 killed, after which the Hagana dissolves the United Resistance Movement.
August 17	Eighteen male Lehi members arrested after the destruction of railway works in Haifa are sentenced to death. Four female Lehi members arrested then are sentenced to life imprisonment. On August 28, the sentences of the men are commuted to life imprisonment.
September 9	Area Security Office (British intelligence) is blown up in Tel Aviv. The commanding officer and two policemen are killed.
September 9	Assassination of Sgt. T. G. Martin, head of the Jewish section of the Haifa CID.
September 22	Attempted assassination of Lt. General E. Barker, commander of British armed forces in Palestine.
September 26	Attack on military vehicles on Lod road.[a]
September 26	Attack on military vehicles on Haifa-Tel Aviv road.[a]
September 30	Two shootings at military vehicles, in Lod and Haifa, injure four soldiers.[f]
October 1	A sergeant is shot and killed near Petach Tikva, the night of Sept. 30-Oct. 1.
October 8	Mines planted on road in attacks on armored vehicles.[f]
October 9	Attack on military train on the Haifa-Kantara line.[f]
October 9	Mine on Jaffa-Ramla road injures six policemen.[f]
October 9	Mine attack on police car in Jerusalem.[a]
October 14	Police car blown up on Bet Lid road.[a]
October 16	Sabotage of military telegraph lines near Haifa.[f]
October 17	Mining of military vehicle near Bet Lid, three soldiers injured.
October 17	Mine attack on military vehicle on Bet Dagan road.[a]
October 18	Mining of military vehicle near Petach Tikva, two soldiers injured. Mines also planted on Binyamina, Hadera and Netanya roads.[af]

October 20	Mining of military vehicle near Rishon Lezion, one soldier injured.
October 20	Mining of communications cable near Hadera.
October 20	Military telegraph lines severed between Haifa and Tel Aviv.[a]
October 21	Attack on train near Betar.[a]
October 21	Attack on military vehicle near Haifa.[a]
October 22	Mining of rail line near Jerusalem disables train.
October 22	Attack on military vehicle near Haifa.[f]
October 23	Attack on military vehicle near Hadera injures soldiers.[f]
October 24	Several mine attacks on military guard posts in Jerusalem, 11 soldiers injured.
October 24	Jerusalem-Beirut and Jerusalem-Cairo military telegraph lines severed.[f]
October 27	Mine injures 18 soldiers.
October 29	Mine attack on military vehicle near Raanana.[f]
October 31	Mining of road near Kfar Sirkin kills two soldiers and injures two.
November 1	Sabotage of rail tracks near Kalkilya derails train.[f]
November 1	Attack on military vehicle near Haifa.[f]
November 1	Attack on Haifa-Lod train.
November 2	Attack on military convoy on the Jaffa-Lod road destroys two cars, injures 18 soldiers.[f]
November 4	Military telegraph line between Hadera and Pardes Hanna is severed.
November 4	Two trains are derailed, one near Rosh Haayin and one near Betar.
November 5	Attack on cargo train and its military guard near Kalkilya.[f]
November 5	Attack on train near Jerusalem.
November 6	Train derailed near Mikveh Israel.
November 9	Mine kills three soldiers attempting to confiscate arms cache in Jerusalem.
November 9	Sabotage of Jerusalem-Beirut military communications cable.
November 11	Dual sabotage of Haifa-Lod rail line, near Kalkilya and near Raanana.
November 11	Jerusalem-Beirut military telegraph line severed near Raanana.

November 13   Mining of road near police station in Jerusalem injures ten policemen.

November 13   Sabotage of Jerusalem-Lod rail line, six policemen killed.

November 13   Mining of Jaffa-Lod rail line derails several rail cars.

November 14   Attack on police cars at entrance to Jerusalem.[a]

November 15   Mine attack on armored train on the Haifa-Lod line, south of Binyamina, destroys tracks, armored vehicles, mortars, and ammunition. One soldier injured.

November 17   Military jeep blown up near Sarona, four policemen killed.

November 25   Attacks on two military vehicles near Bet Dagan.[a]

November 30   Joint units of the Irgun and Lehi attack the Mahane Yehuda police station and the Notre Dame military command post in Jerusalem.

December 2   Mining of Jerusalem-Sarafand road kills four soldiers in jeep.

December 2   Attack on military vehicle near Binyamina.

December 3   Mining of Raanana-Haifa road kills one soldier, injures two.

December 3   Army jeep blown up near Kfar Vitkin.

December 3   Attempted robbery of Polish Welfare Office payroll at Barclays Bank in Tel Aviv. One Lehi member killed by police and one passerby killed in crossfire.[c]

December 5   Car bomb explodes in Sarafand military base, killing 2 soldiers, injuring 40.

1947

January 2   Attack on military command post and police positions in Tel Aviv.[a]

January 2   Mine attack on military jeep near Petach Tivka.[a]

January 3   Military vehicle blown up near Wilhelma.[a]

January 4   Mines planted and soldiers injured on roads in Raanana, Kfar Sirkin, and Haifa.

January 12   Bomb planted in Haifa police headquarters kills six, injures dozens.

January 14   Yitzhak Shamir escapes from detention camp in Africa with two Lehi members and five Irgunists.[a]

January 16   Sabotage of telegraph cable near Hadera.

January 18	Mine planted in Jerusalem is discovered by the British.[f]
February 20	Jerusalem-Ramla telephone lines severed in 14 locations.
February 28	Haifa Shipping Agency, port offices and army cashier office, involved in deportation of immigrants, blown up; two shipping agency employees killed, four injured from the Navy, Army and Arab Legion.[ac]
February 26	Shots fired at Bet Hadar military regional headquarters in Tel Aviv.[f]
March 2	Mining of Hadera road injures three soldiers.
March 2	Mining of Rishon Lezion road injures three soldiers.
March 3	Shots fired and grenades thrown at an army base in Haifa.
March 4	Mining of road near Rishon Lezion injures three soldiers.
March 5	Haifa Tax Assessor's Office and a machine gun nest on its roof are blown up.[a] The machine gunners were protecting vehicles belonging to the airborne forces, which were parked in the building's parking lot.
March 5	Attacks on police positions in Jerusalem.[a]
March 7	British Colonial men's club in London blown up.
March 7	Attack on military vehicle in Jerusalem kills two soldiers and injures two.
March 7	Attack on command car near Hadera.[a]
March 8	Grenade attack on Mobile Police and army camp in Sarona. One soldier killed.
March 8	Mortar and automatic weapons attack on Bet Hadar military headquarters and mining of surrounding streets.
March 8	Shots fired at police headquarters in Jaffa.
March 8	Grenade and submachine gun attack on soldiers in Hatikva neighborhood, Tel Aviv.
March 8	Military vehicle blown up in Tel Aviv.
March 8	Attack on military barracks in Haifa.[a]
March 8	Attack on military base in Hadera.[a]
March 8	Military vehicles attacked in Tel Aviv, Haifa, and Jerusalem.[a]

March 8	Attack on armored convoy near Even Yehuda.[a]
March 9	Moshe Barazani arrested in Jerusalem with a grenade in his pocket.
March 9	Attack on military base #72 near Pardes Hanna kills 11 soldiers and injures 18.
March 10	Mine attack on military vehicle near Ramat Gan.
March 11	Shots fired on British vehicles near Even Yehuda.
March 12	Mining attack on military vehicle near Sarona.
March 12	Exiled detainees transferred to a detention camp in Kenya.
March 13	Mines disable tracks and derail a fuel train between Rosh Haayin and Kalkilya.
March 13	Grenade attack on military vehicles on Jaffa-Tel Aviv road.
March 13	Train derailed near Beit Tsafafa in Jerusalem.
March 13	Robbery of Utility Bank in Tel Aviv.
March 14	Mine attacks damage trains near Rehovot and near Be'er Yaacov.
March 15	Sabotage of rail tracks near Rehovot.
March 15	Attack on military zone in Jerusalem.[a]
March 16	Mine in Jerusalem injures three soldiers.[f]
March 17	Moshe Barazani refuses to recognize the authority of British courts and is sentenced to death.
March 19	Soldiers and police shot at in Zichron Yaacov. One policeman is killed, five soldiers are wounded.
March 24	Robbery of Discount Bank in Tel Aviv.
March 27	Attempted assassination of officer in charge of Jewish section of CID in Tel Aviv.
March 30	Eleven oil tanks blown up in attack on oil storage installations in Haifa. Some 30,000 tons of fuel destroyed in fire that lasts several days.
March 31	Attack on police near Sarafand.
March 31	Mine on Mount Carmel in Haifa injures three soldiers.[f]
April 1	Confiscation of weapons from military base in Wadi Sarar.[a]
April 2	Attacks on trains near Tel Aviv and near Binyamina.[a]
April 3	Lehi sentences to death a Jewish collaborator with British intelligence and shoots him, in Jerusalem.[c]

April 13	Yousuf Abu Gosh and a group of Arabs help Geula Cohen escape from the Government Hospital in Jerusalem. Two of the group are sentenced to a year in jail.[c]
April 16	Bomb planted in the Colonial Office in Whitehall, in London.
April 16	Firebombing of two military vehicles in Tel Aviv.[c]
April 18	Attack on military vehicle near Raanana.[a]
April 20	Attack on military vehicle near Jerusalem.[a]
April 21	Moshe Barazani and Irgunist Meir Feinstein blow themselves up in their death row cell in Jerusalem, hours before their scheduled hanging.
April 22	A military train from Egypt is blown up near Rehovot, killing 5 soldiers and injuring 25.
April 23	Mine attack on two military vehicles near Lod.[a]
April 25	Car bomb blows up police headquarters in Sarona, killing four policemen, injuring five, and destroying offices, an arms storehouse, and a telephone exchange.
April 26	Assassination of CID Haifa District Chief A. E. Conquest.[a]
May 4	Irgun frees underground prisoners from Acco prison. Among them are 11 members of Lehi, including David Hameiri-Begin, Joshua Zetler, Joshua Becker, and Matityahu Shmuelevitz. Lehi members Haim Applebaum and Shimshon Vilner are killed escaping and Matityahu Shmuelevitz and Joseph Dar are recaptured.[a]
May 6	Alexander Rubovitch, who is carrying Lehi literature, is kidnapped by a British squad in Jerusalem and beaten to death with a stone outside the city.
May 11	Fifty detainees from Latrun are deported to a detention camp in Kenya.
May 12	Two policemen are shot to death in Jerusalem.
May 16	CID car is blown up in Haifa.[a]
May 21	Mine explodes under police car in Tel Aviv.
June 3	Up to seventy letter bombs sent to British ministers and officials in London.[d]
June 27	In shootings, three soldiers killed and two injured

in Tel Aviv, one killed and three injured in Haifa.

July 16   Mine attack on army truck near Petach Tikvah.

July 18   Soldiers attacked by mines and gunfire in Jerusalem, Haifa, and Kfar Bilu. One soldier and one policeman killed.[a]

July 19   One policeman killed, two injured in Haifa shootings.

July 19   Military vehicle destroyed and three soldiers injured in Sanhedria neighborhood of Jerusalem; firebombing of a police car in Jerusalem.[b]

July 20   Military vehicle blown up near Raanana, killing one soldier.[f]

July 20   Mines planted on night of July 19-20: damage to cargo trains in Haifa; on Jaffa-Lod line; on Haifa-Lod line; and mines discovered on Lod-Jerusalem, Lod-Kuneitra and Haifa-Zemach lines.[b]

July 21   Military vehicles and soldiers attacked in Haifa, killing one and wounding four.

July 21   Military vehicle attacked on Haifa-Tel Aviv road.[b]

July 21   Attack on police station in Jerusalem.[b]

July 21   Attack on military vehicle near Bet Lid.[a]

July 22   In Jerusalem, three armored vehicles and one R.A.F car are firebombed, grenades are thrown into a military vehicle, and an R.A.F. car is attacked with automatic weapons.

July 22   Attack on Mahane Yehuda Police Billet, hundreds of bullets fired from three positions.[bc]

July 22   Military vehicle blown up in Haifa.[a]

July 23   Mining of road near Mount Carmel injures three soldiers.[f]

July 23   Military vehicle blown up near Ahuza injuring four soldiers.[f]

July 23   Military vehicle blown up near Rishon Lezion injuring two soldiers.[f]

July 23   Military vehicle blown up near Raanana injuring four soldiers.[f]

July 23   Vehicle blown up near Tel Zur injuring one soldier.[f]

July 23   Rail car blown up near Gaza.[f]

July 24   Mine in Jerusalem injures three policemen.[f]

July 24   Attack on military building in Jerusalem.[a]

July 24	Rail bridge blown up between Binyamina and Zichron Yaacov.[f]
July 25	Attacks on army and police in Haifa.[a]
July 26	Mining of telegraph cable near Motza kills two soldiers, injures eight.
July 26	The replacement bridge erected between Binyamina and Zichron Yaacov is burned down.[f]
July 29	Policeman shot and killed in Haifa.
August 7	Sabotage of rail line near Gaza.
August 7	Attack on train carrying oil near Haifa.
August 7	Military vehicles blown up near Hadera.
August 9	Military train from Cairo derailed on the Lod-Haifa line.
August 11	Attacks on three military vehicles near Gedera.[a]
August 21	Mine on road near Netanya injures two soldiers.[f]
September 11	Yaacov Eliav and Betty Knout sentenced in Belgium to a year in jail for possession of explosives.
September 26	Robbery of Barclays Bank in Tel Aviv. Four policemen killed.
September 28	Dov Berman escapes from Latrun.[a]
September 29	Mining of road near Kfar Sirkin injures four soldiers.[f]
October 22	Anshel Spielman escapes from Jerusalem Central Prison.[a]
October 30	Lehi sentences to death and executes a Jewish collaborator with the CID.
November 3	Lehi frees from jail two members arrested for removing a street sign marking "Allenby Street" and confiscates the weapons of the policemen guarding the arrestees.
November 3	A Jewish police sergeant operating against the underground is sentenced to death and executed.
November 11	Soldiers and police open fire on young members of Lehi in a training course in Raanana, killing five.
November 12	In retaliation for the Raanana attack, a police sergeant is killed in Haifa.
November 13	Grenades thrown at a café frequented by the British in Jerusalem, injuring 28 soldiers and policemen. One policeman killed afterward in encounter with the assailants.[c]

November 13 Four British oil officials shot to death in Haifa.

November 14 Two soldiers shot and killed in Tel Aviv.[c]

November 14 Two policemen shot and killed in Jerusalem, one injured. British authorities impose curfew on British civilians, directing them not to leave homes at night.[c]

November 29 Following United Nations vote to partition the country and establish Jewish and Arab states, Arabs attack Jews, killing many and looting Jewish stores, opening an Arab-Jewish front.

December 4 Four British soldiers shot and wounded and their guns confiscated in Tel Aviv.

December 6 Grenade attack on Husseini-backed newspaper in Jerusalem.[f]

December 9 Military jeep attacked near Haifa.[a]

December 15 Attack on Arab Legion vehicle in Jerusalem kills one, after Arab Legion troops kill 14 Jews in a food convoy on December 14.[fc]

December 26 Arab Legion vehicle attacked on Mount Carmel.[f]

December 28 Battles with Arabs fought in Romema and Lifta in Jerusalem.[f]

December 30 Two British detectives attempting to disarm Lehi members are shot to death.

December 30 Fighting with Arabs in Kfar Yazur.[f]

December 31 Sabotage of rail to Jaffa.[f]

1948

January 1 Arab sniper nest in Jaffa blown up.[f]

January 1 Attacks on Arab forces in Katamon and Malcha areas of Jerusalem.[f]

January 4 Saraya headquarters of Arab Higher Committee blown up in Jaffa.

January 5 Sabotage of repaired Jaffa rail.[f]

January 11 Arab sniper positions in Sheikh Badr, Jerusalem, blown up.[f]

January 14 Fighting on the Arab front in Manshieh in Jaffa and Sheikh Jarrah in Jerusalem.[f]

January 16 Battle with Arabs in Jerusalem.[f]

January 18 Ten buildings blown up in Manshieh.[f]

January 21 Buildings blown up in Katamon in Jerusalem.[f]

January 23	Battle in Lifta in Jerusalem.[f]
January 25	More fighting in Manshieh.[f]
January 29	Trial and execution of Jewish woman planning to carry bomb into Tel Aviv in collaboration with Arab forces.[f]
January 29	Fighting in Lifta.[f]
February 1	British-driven car bomb blows up *Palestine Post* offices in Jerusalem and nearby houses, killing 90 Jews.
February 1	Fighting in Katamon.[f]
February 6	British soldier shot in Jerusalem.[a]
February 8	Destruction of building used by Arab forces in Jerusalem and battle with its British guards.[f]
February 9	Sniper position blown up in Katamon.[c]
February 10	Fighting in Katamon.[f]
February 11	Robbery of Electric Company in Jerusalem.[f]
February 12	Moshe Rosner and an Irgunist escape while being transferred from Latrun to Atlit.[a]
February 20	Lehi prisoners dig tunnel out of Jerusalem prison. Eight members of Lehi, including Moshe Svorai and Matityahu Shmuelevitz, and four Irgunists escape.
February 20	Three Lehi members escape from Atlit.[a]
February 22	British escorted car bomb blows up on Ben-Yehuda Street in downtown Jerusalem, killing approximately sixty people.
February 22	In retaliation for the Ben-Yehuda bombing, shots fired at soldiers' residence in Jerusalem, mine attack on military vehicles in Jerusalem, and a British truck attacked on Ramallah-Latrun road. Seven or more British soldiers killed.[afc]
February 23	Mine attack on a military vehicle in Jerusalem injures two.[f]
February 29	In retaliation for the Ben-Yehuda bombing, a military train is blown up near Rehovot, killing 28 soldiers and injuring 35.
March 1	Attack in Kfar Kanir.[f]
March 3	Headquarters of Arab gangs in Haifa blown up, killing 14.
March 4	Attack in Bir Adas.[f]

March 4	Attack on Arab bus and homes in Lifta.[f]
March 5	Eight Irgunists and Lehi members escape from Atlit Detention Camp.
March 5	Abraham Cohen is caught transporting bombs to Shchem and killed. Six people are killed trying to dismantle the bombs, including the two British deserters who took the car bomb to Ben-Yehuda Street on February 22.
March 5	Fighting in Lifta.[a]
March 9	Fighting in Katamon.[f]
March 13	Fighting in Katamon.[f]
March 14	Street signs with British names removed, replaced with Hebrew names.[f]
March 25	Haim Ben-Israel escapes from Atlit.[a]
April 3	Mining of Arab vehicles on road to Bethlehem.[f]
April 9	Irgun and Lehi forces capture Deir Yassin, near Jerusalem.
April 27	Robbery of Barclays Bank in Tel Aviv.
April 30	Yoram Sion and Zev Fuchs escape from Atlit.[a]
May 1	Three Lehi members escape from Atlit.[a]
May 3	Letter bomb sent to Major Roy Farran to avenge the kidnapping and killing of Alexander Rubovitch on May 6, 1947. Farran's brother opens the package and is killed.[g]
May 18	Four female Lehi members are broken out of the Petach Tikva police station by Lehi's combat division.[a]
May-July	Some seven hundred members of Lehi enlist in the newly formed Israeli army. Some fifty had enlisted separately and before the others and some two hundred more enlist through February 1949.
September 17	Assassination of U.N. mediator Count Folke Bernadotte in Jerusalem.[a]

Sources

Unless otherwise noted, the dates above are from Yaacov Amrami and Arieh Melitz, ed.s, *The Chronicle of the War of Liberation* (Tel Aviv: Shelach, 1951) [Hebrew].

a   Nechemia Ben-Tor, *The Lehi Lexicon* (Israel: Ministry of Defence, 2007) [Hebrew].

b   *Lohamey Herut Israel, Collected Writings*, 2nd ed. (Tel Aviv: Yair, 1982) [Hebrew].

c   The *Palestine Post*.

d   Yaacov Eliav, *Mevukash* (Jerusalem: Bamachteret, 1983), 371-381 [Hebrew].

e   Shlomo Okun, ed., *The Kenyan Exiles* (Israel: Amutat Golei Kenya, 1995), IX [Hebrew].

f   Yaacov Banai, *Anonymous Soldiers*, 3rd ed. (Tel Aviv: Yair, 1989) [Hebrew].

g   British Pathé Newsreel, May 13, 1948.

Appendix B

Quick Facts about Lehi:

Nature: Jewish revolutionary underground

Short-term goal: Liberation of Jewish homeland and establishment of Jewish state

Long-term goal: Redemption

Method: Attacks on British Mandatory regime and British imperialism

Dates: 1940-48

Places of Operation: Eretz Israel primarily; also England, Europe, Egypt

Founder: Abraham Stern

Commander, 1940-42: Abraham Stern

Central Committee, 1942-48: Israel Eldad, Nathan Yalin-Mor, Yitzhak Shamir

Number of members: approximately 950

Number of members killed: 127

Killed in war against the British: approximately 50

Hanged by the British: 2

Killed on Arab front or serving in Israeli army: approximately 70

Most famous action: Assassination of Lord Moyne in Cairo, 1944

Frequently Asked Questions

Why was Lehi fighting the British?
The British occupied the ancient Jewish homeland.

Why is that homeland sometimes called Palestine and sometimes Eretz Israel?
The land goes by many names: Canaan, the Promised Land, the Holy Land, Eretz Israel, Judah (or Judea), and Palestine. In this book, they are used almost interchangeably. For convenience's sake, a reader can assume they are the same. For the sake of historical accuracy, though, care has been taken to use Eretz Israel when referring to areas technically outside the borders of Palestine, or when citing Hebrew speakers who used the name Eretz Israel.

The land was called:
Canaan about four thousand years ago.

The Promised Land from about 3,400 years ago until today, referring to God's promise of the land to the Jews.

The Kingdom of Judah (or Judea) and the Kingdom of Shomron (or Samaria) from approximately 1400 B.C.E. until approximately 135 C.E.

Eretz Israel (the Land of Israel) from approximately 1000 B.C.E., until today. The first reference to Eretz Israel is in the biblical book of I Samuel.

Palestine from approximately 135 to 1948. (The Romans renamed the country, changing Judah or Eretz Israel to Palestine, in order to disassociate it from the Jews. The Hebrew name remained Eretz Israel.)

Israel from 1948 until today.

The borders of the territory designated by each of these names are slightly different, because the Jewish kingdoms and state gained and lost territory over the years and foreigners also conquered different amounts of the country. Thus:

The Promised Land that, according to the Bible, was promised by God to the Jews stretches from the Nile River to the Euphrates River.

Judah (Judea) refers to the southern part of the Jewish kingdoms, around Jerusalem.

Shomron (Samaria) refers to the northern Hebrew kingdom, the upper part of what today is often called the West Bank.

Palestine during the British occupation and Mandate (1917-48) refers to the territory captured by the British from the Ottoman Empire in World War I. Approximately one-quarter of it is today's State of Israel including the West Bank and three-quarters of it is today's Hashemite Kingdom of Jordan.

When did the Jews have a state and when did they leave?

The Jews had a state that was destroyed twice. It was established by King David approximately three thousand years ago. After just over four hundred years, in 586 B.C.E., the kingdom was defeated by the Babylonians. Many thousands of Jews were expelled; a small number remained. Some of those who were taken captive to Babylon returned after fifty years, and the Jewish Temple was rebuilt in 516 B.C.E.

This second Jewish state and its Second Temple lasted for close to six hundred years until they were destroyed by the Romans in 70 C.E. The Jews who stayed in the country declared a free Jewish state some sixty years later. The Romans again defeated the Jews in 135.

Many Jews were expelled and they, along with those who had been expelled or taken out before, wandered among the nations of the world for almost nineteen hundred years. The Jews who were not expelled remained throughout the centuries in, among other places, Jerusalem, Hebron and the Galilee. Gaza, too, was a Jewish center in the seventeenth century.

What were the British doing in Palestine?

Palestine was conquered by many, including the Arabs, the European Christian Crusaders of the Middle Ages, and the Ottoman

Empire. The British conquered the Holy Land from the Ottoman Empire in World War I. England was given a "Mandate" by the League of Nations (a forerunner of the United Nations) to prepare it to become a "Jewish National Home."

When was the Israeli War of Independence?

The Israeli government declared that the War of Independence started on November 30, 1947, when Arabs attacked the Jewish community after the United Nations voted to establish Jewish and Arab states. The British left on May 14, 1948, at which point Israel came into being and neighboring Arab armies invaded the new country. The war ended with no agreement on borders, only cease-fire lines.

The Israeli government said the War of Independence was fought only against Arabs. But the Irgun and Lehi undergrounds had been fighting to expel the British beginning in May 1939, when the British essentially barred future Jewish immigration and prohibited Jews from buying land. Some argue that the Jewish community began opposing the British as early as 1920, when Jabotinsky organized the Hagana in Jerusalem.

What did Stern call his group?

At first Stern called it the Irgun Zvai Le'umi B'Israel, which means the National Military Organization in Israel. This name was soon dropped (because it was too similar to the name of the rival Irgun) and the official name became Lohamey Herut Israel, which means Fighters for the Freedom of Israel. But this being too long, it was known by its Hebrew initials: Lehi, or by its English initials, F.F.I. The British called it the Stern Gang. People trying to be more objective than the British called it the Stern Group. Today in Israel it is usually called Lehi. So its most common names are Lehi and the Stern Group.

Its common names are:
Lehi
Lohamey Herut Israel
F.F.I.
Fighters for the Freedom of Israel
The Stern Group
The Stern Gang

Did the Irgun also have many names?
Mostly these:
Irgun
Irgun Zvai Le'umi
Etzel (the acronym of the above)
N.M.O.
National Military Organization

What were the code names of the Lehi leaders?
Abraham Stern: Yair
Israel Scheib: Sambatyon; Eldad
Nathan Yalin-Mor (or Friedman-Yalin): Gera
Itzhak Ysernitzki: Michael; Dov; Shamir
Stern took his name in honor of the leader of the Jewish community at Masada during the Jewish revolt against Rome (66-70 c.e.).

Why haven't I heard of Lehi before?
Ben-Gurion opposed the underground war against the British and he influenced many historians; also, his diaries have been a main source of material for historians. Official Israeli histories and state education curricula reflected the views of politicians who provided funding.

If the Irgun and Lehi led the fight against the British why didn't they take over when the British left?
The Hagana militia was stronger than they were; the leaders of the Jewish Agency for Palestine declared a state and said they would run it. The Irgun and Lehi believed it was not important who ran the country as long as the Jews were free of foreign rule.

What's the difference between the Irgun and Lehi?
The Irgun was founded in 1931 (some say an earlier incarnation was created in 1929) and stopped fighting the British at the beginning of World War II; its members enlisted in the British army to fight the Germans. Lehi was founded when it split from the Irgun in 1940 and continued fighting the British, on the theory that the British were the enemy preventing Jewish independence and also thereby preventing the rescue of Jews from abroad.
The Irgun had about five thousand members and engaged in

military-style attacks. Lehi was smaller and engaged in acts of "individual terror," such as assassinations.

Were the Irgun and Lehi terrorist organizations?

Many in the Irgun or Lehi called themselves terrorists. Today terrorism indicates the wanton murder of civilians. There were many actions by the Irgun in the 1930s that qualify as terrorist. In Haifa, Benjamin Zeroni's bombs killed hundreds of people. In Tiberias, mines did the same. On the road to Jerusalem, Yehezkel Altman was caught and sentenced to death after firing at a bus and a police car. Shlomo Ben-Yosef tried to fire on a bus in the Galilee shortly afterward and was hanged by the British.

These Irgun attacks were all reprisals for Arab attacks against civilians. The Irgun philosophy was not to drive Arabs out of the country by killing their children, but rather that if the Jews did not attack to deter the Arabs, the Jews would be massacred.

Menachem Begin was not in the country during the 1930s. He took over the Irgun in late 1943, and the Irgun then became a different organization. Under Begin's direction, the Irgun put signs on mines warning civilians to stay away and phoned warnings to the people in the buildings it was about to attack so they could be evacuated.

Stern, and later Lehi, supported attacks only on official representatives of the British regime.

In late 1947, following the United Nations' vote to partition the country, things changed; the war became a street fight again. The *New York Times*, for example, wrote on January 4, 1948, that "Fear and grief are both growing in Palestine as Zionists and Arabs kill each other in a struggle that hardly can be dignified with the name of war because it is more like a great mass vendetta." During this period, Lehi planted bombs in various buildings; the targets were military objectives, not civilian, but given the targets' location and the type of Arab "military" forces fighting the Jews, civilian deaths were numerous. The battles between Jewish forces, including those of the Irgun and Lehi, and Arab forces often involved civilian deaths.

Thus one might argue that the Irgun's and Lehi's wars against the British were not terrorist in today's sense, while the Irgun of 1937-39 engaged in terrorist actions. The Arab-Israeli war of 1947-48 was a mess.

In an article entitled "Terror," Lehi's underground paper justified the use of terror, which, Lehi said, "is a part of political warfare in our time and it plays a major role...."[1] The "terror" justified by Lehi is, however, clearly defined as ambush, deception, and assassination, which it contrasts with the knightly battles of yore and wars fought according to sporting rules. The intentional murder of innocents is not even mentioned, much less justified, in this occasionally referenced and never-quoted article.

What made Lehi unique?

They turned the Jewish idea of redemption into a practical action plan.

They fought not to create a refuge for Jews in trouble in other countries, but to liberate the homeland and bring redemption. This meant that the British—and any non-Jewish power ruling over any part of the homeland—was the enemy.

Notes

All translations from Hebrew are by Zev Golan unless otherwise noted.

CHAPTER ONE

[1] Joseph Kremin, interview with the author, August 30, 1990; Yehoshua Ofir, *Rishonei Ha'etzel* (Israel: Amuta Al Shem Hanania Ve'Olga Yekutieli, 2002), 221 [Hebrew]; Yaacov Gilboa (Polani), *As You Walk Through Fields of Terror...* (Tel Aviv: Yair, 1986), 35-36 [Hebrew].

[2] Abraham Stern, *In My Blood, Live Forever*, sixth expanded edition (n.p.: Yair, 1979), 49 [Hebrew].

[3] Ada Amichal-Yevin, *In Purple, The Life of Yair-Abraham Stern* (Tel Aviv: Hadar, 1986), 12 [Hebrew]; and Stern to his father, October 12, 1918, in Abraham Stern, *Letters to Roni*, ed. Aharon Amir (Tel Aviv: Yair, 2000), 223 [Hebrew].

[4] Stern to his mother and father, December 17, 1920, *Letters*, 224-25.

[5] Amichal-Yevin, *In Purple*, 14.

[6] Ibid., 15.

[7] Ibid., 16-17.

[8] Stern to Meir Klaif, March 26, 1926, *Letters*, 228.

[9] Amichal-Yevin, *In Purple*, 24.

[10] Ibid., 25, 28, 30.

[11] Ibid., 32.

[12] The *New York Times* of April 28, 1903, reported that during the three days of rioting, 120 Jews had been killed and over 500 injured, while the police did nothing to stop the pillage.

[13] Amichal-Yevin, *In Purple*, 33-34.

[14] Ibid., 34-35.

[15] Ibid., 38.

[16] Ibid., 39-40.

[17] Ibid., 41.

[18] Ibid., 45.

[19] Stern, *In My Blood*, 57.

[20] Stern to Roni Burstein, *Letters*, July 30, 1928, 9.

[21] Douglas V. Duff, *Bailing with a Teaspoon* (London: John Long, [1953]), 96. According to Duff (189), "In all the Holy Land of 1929 the Government had only about 30 British police officers and 120-odd constables in the British Section, on whose loyalty they could rely," an additional 1,800 mostly Moslem policemen, and not a single garrisoned soldier.

[22] Stern to Roni, October 1, 1929, *Letters*, 12.

[23] Ibid.

[24] Ibid.

[25] Stern to Mrs. Burstein [Roni's mother], October 4, 1929, *Letters*, 229.

[26] Stern to Roni, November 1, 1929, *Letters*, 14.

[27] Amichal-Yevin, *In Purple*, 51.

[28] Stern to Roni, November 15, 1929, *Letters*, 16.

[29] Stern to Roni, December 12, 1929, *Letters*, 20.

[30] Stern to Roni, December 25, 1929, *Letters*, 25.

[31] Ibid.

[32] Stern to Roni, February 13, 1930, *Letters*, 29.

[33] Stern to Roni, April 17, 1930, *Letters*, 31.

[34] Stern to Roni, May 1, 1930, *Letters*, 32.

[35] Stern to Roni, November 20, 1930, *Letters*, 47.

[36] Cited by Stern in Stern to Roni, February 12, 1931, and February 5, 1931, *Letters*, 62, 60.

[37] Stern to Roni, October 30, 1930, *Letters*, 43.

[38] See for example Stern to Roni, February 6, 1934, *Letters*, 123.

[39] Stern to David Stern, April 19, 1930, *Letters*, 231.

[40] Stern to Roni, November 26, 1930, *Letters*, 49-50.

[41] Israel Eldad, *The First Tithe*, trans. Zev Golan (Tel Aviv: Jabotinsky Institute, 2008), 258.

[42] Amichal-Yevin, *In Purple*, 58.

[43] Stern, *In My Blood*, 19.

[44] Roni Stern-Zamir, speech at Hechal Shlomo, Jerusalem, February 19, 2001 [Hebrew].

[45] Amichal-Yevin, *In Purple*, 65-66.

[46] Stern to Roni, November 5, 1931, *Letters*, 75.

[47] Stern to Roni, November 12, 1931, *Letters*, 77.

[48] Stern to Roni, February 18, 1932, *Letters*, 91.

[49] Amichal-Yevin, *In Purple*, 71-72.

[50] Stern to Roni, March 17, 1932, *Letters*, 93-94.

[51] Stern to Roni, February 11, 1932, *Letters*, 89.

[52] For example, the letters of February 6, 1934, and April 3, 1934, *Letters*, 122, 125, 135. In one letter written in his childhood the phrase "Thank God" appears.

[53] See, for example, the letter of April 3, 1934, *Letters*, 135.

[54] Stern to Roni, May 22, 1934, *Letters*, 146.

[55] Stern to Hinda [Sperling], *Letters*, 237.

[56] Stern to Roni, June 19, 1934, *Letters*, 151.

[57] The god of love in ancient Greece. Stern to Roni, February 6, 1934, *Letters*, 125.

[58] Stern to Roni, January 23, 1934; April 10, 1934, *Letters*, 117, 137.

[59] Stern to Roni, June 12, 1934, *Letters*, 148.

[60] Stern to Roni, January 30, 1934, *Letters*, 121.

[61] Stern to Roni, April 10, 1934 and January 9, 1934, *Letters*, 137, 114.

[62] Stern to Roni, January 2, 1934, *Letters*, 111.

[63] Stern to Roni, February 20, 1934, *Letters*, 128.

[64] Stern to Roni, June 12, 1934, *Letters*, 149.

[65] Stern to Roni, May 1, 1934, *Letters*, 142.

[66] Stern to H. Sh. Halevy, [February 13, 1934], *Letters*, 233-35.

[67] Stern to Roni, May 22, 1934, *Letters*, 146.

[68] Stern to Roni, February 6, 1934, *Letters*, 123.

[69] Stern to Roni, June 19, 1934, *Letters*, 150.

[70] Amichal-Yevin, *In Purple*, 90.

[71] Roni Stern, radio interview, "Blood on the Threshold," Arutz 7 [Hebrew].

[72] Stern to Roni, May 16, 1936, *Letters*, 169.

73 Stern to Roni, May 18, 1936, *Letters*, 170.

74 Abraham T'homi, "Why Did the Irgun Zvai Leumi Split?" September 18, 1958, typed manuscript in Jabotinsky Institute, P 77 21/3 [Hebrew].

75 Stern to Roni, April 8, 1938, *Letters*, 189.

76 Amichal-Yevin, *In Purple*, 149.

77 Azriel Bensenberg, interview with the author, November 28, 1998.

78 In 1917, when the Balfour Declaration was issued, Palestine included the territories today called the State of Israel, Judea and Samaria (the West Bank), and the kingdom of Jordan. At the time all these were called Palestine in English, or Eretz Israel in Hebrew, though the geographical boundaries of Eretz Israel extended beyond those of Palestine. In 1922, the British issued the first White Paper, removing most of the territory in order to create an Arab state in Palestine, which later came to be called Jordan.

79 Nathan Yalin-Mor, *The Years Before* (Israel: Kinneret, 1990), 67-68 [Hebrew].

80 *Lohamey Herut Israel, Collected Writings*, 2nd ed. (Tel Aviv: Yair, 1982), 1:47-48 [Hebrew].

81 Amichal-Yevin, *In Purple*, 154.

82 David Sitton, *Free and Behind Bars: From the Diary of an Interned Patriot* (Jerusalem: Bamaaracha, 1978), 119, 121-22 [Hebrew].

83 Ibid., 108.

84 Ibid., 105, 109-11, 128-31.

85 Ibid., 1-2, 38. (Regarding Haj Amin el-Husseini, see for basic data the Encyclopaedia Brittanica online, www.britannica.com/EBchecked/topic/277483/Amin-al-Husayni , accessed November 17, 2010. More detailed accounts note that British High Commissioner Herbert Samuel had pardoned the fugitive el-Husseini and chosen him as mufti over three candidates who garnered more votes, then vested him with the new title "Grand Mufti." The British purpose was to bolster the Husseini clan that was opposed by the equally important Nashashibi clan, and perhaps also to put in place an Arab leader opposed to Zionism.)

86 David Raziel to Arthur Giles, Jerusalem, December 29, 1938; Stern placed a copy of the letter in a time capsule, which was discovered years later.

87 Stern, *In My Blood*, 33.

88 Ibid., 67.

89 Ibid., 114.

90 Sitton, *Free and Behind Bars*, 80.

91 Command Bulletin no. 112, *Lohamey Herut Israel, Collected Writings*, 1:17-18. On July 21, 1940, the Irgunists opposed to Stern issued a similarly numbered bulletin. See *Irgun Zvai Leumi, Collection of Archival Sources and Documents, April 1937-April 1941* (Tel Aviv: Jabotinsky Institute, 1990), 153-54 [Hebrew].

92 Roni Stern-Zamir, in conversation with the author and others, 57 Pinsker Street, Tel Aviv, February 20, 1990.

93 Stern called his organization the Irgun Zvai Leumi B'Israel, while the original Irgun had the additional word "Eretz": Irgun Zvai Leumi B'Eretz Israel. "Fighters for the Freedom of Israel" began to appear in the text of broadsides in November-December 1941 (though these underground messages were still signed "Irgun Zvai Leumi B'Israel") and officially replaced the cumbersome Irgun Zvai Leumi B'Israel after Stern's death.

94 Command Bulletin no. 1, *Lohamey Herut Israel, Collected Writings*, 1:19-20.

95 Heichman, interview with the author, September 13, 1990. Segal was one of those who had brought Stern and Raziel together to negotiate.

96 Abraham Liberman, *Fighters' Stories* (Tel Aviv: Yair, 1991), 22 [Hebrew]. Later, writing in the Lehi newspaper, Nathan Yalin-Mor took a different approach to justifying bank robberies. He argued that: Some of the institutions robbed were British, i.e., the enemy, and their money really belonged to the native residents of the country whose resources and labor the British were exploiting; other individuals and institutions robbed were

capitalists who were exploiting the labor of others and who, in any case, should be glad they were only asked to give their money for the general good and not their lives; and revolutionary movements often steal the funds they need, since they cannot make legal, public appeals. Yalin-Mor mentioned as examples of such revolutionaries Józef Piłsudski [who robbed a train near Vilna in 1908] and Joseph Stalin and Maxim Litvinov, who began with an armed bank robbery [in Tiflis in 1907] and ended up respected members of the international community (*Lohamey Herut Israel, Collected Writings*, 1:217-18). It is perhaps little wonder that the ranks justified the robberies based on their having given everything they owned and robbery being a necessity, not an option with moral value of its own. The ranks were usually disappointed to learn they were being sent to rob a bank or a bank messenger instead of to attack an installation or a police official (see, for example, Joshua Israeli [Becker], *In a Red Uniform* (Karnei Shomron: self-published, n.d.), 12 [Hebrew]).

97 *Bamachteret* no. 3, in *Lohamey Herut Israel, Collected Writings*, 1:41-42.

98 Eldad, *The First Tithe*, 85.

99 Yitzhak Shamir, "The Day I Escaped from Jail," *Maariv Sofshavua*, October 10, 1997, 28 [Hebrew].

100 Nathan Yalin-Mor, *Lohamey Herut Israel* (Israel: Shikmona, 1974), 62 [Hebrew].

101 Moshe and Tova Svorai, *From the Irgun to Lehi, a Personal Story* (n.p., 1989), 216 [Hebrew].

102 Roni Stern, interview with Moshe Zonder, *Maariv Sofshavua*, July 17, 1998, 26 [Hebrew].

103 Moshe and Tova Svorai, *From the Irgun to Lehi*, 219-20.

104 *Lohamey Herut Israel, Collected Writings*, 1:101.

105 Yaacov Orenstein, *In Chains* (Tel Aviv: Hug Yedidim, 1973), 154-55 [Hebrew].

106 Heichman, interview.

107 Gilboa (Polani), *As You Walk*, 80.

108 Ibid., 81-83. (Actually, the Germans were already murdering Jews, but they formulated a "Final Solution" in December 1941 and made the systematic murder of all Jews official policy on January 20, 1942, in a meeting in Wannsee, near Berlin.)

109 Moshe Svorai, *The Libel Trial* (Shaked: Matsoi, 1997), 124 [Hebrew].

110 Moshe and Tova Svorai, *From the Irgun to Lehi*, 246.

111 Israeli, *In a Red Uniform*, 15-16.

112 Ibid., 49. In jail, Becker heard the story from Zetler.

113 Moshe and Tova Svorai, *From the Irgun to Lehi*, 246.

114 Ibid., 248.

115 Geoffrey J. Morton, *Just the Job* (London: Hodder and Stoughton, 1957), 141.

116 Ibid.

117 Moshe and Tova Svorai, *From the Irgun to Lehi*, 334-37.

118 Ibid., 337-38.

119 Ibid., 337; Yaacov Eliav, interview with the author, 1980. In Yaacov Eliav, *Mevukash* (Jerusalem: Bamachteret, 1983), 209-10 [Hebrew], Eliav says he thought he was going to die and so, abandoning caution, told the police that they were shooting and beating men they had not bothered to identify or put on trial, but Lehi would pay them back twice over. The beating stopped only when neighbors appeared at nearby windows and on adjacent porches to watch.

120 Morton, *Just the Job*, 143.

121 Eliav, *Mevukash*, 210.

122 Moshe and Tova Svorai, *From the Irgun to Lehi*, 338.

123 Ibid., 339.

124 Stern to Roni, May 16, 1940, *Letters*, 218.

125 Stern to Roni, January 30, 1942, *Letters*, 220.

126 Ibid. Lermontov's verse is from "The Sail" (1832).

127 Julie Torenberg, interview with the author, August 10 and 15, 1998.

[128] Ibid.

[129] Nelly Lengsfelder, interview with the author, March 19, 2009.

[130] Torenberg, interview.

[131] Svorai, *The Libel Trial*, 124.

[132] Hisia Shapiro, "With Yair in His Final Days," *Hazit Hanoar* 2 (Shevat 5707), in *Lohamey Herut Israel, Collected Writings*, 2:377.

[133] Stern, 25 Shvat 5702 [February 12, 1942], *Letters*, 257.

[134] Shapiro, "With Yair in His Final Days," 2:378; Tova Svorai, telephone interview with the author, September 1, 2000.

[135] Bernard Stamp, interview with Ilana Zur, broadcast on Israel Radio, November 29, 1986. Audiocassette in archives of Lehi Museum, Tel Aviv. See also *Yediot Aharonot*, November 28, 1986.

[136] Saunders' report, Hagana Archives, see files 47/0007, 80/041/P5, 80/041/P3; Morton, *Just the Job*, 145; Roni Stern, interview with Zonder, in which Roni reported that Eliav told her that the ambulance was already there for Stern's body when she arrived; High Commissioner to Secretary of State for the Colonies, telegram 695, May 31, 1942, in Jabotinsky Institute, chaf 20 aleph 112.
Some Lehi veterans reject the veracity of Saunders' account and believe the British were trying to sow dissent among the fighters. Others accept Saunders' account on the assumption that he had no reason to deceive London in an internal, secret document. One possible explanation for a distortion by Saunders is that he might have wanted to avoid telling his superiors that his policemen happened upon the most wanted man in the country by chance and were so unprepared that they had to drive back to the station for handcuffs; instead he preferred to present the case as one of determined, professional police work.

[137] "This is not the absolute truth, if that is even attainable. But this is the legal 'truth' in this case. It is the 'truth' of which I have been convinced based on my consideration of the evidence given by the witnesses, based on my assessment of their testimonies, based on a comparison of the evidence and the support, or lack of it, that can be gained from one piece of evidence or testimony, for another." *Moshe Svorai v. Anshel Spielman*, Tel Aviv District Court decision 126//89 (January 14, 1993), 12 c-d, 17 [Hebrew].

[138] Stamp, interview.

[139] Moshe and Tova Svorai, *From the Irgun to Lehi*, 360.

[140] Ibid., 361. "I don't know how I had the courage to say that," Svorai says today. Tova Svorai, interview with the author, February 6, 2011.

[141] Stamp, interview.

[142] Tova Svorai, interview, February 6, 2011.

[143] Stamp, interview. Decades later, Stamp apparently exaggerated Stern's helplessness and his bent head in his mind and remembered finding him fully crouched.

[144] Moshe and Tova Svorai, *From the Irgun to Lehi*, 362.

[145] Ibid.

[146] Stamp, interview.

[147] Moshe and Tova Svorai, *From the Irgun to Lehi*, 362; "Aimed between…," Tova Svorai, interview, February 6, 2011.

[148] Tova Svorai, *The Last Days of Yair – Abraham Stern* (n.p., n.d.), 7 [Hebrew].

[149] Tova Svorai, interview, February 6, 2011.

[150] Stamp, interview.

[151] Tova Svorai, interview, February 6, 2011; "Wilkin made…," Tova Svorai, interview in *Maaynei Hayeshua* 144 (3 Iyar 5770 [April 17, 2010]), 10 [Hebrew].

[152] Morton, *Just the Job*, 145.

[153] Stamp, interview.

[154] Ibid. As to why the alleged falsehoods in Morton's accounts were allowed to stand, Stamp reported that "An Arab police officer was given the job of investigating the case. A Jew's

been killed, an Arab police officer to investigate his killing? Well, what do you expect? Everyone laughed when they heard." Stamp added, "No one ever came to me and asked me to make any further statement about it."

155 Censored pages sold in Charles Hamilton auction, catalogue 141, October 29, 1981, item 144.

156 "Most Secret" ciphered telegram 1/255 dispatched 22:25, February 12, 1942; S.E.V. Luke to War Office, February 14, 1942. Both in Jabotinsky Institute, chaf 20 aleph 112.

157 "The Lesson of His Life and Death," in *Yair* (25 Shevat 5704), in *Lohamey Herut Israel, Collected Writings*, 1:375-76.

Chapter Two

1 Flavius Josephus, *The Wars of the Jews, or the History of the Destruction of Jerusalem*, trans. William Whiston, chap. 8, 6-7, http://www.gutenberg.org/cache/epub/2850/pg2850.txt

2 *Haor*, January 16, 1978 (Queens College, Flushing, New York), 11.

3 Copy provided by Eldad, in the author's files.

4 Yitzhak Shamir, interview with the author, January 20, 1980.

5 *Lohamey Herut Israel, Collected Writings*, 1:279.

6 Ibid., 1:32.

7 *Bamachteret* 2, in *Lohamey Herut Israel, Collected Writings*, 1:34.

8 *Lohamey Herut Israel, Collected Writings*, 1:219.

9 Ibid., 1:65-66; modern scholarship has corrected various misconceptions and added much information. In order to provide as full and as correct an account as possible, the details here are from Ben Abrahamson and Joseph Katz, "The Persian Conquest of Jerusalem in 614 C.E. Compared with Islamic Conquest of 638 C.E." (2004, draft), 5.

10 Abrahamson and Katz, "The Persian Conquest," 6.

11 *Lohamey Herut Israel, Collected Writings*, 1:220.

12 Abba Ahimeir, "The Great Israeli Revolution" (August 12, 1932), in Abba Ahimeir, *Revolutionary Zionism* (Tel Aviv: Committee for Publication of Ahimeir's Writings, 1966), 241 [Hebrew].

13 Aurelius Victor, *Liber de Caesaribus* 42.11. According to Jerome's *Chronicon* for the year 352, this led to the destruction of Tzippori, Tiberias, and Lod, along with many villages.

14 Abrahamson and Katz, "The Persian Conquest," 11.

15 *Lohamey Herut Israel, Collected Writings*, 1:34.

16 Abrahamson and Katz, "The Persian Conquest," 13-14.

17 Ibid., 15; see also Israel Ben Ze'ev, *Jews in Arabia* (Tel Aviv: Mitzpeh, 1931; Jerusalem: Ahiasaf, 1957) [Hebrew].

18 Abrahamson and Katz, "The Persian Conquest," 16-17.

19 Ibid., 18.

20 *Lohamey Herut Israel, Collected Writings*, 1:34.

21 Abrahamson and Katz, "The Persian Conquest," 18.

22 Ibid, 18-20, 25.

23 *Lohamey Herut Israel, Collected Writings*, 1:66; Yaacov Weinshal, *Giants in the Desert* (Tel Aviv: Shelach, 1952), 47-57 [Hebrew]; Abrahamson and Katz, "The Persian Conquest," 41-42. Various versions of this story are extant, some of which have the name Jacob Ovadia; others have Abu Issa as the son of Jacob Ovadia.

24 *Lohamey Herut Israel, Collected Writings*, 1:66; Weinshal, *Giants*, 35-46; Abrahamson and Katz, "The Persian Conquest," 41.

25 Heinrich Graetz, *History of the Jews*, vol. 5 (Philadelphia: Jewish Publication Society of America, 1895), 330-31.

26 Ibid., 520-21.

27 *Lohamey Herut Israel, Collected Writings*, 1:197.

[28] Ibid., 491-99, 504, 511.

[29] *Lohamey Herut Israel, Collected Writings*, 1:214.

[30] Graetz, *History of the Jews*, 499-511.

[31] Uri Zvi Greenberg, "Masechet Menofim Bakodesh," *Shnaton Yerushalayim Ledivrei Sifrut Vehagut*, 1966, 25 [Hebrew]. (Reprinted in Greenberg's *Collected Writings* 11:166.)

[32] *Lohamey Herut Israel, Collected Writings*, 1:199.

[33] Ibid., 1:873.

[34] Ibid.

[35] Ibid., 1:257-58; Israel Eldad, *The Jewish Revolution*, trans. Hannah Schmorak (New York: Shengold, 1971), 27.

[36] See Anita Engle, *The Nili Spies* (London: Hogarth, 1959; Jerusalem: Phoenix, 1989); Samuel Katz, *The Aharonsohn Saga* (Jerusalem: Gefen, 2007); and for a well-researched novel on the subject, Michael Blankfort, *Behold the Fire* (New York: New American Library, 1956).

[37] Keith Jeffery, *MI6, The History of the Secret Intelligence Service, 1909-1949* (London: Bloomsbury, 2010), 132.

[38] Raphael Abulafia, Israel Television interview (rebroadcast July 21, 2006).

[39] Abraham T'homi, *Between Darkness and Dawn* (New York: Bloch, 1986), 239.

[40] Ibid., 237-45.

[41] As recorded by the physician attending him. Elias Gilner, *War and Hope, A History of the Jewish Legion* (New York, Herzl Press, 1969), 343.

[42] *Lohamey Herut Israel, Collected Writings*, 1:414-16.

[43] Gilner, *War and Hope*, 351-93, 453.

[44] *Lohamey Herut Israel, Collected Writings*, 1:128.

Chapter Three

[1] *Lohamey Herut Israel, Collected Writings*, 1:257-58.

[2] Ibid., 1:258-59

[3] Ibid., 1:159.

[4] Ibid., 1:117.

[5] Ibid., 1:213.

[6] Ibid., 1:116.

[7] Ibid., 1:137.

[8] Ibid., 1:213-15.

[9] Ibid., 1:260-62.

[10] Ibid., 1:159.

[11] Ibid., 1:260-62.

[12] Ibid.

[13] Ibid., 1:213.

[14] Ibid., 1:116.

[15] Ibid., 1:260-62.

[16] Eldad, *The First Tithe*, 52.

[17] Dr. Arieh Morgenstern, interview in *Maariv*, October 5, 2007.

[18] Engle, *The Nili Spies*, 19, 30.

[19] Haim Dviri, interview with the author, April 25, 1982.

[20] Stern, *In My Blood*, 130. For more information on the League of Birionim see Zev Golan, *Free Jerusalem* (Jerusalem: Devora, 2003), 66-80; and, in Hebrew, Joseph Ahimeir and Shmuel Shatzky, *Hinenu Sicricim (Brit Habiryonim, the First Anti-British Organization)* (Tel Aviv: Nitzanim, 1978).

[21] Abba Ahimeir, "Betar as a Worldview" (December 1928), in Ahimeir, *Revolutionary Zionism*, 21-24.

[22] Abba Ahimeir, "A Word to the Betar Youth" (October 1930), in Ahimeir, *Revolutionary Zionism*, 42-44.

[23] Ahimeir, "A Letter to the Betar Youth" (March 1932), in Ahimeir, *Revolutionary Zionism*, 58-60. This letter was written from the Jerusalem Central Prison where Ahimeir was incarcerated.

[24] Joshua Yevin, *Jerusalem Awaits* (Tel Aviv: Y. Ish Bruria, 1932; 2nd ed. Tel Aviv: Herut Yerushalayim, 1939), 85 [Hebrew].

[25] Ibid., 86.

[26] Joshua Yevin, *The Lawgiving Poet* (Tel Aviv: Sdan, 1938), 22, 25-26 [Hebrew].

[27] Israel Eldad, *A Tear and Glow, Blood and Gold* (Jerusalem: Schocken, 2003), 306 [Hebrew].

[28] Uri Zvi Greenberg, "The Earthly Jerusalem," in *Eima Gedola Veyareach, Sefer Poemot* (Tel Aviv: Hedim, 1925), 56 [Hebrew]. He also referred to them as "the kingdom of the barefoot," and "the army of the barefoot," 50, 55.

[29] Uri Zvi Greenberg, "Hunger in the Land of Israel," in *Hagavrut Haolah* (Tel Aviv: Sdan, 1926) [Hebrew].

[30] Uri Zvi Greenberg, *In the Kingdom of the Cross*, trans. from the Yiddish by Benjamin Harshav (Jerusalem: Bet Moreshet UZG and Bet Shalom Aleichem, 2006), 10, 32 [Hebrew].

[31] Greenberg, "The Earthly Jerusalem," 55.

[32] Uri Zvi Greenberg, "Ne'um Ben Hadam\Kategoria," in *Ezor Magen, Ne'um Ben Hadam* (Jerusalem: Sdan, 1929) [Hebrew].

[33] Uri Zvi Greenberg, "Sicricin 2," in *Ezor Magen, Ne'um Ben Hadam*, 4.

[34] Uri Zvi Greenberg, "Judah Today, Judah Tomorrow," in *Sefer Hakitrug Ve'haemunah* (Jerusalem-Tel Aviv: Sdan, 1937), 169 [Hebrew].

[35] Greenberg, "Ezor Magen 2," in *Ezor Magen, Ne'um Ben Hadam*, 6; Stern, *In My Blood*, 41.

[36] Stern, *In My Blood*, 28-29.

[37] Ibid., 25.

[38] "The Messiah," ibid., 130-31. This poem has no set rhyme scheme.

[39] Ibid., 54-55.

[40] Ibid., 58.

[41] Ibid., 91.

[42] "Prayer for the Day of Redemption," ibid., 92-93. In the original Hebrew, all the verses rhyme with "Zion."

[43] *Lohamey Herut Israel, Collected Writings*, 1:27-8.

[44] Ibid., 1:51-52.

[45] Dr. Ze'ev Iviansky, "Index of Lehi Underground Literature: Index of Authors' Names," addenda 8 in Nechemia Ben-Tor, *The Lehi Lexicon* (Israel: Ministry of Defence, 2007), 382 [Hebrew].

[46] *Lohamey Herut Israel, Collected Writings*, 1:69-70.

[47] Ibid., 1:69-72.

[48] Ibid.

[49] Ibid.

[50] Ibid.

[51] Shamir, interview.

CHAPTER FOUR

[1] Israel Tevuah, "Recollections" (typed manuscript, copy in author's files) [Hebrew].

[2] Yaacov Banai, ed., *Sources for the History of the Fighters for the Freedom of Israel Movement* (Tel Aviv: Yair, 2006), 62.

[3] Telegrams of February 17, 1942, and April 27, 1942, in Jabotinsky Institute, chaf 20 aleph 112.

[4] Eliav, interview. Eliav, who had assembled the bomb, was of a different make than Cohen and expressed his regret that Cohen had not detonated the bomb.

[5] Liberman, *Fighters' Stories*, 28-29; Yalin-Mor, *Lohamey Herut Israel*, 92. Cohen thought Stern had the decisiveness of a leader and a practical side on which to stand.

[6] Yalin-Mor, *Lohamey Herut Israel*, 92.

[7] *Lehi: People* (Tel Aviv: Yair, 2002), 482 [Hebrew]; Ben-Tor, *Lexicon*, 286-87.

[8] Criminal Investigation Department (CID) file, personality sheet, Hagana Archives, file 001 477.

[9] Liberman, *Fighters' Stories*, 32.

[10] Yaacov Banai, *Anonymous Soldiers*, 3rd ed. (Tel Aviv: Yair, 1989), 118-19 [Hebrew].

[11] Ibid., 121.

[12] Eldad, *The First Tithe*, 94.

[13] Shamir, "The Day I Escaped."

[14] Yalin-Mor, *Lohamey Herut Israel*, 124-25.

[15] Menachem Schiff, one of Lehi's escapees, lecture during a tour of Latrun led by Modi Snir, December 6, 2010.

[16] Yalin-Mor, *Lohamey Herut Israel*, 115-16.

[17] Schiff, lecture.

[18] Yalin-Mor, *Lohamey Herut Israel*, 112-20.

[19] Liberman, *Fighters' Stories*, 61-63.

[20] *Lehi: People*, 186, 817.

[21] Yaacov Banai, lecture to Lehi second generation at Lehi Museum, Tel Aviv, June 27, 2004; Banai, *Anonymous Soldiers*, 176-78; Yaacov Banai, interview with the author, September 19, 2000; *Palestine Post*, February 16 and 17, 1944.

[22] Banai, *Anonymous Soldiers*, 182.

[23] Daniel Day to Benjamin Gepner, printed in Ben-Tor, *Lehi Lexicon*, 93.

[24] Banai, *Anonymous Soldiers*, 194-98.

[25] Eldad, *The First Tithe*, 142.

[26] Ibid., 142-46.

[27] Ibid., 148-50.

[28] *Lehi: People*, 766.

[29] Banai, *Anonymous Soldiers*, 201.

[30] Itzhak Gurion, *Lawyers for Freedom Fighters* (Tel Aviv: Jabotinsky Institute, 1973), 76 [Hebrew].

[31] Liberman, *Fighters' Stories*, 112.

[32] Banai, *Anonymous Soldiers*, 200-202.

[33] *Lohamey Herut Israel, Collected Writings*, 1:255-56.

[34] Ibid., 1:743-44.

[35] Ibid.

[36] Ibid., 1:743-48.

[37] Ibid.

[38] Ibid.

[39] Ibid., 1:747-50.

[40] Ibid., 1:749-50.

[41] Ibid., 1:750.

[42] Ibid., 1:751-54.

[43] Ibid.

[44] *Lehi: People*, 840.

[45] Gurion, *Lawyers*, 75-76; *Lohamey Herut Israel, Collected Writings*, 1:758.

[46] Joshua Zetler, *Jerusalem's Liberation Fighter* (Tel Aviv: Porat, 2006), 166 [Hebrew].

[47] *Lohamey Herut Israel, Collected Writings*, 1:760.

48 Ibid., 763.

49 Zetler, *Jerusalem's Liberation Fighter*, 167-68.

50 David Shomron, lecture to Lehi second generation at Lehi Museum, Tel Aviv, July 25, 2004.

51 Ibid.; Banai, *Anonymous Soldiers*, 248-51; Ben-Tor, *Lehi Lexicon*, 235-36; Banai, interview; High Commissioner to Secretary of State for the Colonies, August 8, 1944 and "Report on the attempt to assassinate the High Commissioner of Palestine," PRO C.O. 733/457/7516/151C, also in Jabotinsky Institute, chaf 20 aleph 125.

52 High Commissioner to the Secretary of State for the Colonies, August 21, 1944, ref. no. C.S. 679/4 and "Report on the attempt," PRO C.O. 733/457/7516/151C, in Jabotinsky Institute, chaf 20 aleph 125.

53 David Shomron, *We Enlisted for All Our Lives*, 3rd ed. (n.p.: Yair, 1997), 86-87 [Hebrew].

54 Banai, interview; Banai, *Anonymous Soldiers*, 254-58; Shomron, *We Enlisted*, 88-92.

55 Eliezer Ben-Ami, interview with the author, March 2, 2009.

56 Tova Svorai, interview, February 6, 2011.

57 Banai, *Anonymous Soldiers*, 258; Shomron, *We Enlisted*, 92.

58 *HL Deb 09, June 1942, vol. 123, cc 179-210,*
http://hansard.millbanksystems.com/lords/1942/jun/09/recruitment-of-jews#S5LV0123 P0-00335

59 *Time*, June 9, 1961. Brand was put under pressure to recant this testimony and at times did.

60 Shamir, interview.

61 War Cabinet 146 (44), 197, PRO Cab. 65\44, in Jabotinsky Institute, chaf 20 dalet 30.

62 Shulamit Livnat and Naama Volcani, eds., *Olei Hagardom*, rev. ed. (Tel Aviv: Hamidrasha Hale'umit, [2000]; orig. published 1978, Chaya Baranes, ed.), 46 [Hebrew].

63 Ibid., 46-47.

64 *Lehi: People*, 399.

65 Ibid., 149; Livnat and Volcani, *Olei Hagardom*, 39, 43.

66 Livnat and Volcani, *Olei Hagardom*, 49-50.

67 Ibid., 57.

68 Eldad, *The First Tithe*, 184.

69 Livnat and Volcani, *Olei Hagardom*, 63.

70 Ibid., 65.

71 Gerald Frank, *The Deed* (New York: Simon and Schuster, 1963), 301.

72 Rabbi Nissim Ohana, letter to Prof. Joseph Nedava, Haifa, September 13, 1951, cited in Livnat and Volcani, *Olei Hagardom*, 67.

73 CID file, personality sheet, Hagana archives, file 001 476.

74 David Shomron, lecture to Lehi second generation at Lehi Museum, Tel Aviv, June 27, 2004.

75 Ben-Tor, *Lehi Lexicon*, 55-56.

76 Ibid., 168-69.

77 Malka Hepner, *In Thy Blood Live!* (Tel Aviv: Hadar, 1978), 8 [Hebrew].

78 Ibid., 10, 17, 22, 28.

79 Ibid., 51, 53-54.

80 Ben-Tor, *Lehi Lexicon*, 74-76.

81 Arye Efrati, lecture to Lehi second generation at Lehi Museum, Tel Aviv, June 27, 2004.

82 Yael Ben-Dov, interview with the author, November 10, 2009.

83 Eldad, *The First Tithe*, 249-50.

84 Ben-Dov, interview.

85 Ibid.

86 Ben-Tor, *Lehi Lexicon*, 65.

87 Eldad, *The First Tithe*, 253.

88 Ibid.

89 Ibid., 253-54.

[90] Ben-Dov interview.

[91] J. Bowyer Bell, *Terror Out of Zion* (New York: St. Martin's, 1977), 167-68.

[92] *Lehi: People*, 24; Ben-Tor, *Lehi Lexicon*, 65-66; Jabotinsky Institute in Israel's *Institute News* 48 (December 2010), 2 [Hebrew].

[93] *Lohamey Herut Israel, Collected Writings*, 2:157-58.

[94] Ibid.

[95] Ibid., 2:161-62.

[96] Ibid., 2:313.

[97] *Toward a Hebrew Foreign Policy*, in *Lohamey Herut Israel, Collected Writings*, 2:352-58.

[98] Jeffery, *MI6*, 692-95.

[99] *New York Times*, March 29, 1947.

[100] Ibid., March 30, 1947.

[101] Eldad, *The First Tithe*, 320-27.

[102] *New York Times*, March 31, 1947.

[103] Ibid., April 3, 1947.

[104] Ben-Tor, *Lehi Lexicon*, 142.

[105] Shoshana Hilkiyahu, interview with the author, July 1, 2010.

[106] Benjamin Gepner, *With a Beating Heart, With a Sword Drawn-out* (Israel: Sifrei Hashemesh Haolah, 2008), 347-48 [Hebrew]. (The English title is that given to the book by the publisher.)

[107] Eliav, *Mevukash*, 310-13.

[108] Ibid, 310.

[109] Ibid., 314-27.

[110] Avner [Gruschow], *Memoirs of an Assassin*, trans. Burgo Partridge (New York: Pyramid Books, 1960), 115.

[111] Ibid., 114-21. This story is unconfirmed by other sources.

[112] Ben-Tor, *Lehi Lexicon*, 65. (There were not many but there were several Arabs who assisted Lehi, Abu Ghosh being the most prominent. He afforded his relatives and other residents of his village the opportunity to assist as well. The village, located on today's main Tel Aviv-Jerusalem highway, has ever since been known for its friendly relations with Israel.)

[113] Meir Feinstein's speech, quoted in Menachem Begin, *The Revolt*, trans. Samuel Katz, 9th printing (Jerusalem: Steimatzky, 1977), 41-42.

[114] Remainder of Feinstein's speech, as written in his hand, reproduced in Livnat and Volcani, *Olei Hagardom*, 144 (author's translation).

[115] Livnat and Volcani, *Olei Hagardom*, 135.

[116] Eliezer Ben-Ami, lecture to Lehi second generation at Lehi Museum, Tel Aviv, June 27, 2004.

[117] Ben-Ami, interview; Ben-Ami, lecture, June 27, 2004; Banai, *Anonymous Soldiers*, 528.

[118] Ben-Ami, lecture, June 27, 2004.

[119] *Palestine Post*, November 14, 1947; Ben-Tor, *Lehi Lexicon*, 312.

[120] Eliezer Ben-Ami, lecture to Lehi second generation at Lehi Museum, Tel Aviv, July 25, 2004.

[121] Matityahu Shmuelevitz, *In Red Days* (Tel Aviv: Elisha, 1949), 353 [Hebrew].

[122] Ibid.

[123] Ben-Ami, lecture, July 25, 2004.

[124] Ibid.; Menachem Malatzky, *One Truth and Not Two* (Tel Aviv: Ministry of Defence, 1997), 230-33 [Hebrew].

[125] Shimon Raz, unpublished research (the number 200 is often bandied about). Several British soldiers and policemen joined the Israeli forces. One, for instance, John Cooper, was forbidden by his staff sergeant to render assistance to a Jewish convoy to Hadassah Hospital in April 1948, as a result of which 78 people were killed, most of

them burned alive. Soon after, Cooper told Israeli army personnel, "I cannot serve in an army that allows atrocities like that." That summer, he was drafted into the Israeli army's 89th Battalion, coincidentally the battalion into which most of Lehi's members had been drafted. Dalia Karpel, "The Irish Rover," *Haaretz*, December 17, 2010.

126 Banai, lecture.

127 He and his driver drove past their target's vehicle, he checked the license plate number, got out of his car, and shot the four without their noticing his approach. Interview with the perpetrator (name in author's files), March 27, 2011. Writing in its underground newspaper after the fact, Lehi justified the attack both in terms of revenge for its dead and because the oil company officials were not welcome guests in the country. *Lohamey Herut Israel, Collected Writings* 2:815-16.

128 Banai, *Anonymous Soldiers*, 613.

129 David Hameiri-Begin, interview with Abraham Liberman, in Liberman, *Fighters' Stories*, 115-16.

130 Banai, *Anonymous Soldiers*, 616-20.

131 *New York Times*, January 5, 1948.

132 Ben-Tor, *Lehi Lexicon*, 94-96; Yoel Kimchi and other fighters in visit to site of battle, April 1987.

133 Ben-Tor, *Lehi Lexicon*, 71-72; *Maariv*, June 30, 1948; *Maariv*, June 10, 1948; *New York Times*, June 14, 1948. Ironically, Bevin endorsed Bernadotte's plan after the latter's assassination, when the rest of the world was abandoning it. See *New York Times*, September 23, 1948.

134 Uri Scharf, interview with the author, March 14, 2006.

135 United Nations, Department of Public Information, Press Release PAL/298, September 18, 1948; *Palestine Post*, September 19, 1948.

136 Ben-Tor, *Lehi Lexicon*, 242-43.

Chapter Five

1 Yaacov Heruti, *One Truth and Not Two* (Tel Aviv: Yair, 2008), 395 [Hebrew].

2 Yitzhak Shamir, letter to the author, November 28, 1996 [Hebrew].

3 Shamir, interview.

4 Yitzhak Shamir, letter to Shulamit Shamir, November 3, 1946, in Yitzhak Shamir, *Letters to Shulamit* (Jerusalem: Ministry of Defence, 2001), 44 [Hebrew].

5 Yitzhak Shamir, *Summing Up, An Autobiography* (Boston: Little, Brown and Company, 1994), 8.

6 Ibid., 34.

7 Menachem Lewin, interview with the author, December 26, 1997.

8 *Minutes of the Conference of the Fighters for the Freedom of Israel*, March 1949, ed. with an introduction and notes by Pinchas Ginosar (Ramat Gan: Bar-Ilan University, 1985), 97-98 [Hebrew].

9 *Lehi: People*, 24.

10 Eldad, *The First Tithe*, 105.

11 David Shomron, "We Saw Him As the Head of Lehi," in Yossi Ahimeir, *Itzhak Shamir, As Solid as a Rock* (Tel Aviv: Yediot Aharonot and the Jabotinsky Institute, 2008), 103 [Hebrew].

12 Yitzhak Shamir, interview with Israeli journalist Yair Stern (Abraham's son), 1991, first shown in Lehi Museum, Tel Aviv, August 12, 2008.

13 Shamir to Shulamit, September 1, 1946, *Letters to Shulamit*, 11.

14 Shamir to Shulamit, September 22, 1946, *Letters to Shulamit*, 27.

15 Shamir to Shulamit, November 20, 1946, *Letters to Shulamit*, 75.

16 Shamir to Shulamit, December 1, 1946, *Letters to Shulamit*, 90.

17 Shamir to Shulamit, January 12, 1947, *Letters to Shulamit*, 135.

18 The British kept the exiles in detention in Kenya until July. Israeli Foreign Minister Moshe Shertok argued the returning exiles should be made to sign loyalty oaths and considered imprisoning them. See Shlomo Okun, ed., *The Kenyan Exiles* (Israel: Amutat Golei Kenya, 1995), XXI-XXIV [Hebrew].

19 Shomron, "We Saw Him," 104.

20 Shamir to Shulamit, December 8, 194[6], *Letters to Shulamit*, 96.

21 Shamir to Shulamit, December 1, 1946, *Letters to Shulamit*, 88.

22 *Minutes*, 90.

23 Shlomo Nakdimon, "Nine Years in a Governmental Underground," in Ahimeir, *Itzhak Shamir*, 120 [Hebrew].

24 *Minutes*, 94-95.

25 Shomron, "We Saw Him," 103; Nakdimon, "Nine Years," 119.

26 Nakdimon, "Nine Years," 120.

27 Ibid., 125.

28 Shomron, "We Saw Him," 105; Nakdimon, "Nine Years," 122, 121, 125; Nachik Navot, "A Fighter and He Who Laid the Operational Infrastructure in Europe," in Ahimeir, *Itzhak Shamir*, 128-31 [Hebrew].

29 Dov Shperling, lecture at Lehi Museum, Tel Aviv, August 12, 2008.

30 He felt that his position representing the Knesset and government precluded him from voting against.

31 Roni Milo, "By His Side in the Likud and Government," in Ahimeir, *Itzhak Shamir*, 141 [Hebrew].

32 Ephraim Even, "Conversations about Yair, Begin, and More," in Ahimeir, *Itzhak Shamir*, 222 [Hebrew].

33 Ibid.

34 Shamir, *Summing Up*, 257.

35 Israel Eldad, conversation with the author, September 8, 1992.

36 Israel Eldad, conversation with the author, July 28, 1994.

37 Israel Eldad, conversation with the author, September 9, 1992.

38 Israel Eldad, "Berdichevski the Rebel," *Metsudah* 3 (May 1937) [Hebrew].

39 Israel Eldad, *Israel, The Road to Full Redemption* (New York: Futuro, 1961), 14.

40 Israel Eldad, "Christian Support for Israel" (manuscript copy in author's files) [Hebrew].

41 Israel Eldad, conversation with the author, July 8, 1985.

42 Reported by Rabbi Zev Sultanowitz, speech at memorial for Eldad, Bet Haam, Jerusalem, January 5, 1997.

43 Yitzhak Shamir, speech at memorial for Eldad, Bet Haam, Jerusalem, January 5, 1997.

44 *Haaretz*, February 7, 1996.

45 Ibid.

46 Some accounts of Eldad Hadani have him traveling *from* a free Jewish state, bringing reports of the ten lost tribes to Jews elsewhere.

47 Israel Eldad, conversation with the author, September 6, 1989.

48 Eldad, *The First Tithe*, 10.

49 Ibid., 32-35.

50 Ibid., 59, 60, 110.

51 Ben-Ami, interview.

52 Yoram Sion, interview with the author, March 9, 2009.

53 Israel Eldad to Rabbi Arye Levin, 21 Elul 5709 [September 15, 1949] (author's files, unpublished) [Hebrew].

54 Yair Stern (the son), reading the inscription at an evening marking the centenary of Eldad's birth, the Menachem Begin Heritage Center, Jerusalem, October 24, 2010.

55 Eldad, conversation, September 8, 1992.

[56] Israel Eldad to Norman Lamm, 21 Kislev 5747 [December 23, 1986] (author's files, unpublished).

[57] Eldad, conversation, July 28, 1994.

[58] Nathan Yalin-Mor, *Haaretz*, July 20, 1978.

[59] Nechemia Ben-Tor, *Torch Bearers of Freedom* (n.p.: Yair, 2008), 227 [Hebrew].

[60] Ibid., 228-29.

[61] Yalin-Mor, *The Years Before*, 140.

[62] Ben-Tor, *Torch Bearers*, 229-30.

[63] Yalin-Mor, *The Years Before*, 11-14.

[64] Ibid., 23, 26.

[65] Ibid., 84-85.

[66] That the British were engaged in the early war years in stopping Jewish refugees from escaping from the Germans was not merely an assumption on the part of the refugees. In July 1939, "The Secretary of State spoke severely to the Rumanian Minister. We should make sure that his reprimand reaches the Rumanian Government..." (Foreign Office document W10846/1369/48268, cited in William R. Perl, *The Four-Front War* [New York: Crown, 1978], 178). The same document notes a decision to "stop the flow of immigration at the source." Perl cites another Foreign Office document (Register no. WF0371/25241/5185/38/48) that references the "Bulgarian front of our campaign against illegal immigration" (179). In January 1940 the Foreign Office cabled its representative in Belgrade to "prevent assistance" from being provided to one thousand refugees trapped in ice on the Danube River (Registry no. 1087/38/48 1940 W 319/20 Jan. 1940) (190). And so forth.

[67] Yalin-Mor, *The Years Before*, 90-110.

[68] Ibid., 113.

[69] Ibid., 120.

[70] Ibid.

[71] Yossi Ahimeir, "Nathan Yalin-Mor is Dead," *Maariv*, February 19, 1980 [Hebrew].

[72] Nathan Yalin-Mor to the editor of *Hehazit*, 24 Tammuz 5703 [July 27, 1943], in *Hauma* 152 (summer 2003), 73 [Hebrew].

[73] Ibid., 73-74.

[74] Yalin-Mor, *Lohamey Herut Israel*, 235, 237. Uri Avnery reports Yalin-Mor told him that he said every Lehi member would shoot anyone attempting to kidnap him. Uri Avnery, "The Holy Cannon," June 5, 2003, www.faz.co.il/story_1436 [Hebrew].

[75] Uri Avnery, "Federation? Why Not?" November 22, 2009, www.faz.co.il/story_5770 [Hebrew]; Uri Avnery, "The Lover of Eretz Israel," August 9, 2009, news1, http://www.news1.co.il/Archive/003-D-40159-00.html [Hebrew].

[76] Uri Avnery, interview with the author, March 13, 2011.

[77] Shamir, *Summing Up*, 37.

[78] Nathan Yalin-Mor, "Who Is a Separatist and What Is Zionism?" *Davar*, June 5, 1969.

[79] Elisha Yalin-Mor, interview with the author, November 5, 2010.

[80] Ibid.

[81] Joshua Cohen, interview in Liberman, *Fighters' Stories*, 29-30.

[82] Ibid., 24-25.

[83] Joshua Cohen to his parents, published in *Lohamey Herut Israel, Collected Writings*, 1:974-75.

[84] Joshua Cohen to his parents, 29 Nisan 5705 [April 12, 1945] (author's files, unpublished) [Hebrew].

[85] Aharon Dolev, "A Legend in Sde Boker," *Maariv*, August 15, 1986.

[86] Ibid.

[87] Ze'ev Iviansky, *On Resistance and Rebellion* (Tel Aviv: Yair, 1991), 315 [Hebrew].

[88] Geula Cohen, speech at memorial for Abraham Stern, Menachem Begin Heritage Center, Jerusalem, February 18, 2009.

[89] Moshe Meirsdorf, "The Story of the State," *Maaynei Hayeshua* 144 (April 2010) [Hebrew].

[90] Tova Svorai, untitled memoir addressed to author and interview, May 1, 2011.

[91] Tova Svorai, interview with the author, July 6, 2010.

[92] Tova Svorai, ed., *And It Came to Pass during British Rule* (Israel: 2006), 10 [Hebrew].

[93] Testimony of Eliezer Sirkis, who was in the station when Tova was brought in and who was in a car with her after her interrogation, in Liberman, *Fighters' Stories*, 78-79.

[94] Tova Svorai, *And It Came to Pass*, 11.

[95] Ibid., 13.

[96] Ibid., 12.

[97] Ibid., 10.

[98] Ibid., 24.

[99] Ibid., 201.

[100] Ibid., 8.

[101] Ibid., 194.

[102] Ibid., 194-97, 18.

[103] Ibid., 19.

[104] Tova Svorai, interview, July 6, 2010.

[105] Ibid.

[106] Ben-Ami, interview.

[107] Moshe Segal, interview with the author, 1979.

[108] Ibid.

[109] The "Western Wall Conflict" began September 23, 1928, when the British District Commissioner in Jerusalem, Edward Keith-Roach, alerted Haj Amin el-Husseini to the presence of a cloth dividing the Jewish male and female worshippers at the Western Wall on the Day of Atonement. Husseini demanded its removal. The British removed it by force the next morning as Arabs massed to attack the worshippers. Duff, *Bailing*, 170; Nachum Pundal, "The Knight Returns to the Galilee," *Davar*, December 20, 1963 (an interview with Duff).
The Jewish community held many protest meetings around the country in the weeks that followed. On October 20, Arab residents of the Moghrabi neighborhood near the Wall hit worshippers at the site, wounding one seriously. On November 1, Husseini demanded the imposition of limits on Jewish rights to visit the Wall. On November 27, a White Paper was issued in London blaming the Jewish worshippers for putting up the division during prayers, in violation of the status quo. In May-June 1929, local Arabs initiated a new prayer service at the Wall, to interfere, they said, with Jewish prayers. *New York Times*, December 5, 1929.
The full story of the conflict, through the riots of August 1929, is detailed in Zev Golan, *The Shofars of Revolt* (Tel Aviv: Jabotinsky Institute, 2007), 18-31[Hebrew].

[110] Moshe Segal, *Each Generation* (Jerusalem: Ministry of Defence, 1985), 85 [Hebrew].

[111] Segal, interview, 1979.

[112] Moshe Segal, during a tour of the Western Wall, June 9, 1981.

[113] Segal, interview, 1979.

[114] Brit Hashmonaim (League of Hasmoneans) membership card. See Golan, *The Shofars of the Revolt*, 47.

[115] *Tsifiya* 2, Nissan 5745 [spring 1985], 133-37; Zev Golan, conversations with Moshe Segal, 1981-85; Zev Golan, *Awake o' Israel, the Life and Thought of the Late Rabbi Moshe Segal* (Jerusalem: Shavei Zion, 5770 [2010]), 41, 44, 51 [Hebrew].

[116] *New York Times*, October 20, 1981.

[117] Segal, conversation with the author, 1985.

[118] Segal, interview, 1979.

[119] Esther Moldovsky, interview with the author, February 25, 2008.

[120] Moshe Moldovsky, interview with the author, January 3, 2000.

[121] Esther Moldovsky, interview, February 25, 2008.

[122] Esther Moldovsky, interview with the author, March 14, 2010.

[123] Moshe Moldovsky, interview, February 25, 2008.

[124] All data and quotes in this section are from Torenberg, interview.

[125] Julie Torenberg, letter to Mrs. Rosman, n.d. [1989] [Hebrew].

[126] All data and quotes in this section are from Nelly Lengsfelder, interview with the author, March 19, 2009, unless otherwise noted.

[127] Based on Ben-Tor, *Lehi Lexicon*, 143.

[128] *Lehi: People*, 160.

[129] Yael Ben-Dov, speech at Underground Prisoners Museum, Jerusalem, November 10, 2009.

[130] Ibid.

[131] Bowyer Bell, *Terror Out of Zion*, 174.

[132] Ben-Dov, speech.

[133] Benjamin Gepner, at Menachem Begin Heritage Center, Jerusalem, June 13, 2010.

[134] Benjamin Gepner, interview with the author, July 8, 2010.

[135] Ibid.; re: Stern's last letter: David Stern, introduction to *Letters to Roni*, [7].

[136] Gepner, *With a Beating Heart*, 292, 298.

[137] Ibid., 298-300.

[138] Ibid. As Leah Granek remembers the incident, "There were no British casualties. My mission was to ensure the British would not use the road. We stopped them, they got out and started shooting, and we left. It was on the road from the Hatikvah neighborhood [in south Tel Aviv] to Tel Litvinsky." Leah Granek, telephone interview with the author, January 9, 2011.

[139] Gepner, *With a Beating Heart*, 320-24.

[140] Ibid., 330-31.

[141] Gepner, interview.

[142] Ibid.

[143] Gepner, *With a Beating Heart*, 61.

[144] Ibid., 63-64, 199-200, 93.

[145] Ibid., 180.

[146] Ibid., 61-63.

[147] Ibid., 252.

[148] Gepner, interview.

[149] Ibid.

[150] Ibid.

[151] "Rabbi Abraham Ravitz of Blessed Memory: Last of the Lehi Fighters in the Knesset," *Matzavharu'ach*, January 30, 2009, 5 [Hebrew].

[152] Ibid.

[153] Rabbi Abraham Ravitz, interviewed by Moshe Oppenheim, *BeSheva* 108 (September 2, 2004) [Hebrew].

[154] Ibid.

[155] Ibid.

[156] Former members of Knesset at www.knesset.gov.il; Rabbi Abraham Ravitz at he.wikipedia.org [Hebrew]; see also http://en.wikipedia.org/wiki/Avraham_Ravitz

[157] Heruti, *One Truth*, 90.

[158] Ibid., 91; re: Ben-Gurion: David Ben-Gurion, speech to Sixth Convention of the Histadrut, November 20, 1944, reported in *Davar*, November 22, 1944.

[159] Heruti, *One Truth*, 92-93.

[160] Ibid., 140.

[161] Ibid., 134.

[162] Ibid., 147-50.

[163] Ibid., 212.

[164] Ibid., 212-13.
[165] Ibid., 218.
[166] Ibid., 222-23, 232, 234-36.
[167] Heruti, interview with the author, July 8, 2010.
[168] Heruti, *One Truth*, 238.
[169] Ibid., 272.
[170] Ibid., 302.
[171] Heruti, interview.
[172] Heruti, *One Truth*, 320-22.
[173] Ibid., 355.
[174] Ibid., 370.
[175] Heruti, interview.
[176] Heruti, *One Truth*, 386.
[177] Heruti, interview.
[178] Heruti, *One Truth*, 395.
[179] Yair Stern (the son), speech at Hebrew University, December 24, 2007.
[180] Yair Stern (the son), interview with Yehuda Hakohen, Lehi Museum, Tel Aviv, June 8, 2010.
[181] *Minutes*, 108.

Chapter Six

[1] *Minutes*, 40.
[2] Ibid., 123-24. In contrast, Uri Avnery, who worked with Yalin-Mor in the 1950s, believes that Yalin-Mor did not support socialism. Avnery says the economic platform of Semitic Action, which Yalin-Mor helped formulate, bore characteristics of what would come to be called Social Democracy and recognized the importance of entrepreneurship and markets. Avnery, interview.
[3] *Minutes*, 41.
[4] Ibid., 114.
[5] Ibid., 118.
[6] Ibid., 119.
[7] Ibid.
[8] Ibid., 120.
[9] Ibid., 122.
[10] Ibid., 127-28, 133.
[11] Yalin-Mor, "Who is a Separatist and What is Zionism?"
[12] Ibid.
[13] Yalin-Mor to Yossi Ahmeir, cited in Ahimeir, "Nathan Yalin-Mor is Dead" (ellipses in original article).
[14] Yalin-Mor, "Who is a Separatist and What is Zionism?"
[15] *Minutes*, 113.
[16] Ibid., 109.
[17] Ibid., 112.
[18] Ibid., 107.
[19] Ibid., 110.
[20] Eldad, conversation, July 28, 1994.
[21] Ben-Ami, interview.
[22] *Minutes*, 128, 133.
[23] Ibid.
[24] Eldad, conversation, July 28, 1994.

[25] *Kol Ha'ir* (Jerusalem), March 11, 1994, 69.

[26] *Yediot Aharanot*, January 19, 1996.

[27] Israel Eldad, "Principles for a Hebrew Liberation Movement," lecture, Jerusalem, 1953, published later in *Sulam* 53-54 (August 1953) [Hebrew].

[28] Ibid.

[29] Ibid.

[30] Ibid.

[31] Ibid.

[32] Ibid.

[33] Israel Eldad, acceptance speech when awarded "Defender of Jerusalem" prize, New York, published in *Nekuda* 116 (December 1987), 22 [Hebrew].

[34] Eldad, "Israel: The Road," 34-35.

[35] Ibid., 37.

[36] Ibid., 40.

[37] Eldad, acceptance speech, *Nekuda*.

[38] Shamir, interview.

[39] Ibid.

[40] *Minutes*, 116.

[41] Ibid., 94.

[42] Ibid., 102.

[43] Ibid., 97

[44] Ibid.

[45] Ibid.

[46] Ibid., 98-99.

[47] Ibid., 97.

[48] Ibid., 99.

[49] Shamir to Shulamit Shamir, December 8, 1947, *Letters to Shulamit*, 98. Emphasis in the original.

[50] *Minutes*, 103.

[51] Ibid., 45.

[52] Shamir, interview.

[53] Eldad, conversation, July 28, 1994.

[54] Shamir, interview.

[55] Ibid.

[56] Several important writers, include W. M. Thackery, shared this trait of Stern's.

[57] Reported by Uri Avnery, *Maariv*, June 22, 2001.

[58] Ibid. A good analysis of Yalin-Mor's later views that addresses the question of whether he or Eldad was the true heir of Lehi can be found in Yaacov Orenstein, "Semitic Action and Its Partners," *Davar*, August 10, 1958. Orenstein was an early member of Lehi who worked closely with Stern, though he did not share Eldad's views then or later. From 1962 to 1964, he was spokesman for the Mapai party.

[59] *Minutes*, 110.

[60] Tova Svorai, interview, July 6, 2010.

[61] Gepner, interview.

[62] *Kol Hair*.

[63] Abraham Stern, drafts of broadcasts, thoughts, ideas, speeches, broadsides and notes, 1940-1941, Central Zionist Archives, A549\65-75 [Hebrew]. "A revolutionary...," was published by Lehi in February 1944, *Lohamey Herut Israel, Collected Writings*, 1:397-98.

In 1943, Eldad had written in the Lehi newspaper that "we are not turning our movement into a 'party.' We will not participate in elections, we will not hold votes, we will not consult the majority." *Lohamey Herut Israel, Collected Writings*, 1:200.

[64] *Lohamey Herut Israel, Collected Writings*, 1:69-70. See ch. 3, note 47.

65 Elisha Yalin-Mor, interview.

66 Yehuda Hakohen, interview with the author, September 6, 2010.

67 Shamir, interview.

68 Ibid.

69 Ibid.

70 Yair Stern, speech marking the 70th anniversary of Lehi, Menachem Begin Heritage Center, Jerusalem, June 13, 2010. Arieh Eldad, speaking at the same event, took issue with Stern's penultimate sentence, stating that the time has not yet come to disband Lehi; the audience applauded enthusiastically.

71 Stern, drafts, Central Zionist Archives, A549\65-16.

72 David Ben-Gurion, letter to committee on medals and badges, January 3, 1952. Cited in Udi Lebel, *The Road to the Pantheon* (Jerusalem: Carmel, 2007), 237 [Hebrew].

73 Lebel, *The Road to the Pantheon*, 127.

74 Ben-Gurion, addressing the Knesset. *Davar*, May 29, 1958.

75 Lebel, *The Road to the Pantheon*, 168.

76 Colonial Office, "Palestine: Termination of the Mandate," May 15, 1948, section 5, available at www.ismi.emory.edu/Articles/terminationofthemandate.pdf (accessed January 7, 2011).

77 Ynet, November 28, 2007.

78 Shiri Altar, MAPA Mapping and Publishing, Ltd., GIsrael geographic database, email to author, August 25, 2010.

79 *Haaretz*, July 29, 2010.

80 Ahimeir had been sent by the army to guard the campus, which was cut off at the time from the rest of Israel and surrounded by Jordanian troops, but he was also expected to return from his duty with boxes of books for the university's library.

81 Joseph Geiger, speech at Hebrew University, December 24, 2007.

82 *Haaretz*, February 12, 2008.

83 Israel Government Press Office photograph of Prime Minister Ehud Olmert speaking at the session, January 29, 2008, code D 1004-037.

84 Natan Sharansky, speech at the Knesset, Jerusalem, March 9, 2010.

85 Zionist Freedom Alliance website, www.zionistfreedom.org

86 Ibid.

87 Arieh Eldad, speech marking the 70th anniversary of Lehi, Menachem Begin Heritage Center, Jerusalem, June 13, 2010.

88 Ibid.

89 Ibid.

90 Shabtai Ben-Dov, *The Complete Writings of Shabtai Ben-Dov*, ed. Yehuda Etzion (Ofra: Sulamot, [2007]), 2:464 [Hebrew], available at http://www.daat.ac.il/daat/vl/bendov/bendov22.pdf (accessed November 10, 2010).

91 Ibid.

92 Uri Zvi Greenberg, "Those Who Live Thanks to Them Say," *Haaretz*, January 23, 1948, reprinted in Uri Zvi Grinberg (sic), *Collected Works*, ed. Dan Miron (Jerusalem: Bialik Institute, 1994), 7:19 [Hebrew]. In this poem Greenberg plays on the verse in Psalm 30, "What advantage is there in my blood if I go down to the grave? Will the earth thank You, will it tell of Your truth?"

Appendix B

1 *Lohamey Herut Israel, Collected Writings*, 1:141-44.

Index